MULTILINGUAL MATTERS 100
Series Editor: Derrick Sharp

Teaching-and-Learning Language-and-Culture

Michael Byram, Carol Morgan
and colleagues

MULTILINGUAL MATTERS LTD
Clevedon • Philadelphia • Adelaide

Library of Congress Cataloging in Publication Data

Byram, Michael
Teaching-and-Learning Language-and-Culture/Michael Byram, Carol Morgan
and colleagues.
p. cm. (Multilingual Matters: 100)
Includes bibliographical references and index.
1. Language and languages–Study and teaching. 2. Language and culture–Study
and teaching. I. Morgan, Carol, 1943-. II. Title. III. Series: Multilingual Matters
(Series): 100.
P53.B938 1994   93-30783
418'007–dc20   CIP

British Library Cataloguing in Publication Data

A CIP catalogue record for this book is available from the British Library.

ISBN 1-85359-212-9 (hbk)
ISBN 1-85359-211-0 (pbk)

Multilingual Matters Ltd

UK: Frankfurt Lodge, Clevedon Hall, Victoria Road, Clevedon, Avon BS21 7SJ.
USA: 1900 Frost Road, Suite 101, Bristol, PA 19007, USA.
Australia: P.O. Box 6025, 83 Gilles Street, Adelaide, SA 5000, Australia.

Printed and bound in Great Britain by
Marston Book Services Limited, Didcot

Contents

Preface

There are a number of reasons for what might appear to be an over-indulgence in hyphens in our title. For the authors of this book, teaching culture together with language has necessitated a great deal of learning, for we were not professionally trained in the study of culture — for example, in social anthropology — and it has been fundamental to our work that we have had to adapt our professional expertise. The second set of hyphens is a statement of our perception of the 'object' of the teaching and learning process, and simultaneously of the reality of the integration of language and culture on which that process is founded. Since language and culture are inseparable, we cannot be teachers of language without being teachers of culture — or vice versa.

Let it be said here already that, although we are aware of the contentious nature of definitions and descriptions of 'culture', we write from our own perspective as 'teachers of language and culture' for other teachers with similar professional and academic backgrounds. We propose therefore to take 'culture' to refer to the knowledge and practices of people belonging to particular social groups, for example national groups. More of this later, but in the meantime who are we?

Although only two authors are named, other colleagues have contributed in different ways. For this is a book which draws upon various research projects, recently completed or still in progress, carried out at the University of Durham, the Institut National de Recherche Pédagogique in Paris, the Thames Valley University, London, Roskilde University Centre, Denmark and the University of Braunschweig, Germany. Each project is being reported separately but this book is intended to provide links between them and therefore uses the work of all of them in some degree, and that work is the product of many people:

Sylvia Duffy: *Monkwearmouth College, Sunderland and University of Durham.*
Anne Hardwick: *St Leonard's R.C. School, Durham and University of Durham.*
Janet Mayes: *St Aidan's R.C. School, Sunderland and University of Durham.*
Val Minns: *Formerly Wolsingham Comprehensive School and University of Durham.*

Richard Turner: *Peterlee College and University of Durham.*
Ana Barro: *Thames Valley University.*
Hanns Grimm: *Thames Valley University.*
Celia Roberts: *Thames Valley University.*
Brian Street: *University of Sussex.*
Anita Baire: *Collège E. Herriot, Luce and INRP, Paris.*
Claudine Briane: *Lycée Victor Dury, Paris and INRP, Paris.*
Albane Cain: *INRP, Paris.*
Frédéric Fesquet: *Lycée Jules Uhry, Creil and INRP, Paris.*
Mickaële Guillien: *Collège Nocard, Saint-Maurice and INRP, Paris.*
Pierre Heudier: *Collège d'enseignement public et secondaire, Montoire and INRP, Paris.*
Hélène Ladevie: *Lycée Ronsard, Vendôme and INRP, Paris.*
Jeannine Leconte: *Ecole Normale d'Antony and INRP, Paris.*
Marie-Jeanne Trividic: *Collège de la Binquenais, Rennes and INRP, Paris.*
Annie Serre: *Lycée Jean Rostand, Chantilly and INRP, Paris.*
Françoise Vigneron: *Collège Berthelot, Le Mans and INRP, Paris.*
Peter Doyé: *University of Braunschweig.*
Michael Bacon: *University of Braunschweig.*
Ulrike Biermann: *Richarda-Huch-Schule, Braunschweig and University of Braunschweig.*
Bettina Borck: *University of Braunschweig.*
Francis Jarman: *University of Hildesheim.*
Ingo Kümmritz: *University of Braunschweig.*
John Lees: *Formerly University of Bath.*
Arnim Mennecke: *University of Braunschweig.*
Jeremy Vanstone: *Formerly University of Exeter.*
Gisela Wheeler: *Bede Sixth Form College, Cleveland and University of Durham.*
Andrea Winter: *University of Braunschweig.*
Karen Risager: *Roskilde University Centre.*

In addition, others have contributed to our collection of case-studies, either by writing themselves or by providing us with the opportunity to observe and describe their work. We are grateful to:

Dianne Wall: *University of Lancaster.*
Edward Woods: *University of Lancaster.*
Sheila Watts: *University of Dublin.*
Lawrence Raw: *British Council, Ankara.*

The two named authors are responsible for the text and trust that they have not mis-represented the work of others. Carol Morgan is now Lecturer in Education at the University of Bath and was Senior Research Assistant at the School of Education, University of Durham; she was appointed to the project 'Cultural Studies/"Civilisation" for advanced language learners — an experiment in French and English schools', but she gave vital support to other projects on language and culture teaching in the School. Michael Byram is Reader in Education at the University of Durham.

Our thanks are due to many others, who do not appear as 'authors', but without whom there would be no book: to the pupils and students of the schools, colleges and institutions of higher and further education in which projects have been based; to those who gave us permission to work there; and above all to our secretaries Catherine Callan and her successor Sally Wagstaffe.

Although this present volume is an independent work, it is best understood in the context of other publications. Most directly, it continues the attempt made in *Cultural Studies in Foreign Language Education* (Byram, 1989) to demonstrate the coherence and necessity of integrating linguistic and cultural learning in the foreign language classroom. It takes further some of the themes started there — particularly the sketch of a psychological theory of cultural learning — and offers some more concrete realisations of the argument. It also introduces new themes — assessment and evaluation, and teacher education — and indicates their implications for practice. This volume also relates to others: first, to the reports of research on pupils' cultural learning (Byram & Esarte-Sarries, 1991; Byram, Esarte-Sarries & Taylor, 1991); and second, to a collection of articles which stake out the ground for research and development in cultural studies (Buttjes & Byram, 1991). There is a wider context too, in the work of many other authors who will be referred to in the text. Two should nonetheless be mentioned here, for those readers new to the field, as crucial texts: *Enseigner une culture étrangère* (Zarate, 1986) and *Zur Integration von Landeskunde und Kommunikation im Fremdsprachersunterricht* (Melde, 1987).

Michael Byram & Carol Morgan
Durham January 1993

Introduction

The hyphenation of 'language-and-culture' in our title is at once an indication of the recent surge of interest in the cultural learning dimension in language learning, and a reminder that this interest should not lead to a separation, either in theoretical discussion or in classroom practice, of cultural studies from language learning. In this respect our earlier title, *Cultural Studies in Foreign Language Education* (Byram, 1989), had a carefully chosen preposition, and a seminal work by Melde (1987), *Zur Integration von Landeskunde und Kommunikation im Fremdsprachenunterricht*, rightly emphasises the particular need in Germany to combine theories of learning about other countries with theories of communication.

On the other hand there is no doubt that the recognition of the cultural learning dimension opens up unfamiliar ground for many *language* teachers. For they are, indeed, language teachers, most often with an education in the literature of the language(s) they teach, and a training in the discipline of literary criticism and the theory and practice of teaching linguistic knowledge and skills. This means that, although their education and training is still highly relevant, whatever definition of culture is used, they need to become familiar with other disciplines pertinent to cultural learning too. Our earlier book, (Byram, 1989), was intended to contribute to this process, and the present volume is written in the same spirit and for the same readership. Its purpose is to make readily accessible to teachers, who have to spend most of their time in practice, some recent and still developing theory. We do not imply by this, however, that theory and practice are separable. Practising teachers are constantly drawing upon theory, both implicit and explicit, both learned and intuitive. The theory we present here will, we hope, enrich their theory-bound practices. But theory itself is modified by practice and we recognise this in our emphasis, in this book, on case-studies of experimentation with new theory, and on projections of how the theory must be related to wider concerns in teacher education, in assessment and in the role of language teaching in education for a multicultural, multi-class and international society.

For this book is written for teachers of foreign languages working within the framework of general education. We shall not repeat our argument that

1

foreign language learning should be seen as a fundamental aspect of general education with a unique role to play. That view will become particularly evident in our discussion of the notion of 'tertiary socialisation'. Similarly, we do not claim, for the following pages, any definitive note. Where the earlier volume consisted of exploratory essays, this one attempts a more systematic approach. Yet it still draws upon unfinished research and explores theoretical avenues, rather than offering a 'finished product'. There are both advantages and disadvantages in waiting till the 'product' is finished before presenting our ideas and materials. We have opted for the 'interim' presentation in the belief that intellectual endeavour should be shared and co-operation pursued.

Since our earlier volume, it has become evident in a number of ways that theorists and practitioners of language teaching have become aware of the importance of cultural learning. Publications have increased (e.g. Harrison, 1990; Valdes, 1986) and conference organisers have included cultural learning on their agenda (e.g. 'The cultural component in language teaching' at AILA '93). There are signs of more interest in cultural studies as a relevant discipline for language teachers in Britain (e.g. new courses in 'British Studies' being developed at the Universities of Warwick and Lancaster) and a higher profile for cultural studies in Germany (e.g. with the founding of a new journal, *Journal for the Study of British Cultures*) and in France. In the education system of England and Wales, the introduction of a National Curriculum for primary and lower secondary schools includes, in the curriculum for 'Modern Foreign Languages', the new element of 'cultural awareness'.

There have also been advances in empirical and conceptual research. Melde (1987) — published as our first volume went to press — has presented a notable discussion of the concept of *Landeskunde* to which we shall return in later pages; and there are others of similar significance (Doyé, 1992; Baumgratz-Gangl, 1990; Ertelt-Vieth, 1991). Empirical research of a non-interventionist kind has been carried out in France (Cain, 1991) and in our own university (Byram, Esarte- Sarries and Taylor, 1991; Alred, Byram, Esarte-Sarries & Ruane, 1990). Zarate has continued the work adumbrated in her account of theory and practice (1986) by developing new methods and materials (Zarate & Troutot, 1990; Arruda, Zarate & van Zundert, 1985) and by initiating discussion on the evaluation of cultural learning during residence in the foreign country (Zarate, 1991b). The significance of evaluation studies has also been recognised in the analysis of textbooks led by Doyé and Byram (Doyé, 1991; Byram, 1993b).

In 1989, we suggested four 'areas of enquiry' for cultural studies:

- the educational value of Cultural Studies within language teaching and within the secondary school curriculum as a whole;

- the structuring of Cultural Studies in a pedagogical manner which takes account of ways of structuring our knowledge of the world and in particular of other cultures, which is influenced by knowledge of cognitive and affective learning processes and which can be expected to lead to specific psychological outcomes; this pedagogy to be related to other aspects of foreign language learning;
- the methodology and techniques of Cultural Studies teaching;
- the evaluation of Cultural Studies teaching and assessment of learning.

Empirical research has shown that the educational potential of language-and-culture teaching is not being fulfilled. Our research demonstrated that young people acquire some *information* but very little *knowledge* of the foreign culture through language classes; the influence of extra-curricular forces such as the media is greater — and more insidious — than the intuitive and unsystematic efforts of the teacher. Cain and her associates have shown that stereotypical views of other cultures and peoples are tenacious and scarcely differentiated during the process of language learning in the classroom (Cain, 1991). Yet conceptual research has argued most convincingly that language teaching has a significant role in developing young people's critical awareness of their own and other societies (Melde, 1987) and in moving them into more advanced thinking as citizens with political understanding (Doyé, 1993).

Conceptual and empirical research have also further clarified the pedagogy and methodology of cultural studies. And it is in this area of enquiry that the present volume will be mainly focused. We shall give examples from work in progress as well as extending our earlier survey of learning theories. We shall also draw upon recent and current work on evaluation and assessment, both areas — but particularly the latter — being crucial to a full integration of language and culture teaching. The truism that only that which is assessed is taught seriously and systematically, holds true here too.

Our overriding purpose — we repeat — is to make this new and varied research and development accessible to fellow teachers. It is for this reason that we have translated all quotations into English; some illustrative teaching material remains however in French or German. Although we shall refer above all to those contexts and situations with which we are most familiar, especially in West European countries, we believe that the essence of the following pages will interest language teachers whatever their situation. Our current research involves teachers fully as researchers in a team. In this way we benefit not only from 'objective' knowledge acquired by scientific principles but also from the subjective 'craft' knowledge inherent in professional practice. By writing this book we wish to add to that valuable exchange.

1 Developing a Theory of Language-and-Culture Learning

It is a commonplace worth repeating that theories of language learning can be seen in practice in every language-teaching classroom. Teachers rely upon a mixture of intuitive theories of how different pupils learn, their recollections of their own language learning, and formal theories expounded to them during professional training. Their intuitions are doubtless acquired partly through experience, partly through discussion with others in the profession and partly through the more or less implicit guidance of textbooks and other pedagogically-structured materials. It is often difficult to distinguish the theoretical origins of their practices, but the latter are largely systematic and therefore driven by their theories.

Insofar as there is system in teachers' presentation of a *cultural* dimension in their teaching, it is evident that they hold theories of culture learning too. They believe that knowledge of the grammatical system of a language has to be complemented by understanding of culture-specific meanings; here, they use comparison and contrast to elucidate the culture-specific element. They also believe that information about social institutions and geographical features of the country — family structures, education systems, political parties, regional industries, for example — is necessary support or 'background' to knowledge of grammar and meaning. The sources of these theories are however much less evident, and the role of professional training and discussion within the profession is less significant, although this varies according to the particular language-teaching tradition and is more prominent in Germany than Britain or France, for example.

The purpose of this chapter is to begin to correct the imbalance in the professional discussion of culture learning theory and language learning theory. We shall nonetheless begin by examining some presentations of language learning theory for it is important to maintain links between the two. Melde is broadly correct in her view:

4

Language acquisition research cannot (yet) make reasoned statements about the contents of foreign language teaching, since it does not yet have a grasp of the connections, relevant to the contents, between communicative action and the foreign language way of life (*Lebenswelt*). (1987: 118, our translation)

There is however a danger, which Melde does not entirely avoid, in ignoring theories of language learning — particularly of vocabulary learning. It can lead to a reduction of the uniqueness of cultural learning through learning a foreign language. It is axiomatic in our view that cultural learning has to take place as an integral part of language learning, and vice versa. The mere acquisition of information about a foreign country, without the psychological demands of integrated language and culture learning, is inadequate as a basis for education through foreign language teaching (Byram, 1989).

In a second section, therefore, we shall consider theories which might support teaching and learning in the classroom, turning to developmental psychology to ask whether theories of cognitive and moral stages are helpful. We can also consider how such theories are useful in other school subjects, in particular history and geography. And thirdly we consider proposals for applying such theories to language and culture learning.

Culture in Language Learning

If we look at the way cultural learning is treated in secondary texts on language teaching and learning, it is useful to categorise this relationship in terms of what is designated as 'successful' language learning. Kramsch, in her overview of different views of culture and language in the US, Germany and France, also points out that these views *themselves* are culture bound (1991: 221). A number of texts perceive this in purely linguistic terms (fluency, accuracy, breadth of lexis etc.) and cultural learning is then evaluated in terms of how much it contributes to this success. 'Culture' is subsumed in a range of variables which could affect learning and is interpreted primarily in terms of the affective. Seliger for example writes:

Since language is used in social exchanges, the feelings, attitudes, and motivations of learners in relation to the target language itself, to the speakers of the language, and to the culture will affect how learners respond to the input to which they are exposed. In other words, these affective variables will determine the rate and degree of second language learning. (1988: 30)

McDonough (1981: 134–5) and Krashen (1981: 23, 29–33) also include a variety of personality factors which are considered to be equally influential as attitudes towards culture: extroversion/introversion, tolerance for ambiguity, ability to empathise, self-confidence etc. There are some hints that other values may accrue through the learning of culture but essentially the goal is seen as one of improved linguistic performance. Littlewood for example applauds the value of cultural learning inherent in language learning itself (although he does not develop this), but keeps linguistic proficiency as the overall aim of communicative competence:

> When we try to adopt new speech patterns, we are to some extent giving up markers of our own identity in order to adopt those of another cultural group. In some respects, too, we are accepting another culture's ways of perceiving the world. If we are agreeable to this process, it can enrich us and liberate us. (1981: 55)

(Similar views are expressed by Seliger (1988: 31) and McLaughlin (1987: 110).

Two models in particular are used in the culture/linguistic success approach: Gardner and Lambert's three-tier model of motivation: integrative, instrumental and manipulative (Lambert et al., 1968), and Schumann's eight dimensions of social distance (Schumann, 1978). Gardner and Lambert's taxonomy focuses on the attitude and learning of the individual according to his own motivation and learning with regard to the target culture, but generally only the first two categories of this model are given attention (Izzo, 1981: 12). Some scepticism is expressed by language learning theorists as to the validity of Lambert's tests (where both integrative and instrumental motivation were found to have an effect on linguistic success). Both McDonough and Bley-Vroman for example opt out of a definitive acceptance:

> There is a basic difficulty with all these studies [Gardner and Lambert, Gardner and Smythe, Spolski, Lukmani] which makes causal inference impossible. (McDonough, 1981: 152)

> Affect may be conceived of as influencing acquisition more or less directly, or it may be combined in an interesting way with... [Krashen's] filter hypothesis... Again, at this stage of their development the ideas here are still too nebulous to bear scrutiny. (Bley-Vroman, 1989: 59)

McDonough also suggests that success and positive attitudes to the target language and culture are interdependent: 'it is quite likely that most if not all of the orientations to the learning experience reported could have been the result and not the cause of successful progress' (1981: 153). Both he and Littlewood point to the research done by Green and Burstall in 1975 where success was seen to have a more influential affect on attitudes than vice versa (McDonough, 1981: 53, Littlewood, 1981: 56).

Schumann's (1978) model of social distance describes the relationships of the learner's group to the target culture group and identifies different factors which bring about the best language learning context: dominance (relative status), congruence, attitude, integration and also factors relating to the learning group: enclosure (open/closed attitudes), length of stay in target culture, size and cohesiveness. 'Psychological distance' relates to individual attitudes and experiences (language shock, culture shock, motivation and ego permeability). 'Acculturation' (learning to function within a new culture, while maintaining your own identity) is one of three integration strategies offered by Schumann, the other two being assimilation/total adoption or preservation/total rejection. 'Acculturation' depends on positive factors in terms of social distance and psychological distance and would seem to offer a fruitful possibility for appreciating *cultural* values.

It is however primarily linguistic factors again which are taken up by theorists. McLaughlin (1987: 111–15) for example looks at work on pidginisation by Schumann and others where the formation of a pidgin language is seen as an indicator of non-acculturation: 'learners who do not acculturate remain fossilized in this pidginized stage' (1987: 115). Izzo considers pidginisation to be an active refusal to acculturate: 'learning the language imperfectly precludes merging with the different culture and therefore allows one to maintain one's own identity' (1981: 20). McLaughlin also considers attitude and linguistic success, linked to Schumann's model of acculturation, to be bi-directional (see McDonough's bi-directional interpretation of motivation cited above):

> Most likely the line of causality [attitude — second language acquisition] is bi-directional. Perceived distance affects second-language acquisition and is affected by success in second-language acquisition. (1987: 126–7)

Understanding the target culture *is* appreciated in these theoretical approaches but generally only as a support to linguistic proficiency. One exception is the interpretation of the Schumann model given in a paper by Cortazzi & Jin (1993) where the model is used to assess 'cultural synergy' between Chinese research postgraduate students and British university supervisors. The difference in approach here is that students are already highly proficient L2 speakers and that the Schumann model is used to measure *cultural* misunderstanding on the part of both supervisors and students. Here cultural learning is valued in its own right; success is not linked, as in most interpretations of Schumann or Lambert and Gardner, to linguistic success but to inter-personal understanding.

Another interpretation of 'successful' language learning which develops beyond linguistic proficiency is that which manifests itself in communicative performance (recognition of linguistic cues, maintaining a balance of input/power in discourse, skills in negotiation etc.). Here cultural learning is in Wringe's words 'instrumental to the processes of communication' (1989: 14). Linguistic competence has been defined more broadly here to include culturally-determined behavioural conventions but does not include analyses of the value systems or ideological expectations of different cultures. Most of the analytical work focuses on second language acquisition, in other words on cultural clashes within the one country. Ellis & Roberts for example look at Asian interviewees in job interviews in Britain (1987: 21–2) and Ellis analyses talk from Portuguese and Punjabi-speaking pupils in an English school (1984: 121–7). Many of the findings are readily transferable to the field of foreign language teaching, although in situations of second language acquisition it is likely that the learner will belong to a minority group in an inferior power position.

As with the mainly linguistic approach to culture, the communicative competence approach considers cultural mismatching as only one of the factors in communicative encounters and misunderstandings. Preston (1989: 131–2, 179–83) for example looks at the size of the communicating group, the topic, and the emotional involvement as equally important contributory factors. However, many useful behavioural conventions are identified in communicative competence theories which are culture-specific and which may be responsible for misunderstanding: the use of silence (Japanese conventions are particularly relevant here: Odlin, 1989; La Forge, 1983: 70–81), acceptability of different levels of volume (Odlin, 1989: 56–7), expected length of turn and frequency of turn-taking (Preston, 1989: 128–31, Odlin, 1989: 55), general formality of style (Odlin, 1989: 56) and expressions of politeness, for example in requests and apologies (Odlin, 1989: 49–54).

Ellis & Roberts go beyond these external behavioural conventions to deeper schematic differences which may exist, identifying not only personal schemata but also those shared culturally. They recognise that, where interactants come from different cultures, gross differences in schemata may lead to an impasse (as explored in the Cortazzi and Jin article cited above):

> Studies of interethnic communication suggest that lack of shared schemas in interaction are more likely to lead to communication breakdown than differences and difficulties at the level of linguistic code. (1987: 24).

Although these theoretical works provide useful cultural pointers, they focus on oral skills in language learning and remain in the main at the analytical level without providing suggestions for teaching or learning. Ellis & Roberts do suggest that practice in interaction will improve skills:

> What we can say is that it is only in interactional contexts that users have the opportunity to develop their communicative resources and that these contexts not only enable specific forms and communicative styles to be developed, but they in part determine what is acquired and used. (1987: 23)

Nonetheless, the skills acquired in such interactional practice could represent conversational survival skills rather than deeper cultural understanding.

La Forge (1983) in his adoption of Curran's Community Language Learning (1972) does seem to offer a possible intercultural teaching approach. His is a dual teaching method based on 'interpersonal security' ('the supportive atmosphere among the participants fostered by the teacher') and 'cultural security' ('a learning atmosphere characterized by learning exercises which are unique to groups of students from different racial or ethnic backgrounds', 1983: 65). The 'learning exercises' he incorporates align with the cultural expectations of the Japanese students he teaches, particularly the use of silence which allows for reflection. Here a supportive personal and intellectual context is created to minimise conflict but there is no systematic examination of cultural differences. The adoption of cultural rituals from the learners' culture is seen as a smoothing-over process rather than an opportunity to relativise and discuss different cultural behaviours:

> By establishing interpersonal and cultural security, the teacher has appealed for psychological rather than mere physical presence. (1983: 66)

Brown's analysis of the 'set of behaviors' and 'modes of perception' (1987: 123) which characterise different cultures goes considerably further in tackling the problem of cultural differences and the relevant teaching and learning process. He identifies four stages of acculturation (euphoria, insecurity, recovery and acceptance) which occur in cross-cultural encounters. He also usefully identifies 'a feeling of homelessness, where one feels neither bound firmly to one's native culture nor fully adapted to the second culture' (cited as Lambert's use of Durkheim's term 'anomie'). Brown links anomie to the beginning of the third stage of acculturation, 'recovery', and suggests that this is the moment when most fruitful language learning takes place: 'mastery of skilful fluency in a second language (within the second culture) occurs somewhere at the beginning of the third — recovery — stage of acculturation' (1987: 135). This is then a useful pointer for teachers, indicating different stages through which pupils need to have progressed. Students need to have covered a range of affective responses to the target culture, both excitement at the newness and shock at the difference, before linguistic progress can be made. Thus, although Brown values linguistic proficiency, cultural learning is placed on an equal footing.

In the two interpretations of 'success' (linguistic and behavioural) cultural awareness and positive attitudes to the target culture are valued, but only insofar as they contribute to other aims. In some other works, notably Robinson (1988), cultural competence is treated as a valuable subject in its own right but with little reference to linguistic skills. Robinson, for example, examines issues of differing behaviour, perception, presentation, schemata and others in a comprehensive analysis of the complexities involved. Her emphasis however is one of social learning rather than culture and language learning.

In only a handful of texts is cultural learning valued as an equal complement to language learning and as an activity valid in its own right. In three key works which seek to combine cultural and language learning (Seelye, 1974; Brown, 1987; Pfister & Poser, 1987) behaviour and language are areas of focus but here cultural learning is seen as a crucial key to understanding the meaning of what is taking place. Seelye, for example, sees the language teacher as the facilitator in this learning exercise:

> One cannot understand a native speaker if his cultural referents, his view of the world, and his linguistic forms are novel. The language teacher can build bridges from one cognitive system to another. (1974: 22).

Pfister & Poser focus more sharply on behavioural differences and in particular on how this may help cross-cultural understanding in reading comprehension, pointing particularly to possible clashes between the culture of the reader and the culture embodied in the text:

> The cultural framework surrounding a text…functions as a connective tissue which binds the specific techniques and activities into a unified organizational scheme. Cultural factors are inherent to the reading act and therefore influence the reader's control over the input. This becomes obvious when the cultural background of the reader and that of the text fail to intersect in the FL classroom…it is imperative that FL teachers deal directly with cultural factors influencing communication. This implies that reading instruction must focus on modifying and expanding the reader's cultural filter in an organized and consistent manner…readers need a concrete set of tools for assessing how the target culture categorizes experience which in turn influences how well the reader modifies expectations and comprehends the text. (1987: 3)

Examples of pre-reading, reading and post-reading activities are provided, illustrating a possible set of cultural tools, but disappointingly prove rather pedestrian with somewhat stereotypical judgements. In a text on driving through a German town, for example, after an explanation of the relative novelty of the family car in Germany, of the occurrence of narrow streets and two-lane motorways, the following cultural comment is offered:

> Taking this all into consideration, it is not surprising that the Germans developed a driving etiquette that varies from the American. The German driver is aggressive. (1987: 18)

It would have been helpful to add that the cultural difference leads to an American interpretation of German behaviour as aggression.

Seelye emphasises the general educative value of cultural learning:

> If he [the student] avoids contact with native speakers and if he lacks respect for their world view, of what value is his training? Where can it be put to use? What educational breadth has it inspired? (1974: 21)

Brown also comments on the different contexts for learning a foreign language, some of which will rely less on cultural learning:

> The *foreign* language context...produces diverse degrees of acculturation since people are attempting to learn a foreign language for a variety of possible reasons. Some people learn other languages simply out of an interest in languages ranging from a passing curiosity to a technical linguistic fascination. Others may learn a language in order to communicate some day with people in another country. Still others learn for specific purposes: say a foreign language requirement or a need to gain a reading knowledge in a field of specialization. It is possible in such settings to function without the foreign language although that foreign language provides advantages in educational advancement, work or social status. (1987: 136)

Although it could be argued that the target culture may be seen as peripheral here in that a communicative urgency is diminished, nevertheless a thorough *understanding* of the language can only be gained by understanding the cultural context which has produced it. This point has been made by Brown earlier:

> Misunderstandings are...likely to occur between members of different cultures;...differences are real and we must learn to deal with them in any situation in which two cultures come into contact. (1987: 123)

Germany and France already have a strong tradition of teaching culture in the form of *Landeskunde* and *civilisation*. In both these countries there is a strong annexe of supportive critical and theoretical writing which accords equal validity to culture and language. Zarate, some of whose work is analysed in more detail in Chapter 4, makes this very clear in her seminal work *Enseigner une culture étrangère* (1986).

Melde, quoted above, and other Ludwigsburg colleagues, notably Baumgratz, have promoted culture and language learning in their prepared classroom materials on schooling in France, French regional identity and the relationship of France to Germany and Europe in general (Schumann, 1986; Melde *et al.*, 1987; Baumgratz *et al.*, 1988; Melde, 1988). Two publications of conference papers also give some indication of the range of interests currently being pursued in these two countries and also in Austria. Papers were published after the Triangle 7 conference (1988) organised by AUPELF, the Goethe Institut, and the British Council. These were given by 12 speakers with equal representation from France, Germany and Britain. The French papers concentrate on cultural difficulties experienced by adult learners of French either as immigrants in France or in Francophone countries, with two models also offered by Zarate of an old-style model of *civilisation* teaching based on authority and transmission of knowledge and a new suggested model based on experiential learning and comparison of mother and target cultures:

> Model 1 is constructed from a definition of cultural competence conceived as a sum of knowledge...didactic tools which reinforce what P. Bourdieu calls the 'language of authority' dominate this model.

> Model 2 aims to provide the pupil with tools for interpreting a foreign culture and to teach him or her how to put these to use...In Model 2 the approach to a foreign culture is mainly pursued through the relationship between the pupil's own culture and the culture or cultures being taught. (1988: 24–5, our translation)

The German papers give accounts of trials with students responding to textbook materials, focusing particularly on the cultural deficiencies of current foreign language textbooks (French textbooks for Germans, German textbooks for the French). Buttjes, in his presentation of cultural learning as a process involving distance and content, highlights the importance of contact with the target culture through visits and exchanges and the distance or relativisation that can be achieved *vis-à-vis* one's own culture: 'The development of critical distance to one's own world remains the pedagogical and political aim' (1988: 56, our translation). The British papers focus on classroom practice (experiments in EFL and multicultural classrooms and observed attitudes in French FL classrooms), with Widdowson identifying different relationships between language and culture: 'Symbolic meaning, the way language *represents* culture...[and] indexical meaning, the way language *refers to* culture' (1988: 14–15), questioning the validity of symbolic meaning and the place of teaching indexical meaning in a language classroom.

The second publication, also published in 1988, is a selection of papers from two conferences in Austria (Klagenfurt) from colleagues working in Germany and Austria in the field of further and higher education. There are two main points of focus here: trips to Britain (Newcastle, Preston and Covent Garden) and the US (Ohio) undertaking project work of different kinds, and a variety of different methods of teaching culture trialled at home. The latter included the creation of a 'cultural' board game, simulation tasks with mixed cultural groups, the use of distance learning, and the use of Commonwealth literature and popular culture (focusing on the best-seller, pop music and Hollywood). Gibson offers an introductory overview of the teaching of culture. In his listing of aims of cultural studies he places 'to support language learning' first, adding that 'communicative competence requires cultural competence' (1988: 13).

In both these collections it is clear that culture is considered not only valid in its own right but also as coming *before* language as a priority. Wright in her preface to the Klagenfurt papers underlines the primacy of content: 'language courses must have meaningful and true content in order for any real learning to take place' (1988: 8). Buttjes sees cultural content as a prime *motivator* for language learning:

> Cultural content (because, first of all, it creates the motivation to learn a foreign language), also indirectly promotes interlingual competence. (1988: 52, our translation)

The extent to which current British pedagogical theory in general lags behind this American and European work may be illustrated by citing two recent works, from Wringe (1989) and Pickering (1992). Both claim to give an overview of language teaching and both include cultural awareness as an integral part, but still in a somewhat tentative and ancillary mode. Pickering focuses on the content of a foreign language course (here upper secondary French) and suggests that criteria should be 'not only those of current interest within our own country, but those which are important to the French' but he then effectively refutes this by suggesting a list of supposedly student-orientated topics, none of which seems particularly French in orientation: 'we should look closely at what works and what does not, and try to include topics which do (or should) excite them [the students]: animal rights, ecology, discrimination, politics' (1992: 7). With no mention of cross-cultural comparison or difficulties in decoding other value systems, Pickering assumes that 'if the programme is balanced and varied and the source material authentic, it is probable that it will automatically give a good insight into the foreign culture'.

Wringe does recognise the existence of cross-cultural misunderstanding but phrases this in a way which makes it appear very unlikely:

> It would certainly be possible…to constantly be at cross-purposes with native speakers…if we had no understanding of their daily concerns or the way in which life in their countries is organised. (1989: 5)

The difficulties of acquiring such relativising techniques are not pursued and the implicit suggestion is that the channels for cultural communication are transparent with no inherent difficulties in understanding culturally encoded meanings:

> the aim [of modern language teaching] must be...to encourage the welcoming of unfamiliarity and accurate information and...the forming of balanced judgements on the basis of knowledge rather than prejudice or hostility. (1989: 19–20)

It is clear from this brief review that, although there are some indications of concern with theories of cultural learning, most theorists influential in foreign language teaching have not yet provided an adequately developed understanding on which practitioners can base their teaching. In the following section we have therefore decided to turn to general theories of psychological development, which might help theorists and practitioners alike to consider how teaching strategies can be linked to issues in attitude change, and moral and cognitive development.

Theories for the Classroom

Educational aims for language teaching in many education systems are based on assumptions that through learning a foreign language students will undergo some kind of mental change. The change may be cognitive or affective or both. Consider the following statement taken from French policy and curriculum documents:

> **German**
>
> *Nature and objectives*
>
> The objectives in the teaching of German are cultural, educational and linguistic.
>
> The teaching of German brings pupils into contact with the cultural facts particular to German-speaking countries. (...)
>
> The educational objective is closely linked to the cultural objective. The discovery of a number of works which are representative of German culture awakens pupils' intellectual curiosity and refines their sensitivity.
>
> Pupils' realisation of the diversity of cultures and the behaviours which are within them, allows them to accept differences more readily in a pluralist spirit. The teaching of German thus contributes to the development of judgement and reasoning.
>
> The linguistic objective of the teaching of German is to be found, first, in the acquisition of automatic control of a substantial number of characteristics of language. Once they are familiar with the learning process in the German language, pupils will be better armed to learn

other foreign languages. (Ministère de l'Éducation Nationale, 1985: 95–6, our translation)

In England and Wales, the advent of a National Curriculum has introduced an explicitness in statements of educational purposes which allows us to examine more closely the assumptions with which teachers have worked for many years. Now, instead of tacit agreements that language teaching should 'broaden pupils' horizons' and 'make them more tolerant', we have the following statements about the educational purposes of FLT:

- to offer insights into the culture and civilisation of the countries where the language is spoken;
- to encourage positive attitudes to foreign language learning and to speakers of foreign languages and a sympathetic approach to other cultures and civilisations. (DES, 1990: 3)

We shall return to the question of attitudes later and concentrate here on the implications of pupils' acquiring 'insights'. In the preparatory work for the National Curriculum, a Working Group was charged with producing a full discussion of language teaching and this remains a significant document, even though their recommendations underwent some change of detail as they became law. The Working Group introduced a new 'educational purpose' to those which had already been accepted in national policy documents, namely:

- to develop pupils' understanding of themselves and their own culture. (DES, 1990: 3)

This reflexivity was then carried through into their discussion of teaching and learning processes. Like others we shall discuss later, they propose a comparative methodology:

Learners should therefore have frequent opportunities to (...)

- appreciate the similarities and differences between their own and cultures of the communities/countries where the target language is spoken;
- identify with the experience and perspective of people in the countries and communities where the target language is spoken;
- use this knowledge to develop a more objective view of their own customs and ways of thinking. (DES, 1990: 36)

It would not have been appropriate for the Working Group to provide research evidence to support the assumptions within this statement but it is evident that their terminology takes much for granted. 'Appreciate similarities and differences', 'identify with' and 'develop a more objective view' beg a number of questions. What evidence is there that learners in the age-group 11 to 16 can in fact 'identify with' the experience and perspective of people from other countries? What stage of affective and attitudinal development should young people have reached before they can 'appreciate' similarities and differences? Should pupils be able to 'decentre', in order to be able to take 'a more objective view of their own customs and ways of thinking'? If the evidence suggests that, say, 11-year-old learners have not reached the necessary stage of development, should we have different aims for different age groups? It is clear from the final document defining the National Curriculum for Modern Foreign Languages that there is indeed a belief that older learners are different. For it is only 14 to 16-year-olds who are to be offered opportunities to 'investigate, discuss and report on aspects of the language and culture of these [target language] countries and communities' (DES, 1991: 26).

Cognitive and moral development

It will have been noticed that we have introduced into the discussion the vocabulary of developmental psychology and the notion that children and young people pass through specific 'stages'. Theorists and practitioners of language teaching have, however, been little concerned with the work of Piaget, Kohlberg and others. They have looked to psychology to explain the acquisition of knowledge and control of syntax, morphology and other aspects of grammar. Littlewood, McDonough and MacLaughlin, for example, make no reference to Piagetian or comparable psychology. Our own earlier volume referred only to work in the Vygotskian tradition. It is one of the merits of Melde's approach that she does draw upon developmental psychology and we shall return to this below.

Let us first consider how developmental psychology can help teachers of other subjects which aim to promote understanding of other people. One of the problems, pointed out by Langford (1987: 54) in his discussion of concept development in social science subjects, is that 'research has tended to concentrate on the pre-adolescent age-group'. In their work on young children's knowledge and understanding of places, Piaget & Weil (1951) postulate a model of understanding places and the paradox that, before acquiring an understanding of their own country, children must be able to 'decentre' and understand points of view different from their own. They are said to pass through three stages: 'egocentricity', in which their utterances about their own and other countries are arbitrary and based on momentary preferences; 'sociocentricity' in which they express opinions reflecting the views of their immediate social environment; 'reciprocity' when they can perceive others' views of themselves and that they themselves could be seen as 'foreigners'. This stage can be reached by age 10/11. This augurs well for language teachers who work with children from the beginning of lower secondary and would lend support to the assumptions identified earlier.

The revival of interest in Europe in the teaching of foreign languages in primary education also requires a consideration of young children's psychological development and the development of appropriate theories of cultural learning. Earlier attempts to introduce foreign language learning were founded on theories that linguistic learning could take place more readily in young children before they lost a certain flexibility and readiness (Penfield & Roberts, 1959; Lenneberg, 1967). There was little or no interest in cultural learning and children's perceptions of and attitudes towards foreign countries and cultures in the primary school period. In the evaluation of the teaching of French in primary schools, for example, the brief discussion of teachers' views of the objectives of French teaching only mentions that learning about 'France and its people' was thought to be appropriate for less able pupils (Burstall et al., 1974: 70). It was in a wider context of concern for international relations that UNESCO commissioned a survey of children's perceptions in the 1960s (Lambert & Klineberg, 1967) but there was no direct link made with the role of language learning in preparing children for life in an international world. Similarly, the current revival of language teaching in the primary school does not appear to have sought to establish a firm psychological foundation for introducing young children to other cultures through learning a foreign language.

It is therefore useful to turn to work in other disciplines. Wiegand (1992), a geographer, takes as his starting point the Piaget & Weil theory of three stages but points out that there have been criticisms of Piaget's methods. He takes the discussion further in his account of how primary school children understand space and place and their sense of their own national identity and national symbols. Young children have difficulty with relationships between geographical units. The realisation is not immediate that there is a 'nesting' arrangement in which towns are within counties, which in turn are within countries, which are also within continents etc. Conceptions of the shape of the earth include 'flat-earth' theories, and others that maintain that 'the Earth is a huge ball made up of two hemispheres. People live *inside* this ball on the flat planar surface of the lower hemisphere' (Wiegand, 1992: 45)

Wiegand also summarises research on young children's sense of their own national identity, some of which involves elaborations of a number of stages. In his summary table, he concentrates on this aspect of development rather than perceptions of foreigners, but it is important for language teachers to know that their pupils are still very much in the process of acquiring 'adult' perceptions of themselves and their country.

Table 1.1 (from Wiegand, 1992: 54)

Generalised 'level of development'	Children are generally found to:
I(age 6–8)	have no understanding of part-whole relationships (for example, Glasgow–Scotland–Britain) and prefer their own country but for no rational reason
II(age 7–9)	have imperfect understanding of part-whole relationships, and prefer their own country for family and 'immediate social' reasons
III(age 9–11)	understand part-whole relationships, prefer their own country by reference to collective ideals and recognize and understand the significance of national symbols

Furthermore, given the elasticity of the postulated stages, the recognition that the ages cited are not universally applicable and that shift from one stage to another is not sudden and without 'slippage' back into earlier stages, language teachers need to be aware that their younger pupils may not have a fully developed conception of the country whose language they are learning. We shall return to this in our discussion of children's attitudes below.

What is clearly lacking in this research, and of particular interest to language teachers, is some account of how young children understand what it is to speak a foreign language. Our own research provides some insight into what primary school children expect foreign language learning to consist of when they move into secondary education. In interviews with children in the final year of primary school, we asked about their expectations of the new subject they would learn in secondary school, 'French'. They had views on what it would be like to hear and speak French, on why one should learn French, on why girls are better at French than boys, and so on. We then compared these with the views of children who had been learning French for three years in the same schools which our primary pupils were expecting to attend. It is clear that pupils come to foreign language learning with detailed expectations, often promoted by the accounts of older siblings, and that language teachers need to take these into account (Byram & Esarte-Sarries, 1991: 70–96).

Turning now to secondary-age children, we might expect, as language-and-culture teachers, to find common interests with those subjects where children and young people are asked to study social issues and the lives of other people. If language learners are to gain some insight into foreign cultures and countries, and some understanding of foreign people's viewpoints, there might be comparable teaching and learning processes in the social sciences and humanities. The study of history, in particular, in which students need to understand the culture of a different age, is at least superficially similar to the study of the culture of a different place.

In his review of 'concept development' in the secondary school, which not surprisingly does not include any reference to foreign language learning, Langford (1987) suggests three aspects of adolescent thinking which can be said to represent something new. Two are mathematical or scientific — the acceptance of ideal entities and the notion of a function — and one is more general: 'in the area of schematic organisation of knowledge...thinking becomes more systematic' (p. 7), on which however there is little research. He takes the general view that Piagetian theory should not be applied mechanically to the learning of mental models or subject content, and this is worth bearing in mind when language teachers propose an image of a foreign culture or, as we suggested in an earlier volume, introduce learners to experience which changes their schemata, their modes of conceptualising foreign cultures and their own (Byram, 1989: 102ff).

Reviewing research on social cognition, Langford turns first to Kohlberg's, and others' work on moral development and social thinking. He identifies several traditions of research which might be helpful to social science teachers. They need a knowledge of the different stages of moral development postulated by Kohlberg, and an awareness of the possibility that individuals are not 'fixed' in any given stage at a particular age. In particular Elleund's proposal (cited in Langford, 1987: 39) that adolescent social cognition may be still egocentric and entertain notions of personal uniqueness and indestructibility may temper teachers' views of adolescents as young adults with a well-developed understanding of others' viewpoints. This also suggests that the optimistic Piagetian view of the young secondary-school pupil reaching a stage of 'reciprocity' and being able to 'decentre' has to be treated with care.

One of Langford's and others' concerns is to consider how psychological theory can help teachers to formulate appropriate methods. Rest (1979: 211–22) has suggested a number of factors and techniques which might be used. He discusses experimental intervention studies with various kinds of short-term treatments and concludes that these lead to very little measurable change. In reviewing studies of correlations between different kinds of experience and moral development — for example, discussion of controversial problems, the assumption of new responsibilities for taking care of others, 'broadening experiences' like travel, art, reading, or meeting new people who have a drastically different perspective — he concludes that there is much speculation and little longitudinal evidence. It is however at least noteworthy that travel and confrontation with different perspectives are considered potentially useful.

The question which arises for foreign language teachers is whether they should take active steps to promote moral and social development. Certainly for teachers wedded to using the foreign language exclusively in their classroom, the notion of 'discussion' with young learners in the early stages of foreign language learning seems out of the question. It may be argued that, within the classroom, teachers have to concern themselves with promoting experiential learning intended to challenge learners' existing concepts and perceptions, their existing schemata. Similarly, one might argue that an organised visit, or 'fieldwork', in the foreign country should be above all experiential. There is however a danger of self-imposed limitations reducing the opportunities for purposeful teaching if teacher–pupil interaction has to be solely in the foreign language. We shall return to this issue later.

It is appropriate to acknowledge at this point that developmental psychological theory is much debated and highly contentious. Piaget's work has excited both consensus and controversy (Modgil & Modgil, 1982). Kohlberg has also been criticised from a number of perspectives — including a feminist one — and has provided some responses (Kohlberg, Levine & Hewer, 1983). Language teachers are as familiar as others with this kind of situation with respect to language learning theories. There is equal danger in accepting the 'certainty' of a simplified version of complex and continually developing theory and total rejection of theory because it offers no simple solutions. The notion of 'stages' of development has perhaps been over-exposed and should be approached as a heuristic tool rather than a dogmatic categorisation of children's development. Despite these difficulties, the stimulation of thinking about foreign language learning in the context of general development is worthwhile.

Melde (1987) and Baumgratz-Gangl (1990) appear to be the only theorists of foreign language learning who have given serious attention to developmental psychology. Melde does so from within a philosophical framework — based on the writings of Habermas — which requires that foreign language teaching, as part of general education, should create in learners a 'critical awareness' (*kritisches Bewußtsein*) of social life. This means that though she sees the attainment of a Piagetian stage of formal operational thinking as a necessary condition for such awareness, it is not sufficient (Melde, 1987: 127ff). Thinking at this level has to be given direction, towards a critical rather than a conservative awareness. When the individual acquires a capacity for understanding the perspectives of others and reflecting on his/her own perspectives, through a process of decentring and a level of reciprocity, there arises a moral dimension, a judgmental tendency, which is not defined purely on formal, logical grounds.

She turns therefore to Kohlberg and to Habermas's reflections on Kohlberg. Since she is ultimately concerned with the teaching of French as a second foreign language in Germany — therefore with students in the age-range 12–20 — she assumes that both formal and concrete operational thinking will be represented in most classes and, similarly, that all three major stages of moral thinking defined by Kohlberg will be present among students. She argues however, with Habermas, that the most developed moral thinking is dependent on learners moving from a capacity for communicative action to a reflexive stage of discourse and a capacity for argumentation (p. 133). Let it be noted in passing that this appears to correspond to the requirement in the English and Welsh National Curriculum, cited above, that discussion should be delayed until pupils are aged 14–16 years.

The first conclusion Melde draws from her discussion of developmental psychology is consistent with her philosophy but raises some concern. For in her summary (pp. 149–50) she states that the attainment of the stage of formal-operational thinking is a prerequisite for the development of a critical social awareness. There is evidence however that 'a majority of (British) adolescents have concrete — whilst only a minority have formal — operational abilities' (Shayer & Adey, 1981, cited in Smith, 1986). On the other hand Tamburrini (1982: 322), in a review of the educational implications of Piaget's theory argues that 'formal operational thinking is contextually bound and that differences in levels of functioning are of intra-individual as well as inter-individual kinds'. In this situation, what role is there for language and culture teaching? Melde's answer is implied in her recommendations that language and culture teaching must find means of encouraging the shift to formal-operational thinking — and to higher levels of moral development — through the process of decentring. This, she says, is central to language teaching for it provides the link with communication. Through acquiring communicative ability in a foreign language and culture, learners are brought into contact with other people's perspectives:

> Bearing in mind the age of our pupils, subject-specific teaching must be so structured that, from a cognitive point of view, it stimulates the transition from the concrete-operational to the formal-operational stage of development and offers sufficient opportunities to apply and practice formal thinking on subject-specific contents, in order to guar-

antee a secure anchoring. Simultaneously, with respect to moral development, it has to support the process of decentering and co-ordination of perspectives so that an optimal development of moral consciousness is guaranteed. This process should be at the centre of foreign language teaching, for this offers the link we seek between communicative skill and critical social awareness. Foreign language communication skill can thus not be reduced to a 'language competence'. (Melde, 1987: 151, our translation)

This then is Melde's answer to the question posed earlier. It is indeed the task of the teacher of language and culture actively to stimulate cognitive and moral development. This can be done through methods which involve active learning — for example through role-play and simulation — and above all confrontation with the values and meanings present in the viewpoint of a foreign interlocutor. In particular, learners need to take the role of the foreign interlocutor in simulations of confrontations in order to develop that higher level of discourse and argumentation from which higher moral development can take place. These recommendations represent, in the German tradition of language teaching, a rejection of the mere provision of information about institutions. Melde nonetheless recognises the need for knowledge of the foreign culture so that learners can understand the assumed values and meanings which his/her interlocutor has acquired from and shares with the society to which he/she belongs.

Excellent though Melde's work is, her use of highly abstract theory — particularly Habermas — and her rapid dismissal of language learning theory as a source of understanding cultural learning lead her to neglect the detail of the linguistic dimension of decentering and shift of perspective. For, although she points to the interdependence between communication in a foreign language and critical social awareness, she does not give sufficient attention to the relationship between acquisition of the structures and vocabulary of a foreign language and the learner's capacity to take the perspective of a foreign interlocutor. She accepts Piaget's view that there is no structural difference betweeen perception and evaluation of one's own society and of foreign societies (Melde, 1987: 150). Whatever the merits of this at a structural level, the means by which individuals decentre and perceive other perspectives in the foreign language classroom are specific and depend on the acquisition of a new language which duplicates but does not replicate the means of conceptualising and referring to the social and physical world available in learners' language(s).

This was our argument in an earlier volume (Byram, 1989: 103ff), based in part on Vygotsky's view that children internalise an existing socially-shared perception of the world as they acquire language. We argued there that language learning can bring experience which produces modifications of existing culture-specific schemata acquired by children through their first language. The confrontation and argumentation, to use Melde's terminology, with another culture in the person(s) of foreign interlocutor(s) requires a re-ordering of perceptions at a level of socialisation which is structurally different from primary and secondary socialisation. It is no doubt also possible for learners to encode many but not all of their existing schemata in another language but in that case they are not learning a new language but a new code. It is if and when they recognise that the foreign language embodies a different set of beliefs, values and shared meanings, that they begin the shift of perspective which leads to reciprocity and reflection on both others and self.

Baumgratz-Gangl (1990: 103ff) also argues that language learning, and especially the acquisition of specific meanings, is closely related to shift of perspective and understanding of a foreign culture and society. She suggests that, for example, *Schule/école, Mann/homme, Frau/femme, Partei/parti, Umwelt/environnement* are in lexical terms equivalents, but only at a high level of generalisation. In the reality of daily use such words have very particular constellations of meaning binding them to a particular time and place in a specific country. It is therefore all the more important that a differentiation of the concepts in the native and foreign language should be made. She suggests that this should be done through conscious comparison.

Baumgratz-Gangl goes on to suggest that, when learners have integrated new meanings into their consciousness through comparative methods, there follows a neutralisation of negative emotions through recognition of cognitive dissonance. This corresponds to the reduction of aggression in interpersonal relationships as learners recognise the justification of another viewpoint and consciously draw back from their own as an absolute. We shall return to the question of the relationship between language learning and attitude-formation below.

We suspect that Melde would agree with this view of the detail of the relationship between communicative ability and awareness of others and self. The question arises, however, as to whether learners must first attain a stage of formal operational thinking before they can reflect upon this experience. Melde's argument would no doubt be that it is only at this level, and through the direction given in stimulating moral development, that that awareness can become critical and fully conscious. Should learners not reach a formal operations stage, however, our interpretation of the *experience* of language learning — and our model of language and culture learning proposes the inclusion of 'cultural experience' (Byram, 1989: 137ff)

— suggests that there is still considerable educational value in language and culture teaching. In order to recognise the significance of this educational role, we coined the term 'tertiary socialisation' (Byram, 1989b: 5) as an extension of our discussion of the role of the first language in primary and secondary socialisation and the generation of new schemata through foreign language learning (Byram, 1989b: 113).

Another perspective is offered by our earlier suggestion that, of other subjects in the school curriculum, there appears to be most similarity between language and culture teaching and history teaching. There has been considerable debate within the teaching of history about the development of learners' 'empathy' with other historical periods. This has not been related directly to stages of developmental psychology, and there are clearly divergences, too, in the emphasis in language and culture teaching on experiential learning and communicative interaction with members of another culture. There is nonetheless some value in analysing the notion of 'empathy' and its possible use as a theoretical concept with which to clarify our understanding of culture learning.

Empathy

We saw above that in the English and Welsh National Curriculum it is intended that learners should 'identify with the experience and perspective of people in the countries and communities where the target language is spoken'. Superficially at least, this is comparable to identifying with the experience and perspective of people of another age. In the teaching of history, the notion of 'empathy' has been much debated and may throw some light on what 'identifying with the experience and perspectives of (foreign) people' could mean for language teachers. It is also the case that 'empathy' is a key concept in social training or therapy. Eisenberg and Strayer suggest a desired link with prosocial behaviour although this is by no means automatic:

> One reason for the considerable interest in empathy and related constructs is the assumption of many psychologists and philosophers that empathy (or sympathy) mediates prosocial behavior...[but] the relation between empathy and prosocial behavior is neither direct nor inevitable. (1987: 10–11)

'Empathy' is a comparatively new term in the English language (appearing only after 1928 in the OED); it seems to be interpreted differently according to the context in which it arises and may on occasion be identified with 'sympathy' or 'imagination'. Generally, though, the notion of 'placing oneself in someone else's shoes' represents the overall desired aim. The desired results or purpose of encouraging empathy also seem to vary according to context.

Looking firstly at *who* is involved in the empathetic process, there is an important distinction to be drawn between the student operating on a personal, interactional level, and operating in a pedagogical situation. Clearly in social and therapy training, the emphasis is on personal inter-action and the interpretation of physical, non-linguistic and linguistic cues, in order to understand other interactants. In history teaching there is no such personal interaction, but rather a combination of cognitive skills in understanding certain contexts, together with the affective demands of imagining oneself operating in those contexts. In the teaching of language and culture there can be an amalgamation of the two: the possibilities of personal contact with those from another culture and the observational training that is necessary to decode and understand that contact as fully as possible, plus the need to understand the overall cultural context within which an individual operates, and the imagination that is necessary to transcend cultural boundaries in order to achieve this understanding.

It is perhaps useful to outline four elements needed for empathetic understanding, since not all four are present to the same degree in the three different disciplines. In order to empathise with another individual one needs to take into account personality, situation, social groups and national identity. In social training it is likely to be the first three factors which are most important, with perhaps personality the key factor in the interaction; in history teaching, personality is likely to feature less, since this can be the least identifiable feature. Even though it may be colourful to speculate on the moods of certain historical characters, the aim of historical empathy is the understanding of the range of possibilities that would have been available to individuals in certain contexts; here situation is of prime importance. In teaching language and culture, social and national groups claim more attention, because the discipline focuses on inter-group com-munication, although clearly in any context personality and situation will also be influential. In trying to place oneself in the situation of another there are thus likely to be differences in emphasis according to the context and the level of personal or professional involvement of the participants.

The other important factors in considering who is involved in empathetic process are the age, gender, ethnicity and regionality of the participants. This can be seen to operate on two levels: choice of material and visibility of ability to empathise. The first factor does not apply to social training where the process involves personal interaction. In teaching history and language and culture though, some process of topic selection, for empa-thetic treatment by the teacher, is necessary and here the ethnic and gender identity of the class may be considered. Certain topics may be avoided because they do not seem to relate immediately to the students, whilst others may be chosen for that very reason. Opinion seems divided as to which course is the most beneficial here. Historians such as Gard & Lee for example criticise exclusive emphasis on local history. 'Evidence for local history is not necessarily easier for the pupil to understand as evidence, than that for national or foreign history…it may be that younger pupils' interest is aroused just as well by historical situations remote from their own experience' (1978: 35). Partington, on the other hand, warns against the danger of assuming that a 'national history is more relevant to the needs of citizens', since such citizens are likely to belong to different cultural groups with differing roles within that history, reminding us that 'heritages are not shared unambiguously' (1980: 125–6). Earlier Partington also rejects the 'familiarity and unfamiliarity' axis as a selection criterion since 'such relevance referenced claims are of little help in determining content' (1980: 115).

In the teaching of language and culture, as in the teaching of history, it seems likely that a middle course needs to be steered where some account of student interest is taken, but without distorting important content criteria within the discipline itself. Even within a discipline, judicious discrimination is needed to select truly representative areas (cf. Partington's comments on the 'significant' (1980: 100–3)) and not to be restricted to traditional areas of focus. Barker for example suggests rethinking the usual divisions in the history syllabus:

> The traditional criteria for selecting subject matter (e.g. period, reign) have been too insensitive to their own context to assist in the choice of events for study. A more promising possibility is for teachers to construct their own patterns or concepts, selecting events, topics or themes likely to communicate the variety and significance of human experience in the past. (1978: 123)

In teaching language and culture some recent areas of focus in Britain have reflected the tourist's outsider experience of a culture: food, places and buildings of historical interest, historical personalities etc. In order to empathise more closely with natives of a particular culture these should be replaced by topics that relate more directly to individuals' experiences within that culture: the home, the workplace, the social norms and expectations.

Another key factor is gender. In social training experiments it has been shown that female participants display a higher degree of empathy than males. Bryant in her overview of empathy testing shows that gender is a much more discriminating factor than age (1987: 250). In testing cultural

attitudes too, where a degree of empathetic transference is involved, classroom tests revealed a higher level of awareness amongst girls (Byram,
Esarte-Sarries & Taylor, 1990: 166–8). However these differences may be a
question of voiced rather than actual opinion. In commenting on the use of
self-reported levels of empathy, Batson notes that males often report less of
either empathy or empathy-related personal distress but believes this may
be misleading.

> That this sex difference is due at least in part to self-presentation
> concerns and not to sex differences in emotional experience is sug-
> gested by the fact that these sex differences tend to disappear when one
> takes less obtrusive, physiological and facial expression measures of
> emotion. (1987: 359)

The suggestion here then is that empathy is not as gender-discriminated as
is generally thought, but that perhaps particular kinds of testing are necessary in order to reveal its presence amongst male participants.

In both history and language and culture teaching, the teacher is important on two levels in the development of empathy: both as a model and as
a source of information. Portal singles out the importance of the teacher's
attitudes in determining the level of pupils' commitment to empathy as a
valid exercise:

> History teachers are often, perhaps as a result of their own training,
> unduly modest about their own powers of imagination. It is hardly
> surprising if pupils dismiss as marginal frills the responses that teach-
> ers seldom employ orally or demonstrate to the class. (1983: 308)

Clearly the teacher's own approach will set the tenor of the classroom but
it also seems likely that a more modest role in terms of opinion or informa-
tion-provision can promote higher levels of input from the students. Conclusions drawn by Dickinson & Lee after classroom observation of group
empathy exercises showed that pupils attempt more away from direct
teacher influence:

> Pupils...seem more willing to articulate problems and seek clarification
> of difficult points from their peers than from their teachers. (1984: 148)

When one moves on to what exactly is involved in the teaching of
empathy, then it is clear that, although the terminology may be comparatively new, the process of anticipating and understanding the behaviour of
others is something which is engaged in from a very early age. Hofmann
in his survey of social and physical cognition shows that anticipating
behaviour is a far more difficult process than understanding, based as it is
on probabilities. However it is more deeply ingrained and focal because of
the constant corrective feedback received by the child (1981: 67–70). He cites

examples of even very small children adjusting their behaviour to the cues of others, in other words demonstrating a form of empathetic awareness in recognising the otherness of others (1981: 71–2). Sutherland, in her overview of the problems of empathy in education, points up the recognition of the limits of empathetic understanding, familiar in such cases as the inappropriate birthday or Christmas present (1986: 149). In teaching empathy therefore, one is not treading on virgin soil. It is likely that pupils will understand some of the process and limits of empathy even though these may be at an unconscious and unnamed level.

Let us now consider more closely empathetic processes: what levels of cognition and affect are involved and how empathy relates to sympathy and imagination. There is often conflation of the terms 'empathy' and 'sympathy' and the Working Party on the National Curriculum for England and Wales, for example, use the phrase 'a sympathetic approach'. Eisenberg & Miller draw attention to the difference between empathy and sympathy in terms of an identification process: 'sympathy (…) that is not identical to the other's emotion (…) empathy (…) the apprehension of another's emotional state or condition and that is congruent with it' (1987: 292). In practice though in their own report on empathy and altruism they conflate the two since their interest is in 'empathic concern (i.e. sympathy)' (1987: 300). The degree of identification is perhaps less important than the level of emotional involvement and/or approval. Sympathy *for* someone is generally interpreted as synonymous with compassion and limited to situations of personal suffering (see Sutherland, 1986: 147). Sympathising *with* someone extends to a wider emotional and cognitive frame where someone's thoughts and views are recognised as appropriate in a particular situation (see Lee, 1978: 97).

If we translate this process to the cognitive level of understanding (for example, of an historical period) then the altruistic–egoistic differentiation becomes redundant. It is replaced by a scholarly and scrupulous desire for professional validity: that the subject under scrutiny should be seen as clearly as possible for what it is, with the minimum distortion from the students' local and twentieth century perceptions. In this context 'sympathy' may be positively damaging since it can suggest too close an emotional identification: 'identification and even sympathy are signs of partiality, lack of detachment, or just plain bias' (Lee, 1984: 98). Critical distance is necessary in empathetic understanding of an historical period.

In the teaching of language and culture, both the personal and the scholarly come together. The sympathetic understanding of others' feelings and perspectives are necessary in personal contact with individuals from other cultures. Critical perspicacity and a neutral empathetic construction of cultural norms is necessary to appreciate the relevant cultural context.

It is also important to clarify the relationship of 'empathy' to 'imagination', a source of much debate in the teaching of history. Clearly to put oneself in someone else's shoes does require imagination, and in social encounters it could be argued that by using the information gained in the contact with other individuals this is what is happening in an empathetic process. However, in the context of history teaching, 'imagination' does not necessarily mean free-ranging creative flights of fancy inspired by such examination questions as 'Imagine you are a...'. This kind of 'imagining' is criticised for producing descriptive rather than empathetic processes (see for example Southern Examining Group, 1988). 'Imagination' can be classified in three different ways: as creative freedom, as informed supposition, and as vivid presentation. Lee indicates similar categorisation in his investigation of historical imagination, noting particularly the divergence between the creative activity found in the arts and the imaginative processes useful in history.

> In central cases of historical imagination the latter must be tied to evidence in some way, and so in history imagination cannot be creative in the same way as in literature, painting or music. (1984: 85–6)

Clearly creative initiatives can engage pupils' attention and involvement, allowing them to feel that they contribute to the learning process, but weighed against this is the problem of the resources which fuel this kind of activity. In free expressive writing, painting or composing, the student will draw on his or her own experiences as resources. In historical and cultural learning, it is crucial that the pupil attempts to transfer into different contexts and tries to imagine what it would be like to be someone different. Personal experience and observations of others obviously contribute to this transference but it will also be necessary to furnish a considerable amount of structured information to allow students to recognise the differences in context. 'Informed supposition' more closely reflects the kind of process desirable in the teaching of history and of language and culture.

Running below the processes of personal empathetic interaction and more scholarly empathetic interpretation of historical and cultural contexts are the two strands of the cognitive and the affective. Empathy is generally presented as a process of *feeling*, with some uncertainty as to the cognitive content of this process. Sutherland indicates some of the elements of this uneasy marriage:

> Can empathy as cognitive awareness count as true empathy? (...) the intrusion of cognitive data may so easily reduce or destroy the emo-

tional involvement in the situation. Yet the cognitive element must be recognised. (1986: 148, 150)

It would seem plausible that in the area of personal interaction and social training, the training and education necessary is of an emotional nature, and that in the areas of history, and language and culture the focus of learning is cognitive. However the new initiatives in history teaching to introduce a more imaginative or emotional dimension, with examination questions involving empathy, postulate an enhancement of the cognitive through the affective.

Experiments by Natale with extra-mural university students however demonstrated the reverse. By teaching a course in two different ways, Natale found that students given specific training in critical thinking (i.e. in refining their cognitive skills) were able to respond more empathetically to others than students in control group following a more 'normal' course (1972: 68). Mutual benefit therefore accrues from the concurrent operation of the cognitive and the affective, and thus empathy in all disciplines will sensibly involve a combination of the two.

There are however some cognitive processes which can frustrate the development of empathetic understanding. There may be a desire to regularise the specific subject under scrutiny according to general principles or laws. Thus in a social encounter participants may feel that the other protagonist is just another example of a particular group already encountered (a dogmatic teacher, an aggressive German, a bored housewife etc.). This can operate whether the encounter is within a culture or across cultures. On a broader scale, when interpreting situations or events, a similar kind of supposition can be made: that the particular belongs to a general or 'covering' law (see Lee, 1978: 73–4). This stereotyping or paralleling of information into manageable categories, although clearly of use for general understanding, needs some dismantling in order for the specificity of the particular and the role of the accidental to be recognised. Most damaging here is the dismissing of actions or people as inferior because of lack of understanding or differentiation: 'They believed those things because they were thick/stupid/a bunch of dimmos' (Shemilt, 1984: 76). Although these statements were offered as explanations for a historical phenomenon (in this case the putative healing power of the monarch in the thirteenth century), cross-cultural stereotypes are liable to operate in a similar way in foreign language teaching.

We have thus returned to one of the widely-held beliefs about foreign language teaching, namely that by giving learners greater insight into another way of life, there will be a reduction of simplification and stereotyping. This is usually thought of in terms of negative or derogatory stereotypes and we have seen already that there can be no separation of insight and attitude, of the cognitive and the affective. It is nonetheless worthwhile to turn in our next section to a closer focus on attitudes.

Attitudes

The relationship between attitudes and knowledge, between affective and cognitive aspects of young people's development is a complex one at the very heart of language and culture teaching. Referring again to the English and Welsh National Curriculum, we saw above that the Working Party, and others before them, believe the educational purposes should include developing positive attitudes, as well as providing knowledge and insight. These are however simply part of a list of items whose relationship is not discussed.

As we have seen in the previous section, research suggests that a relationship does exist between attitudes, insight and knowledge, but whether it is a causal one and, if so, in which direction, is far more difficult to ascertain. The research with respect to younger children is reviewed by Wiegand who reminds us that:

> in the primary school we are dealing as much with attitude formation as attitude change. Before learning about other countries many children are neither positively or (sic) negatively disposed towards those countries. They simply haven't thought much about them at all and don't have any clearly developed view. (1992: 55)

After reviewing the relevant research for primary school children Wiegand concludes that the intimate relationship between cognitive and affective aspects of understanding of distant people and places imposes certain limitations on Piagetian theory that children proceed through to a stage of reciprocity allowing them to adopt others' points of view. Likes and preferences may prevent them adopting some viewpoints and encourage them to adopt others. We can only speculate on the relationship of attitudes to stages of moral development, which Wiegand does not consider, but it is certainly reasonable to assume a similar complex relationship. Wiegand again provides a useful summary of levels of development of evaluative ideas about distant people and places in the primary schoolchild.

Wiegand also cites evidence that there is a 'downward curve in international and interracial goodwill' during adolescence, due in part to the adoption of prevailing adult stereotypes (Carnie, 1972, cited in Wiegand, 1992: 57). This suggests then that there is indeed a need to 'encourage positive attitudes' through language and culture teaching and is clearly of significance for language teachers in primary education. They may have an advantage over their colleagues in secondary schools teaching children

Table 1.2 (from Wiegand, 1992: 58)

Generalised 'level of development'	Children generally found to:
I(age 6–8)	select 'favourite countries' on the basis of exotic features; stress differences between themselves and foreigners; deny that they themselves could become foreigners.
II(age 7–9)	select 'favourite countries' on the basis of stereotypes; have an imperfect understanding of the concept 'foreigner'.
III(age 9–10)	accept more similarities between themselves and other peoples; are increasingly able to see the point of view of other peoples; understand that foreigners are people out of their own country.

who are likely to be acquiring more negative attitudes precisely at the point when they are being encouraged to be positive.

The distinction between forming and changing attitudes, though appropriate to the primary school, becomes more confused in the secondary school. What evidence is there, then, that teachers can in fact influence attitudes? The research reviewed in our earlier section in the field of psychology and modern languages has tended to focus on the cognitive and affective problems of *language* learning rather than the acquisition of cultural understanding and positive attitudes. More recent works have shown how language learning theories may be extended and modified to incorporate cultural learning theories (Byram, 1989) and how cultural learning can involve processes of an entirely different kind (Valdes, 1986; Robinson, 1988). This research, however, does not fully examine the implications of notions of attitude and belief and how these are affected in the process of cultural learning. In order for a language teacher to assess the options which are available, it is necessary to identify the factors which are influential in forming and changing attitudes, and to consider the results of research on attitude on a broader front.

Although originally the term 'attitude' referred to the disposition of the body, it is now chiefly used for behaviour, feeling and thought ('settled behaviour or manner of acting as representative of feeling or opinion; *attitude of mind*: deliberately adopted of habitual mode of regarding the object of thought' OED). This disposition, whether mental or emotional, is generally thought of in terms of an evaluative scale: the 'positive attitudes', urged upon us by the report on language teaching cited earlier, set against counterbalancing negative attitudes, with some area of neutrality between the two extremes.

Allport, in his work on prejudice, goes even further, suggesting a tripartite categorisation of attitudes (in this case towards racial issues), which is integrated with different character-structures. He identifies the following types:

> the individual...[whose] attitudes are flexible...and...friendly...the second class of attitudes is...self-serving, rigid, sometimes neurotic...finally and frequently we find the ethnic attitudes of many individuals lack internal integration. They are shifting and amorphous and for the most part are linked to the immediate situation. (1979: 505)

If we accept Allport's suggestion that the second category of attitudes is virtually ineradicable ('nothing short of upheaval in the character structure will change them', 1979: 505), then the role of the language teacher seems to be to encourage positive acceptance of other cultures with the first group, to accept as inevitable the negativity of the second group and to concentrate on encouraging positive attitudes amongst the third more ambivalent category. There is a danger however that premature attribution of learners to the second group will exclude them and categorise them as 'uninfluenceable'.

Research evidence shows that there are several dimensions of teaching and learning which can have influence on attitudes. Hovland & Weiss (1951) illustrated the value of credibility in the communicator. The more credible the presenter, the more acceptable was the message. However the beneficial effects of high credibility messages could decrease in impact over time and that of low-credibility could increase, producing the so-called 'sleeper effect'. The initial influence of credibility could also be reinstated by reminding the audience of the communicator. Here, familiar aspects of pedagogical practice are evident: the teacher as a source of knowledge has to be thoroughly prepared and credible in learners' eyes.

Other experiments have shown the importance of the attractiveness of the communicator. In American college groups, altering the appearance of a female student to make her more or less attractive was shown to have a significant effect on her persuasiveness (Mills & Aronson, 1965). In a teaching context, although pupils and teachers both live in an environment where attractive presentation is accepted as the norm for 'selling' a product, there is perhaps some unease in directly transferring such an affective-orientated approach into the classroom. However, the visual impact of the teacher should not be underestimated, and indeed we find exhortations to exploit one's personality in textbooks on language teaching:

[the teacher] should have something which will engage the class, he must have a strong personality and...students should be susceptible to the fascination of that personality. Furthermore he must manifest this personality in the best possible way, thus controlling the class through personal impact... (Leontiev, 1981: 119)

As well as credibility and attractiveness, an atmosphere of security was also seen to help change attitudes. Announcing intentions in a non-threatening way was found to reap beneficial rewards. Observations of these techniques as used by fundamentalist preachers showed positive results (Hass, 1975). Translated into classroom terms for the language teacher, to announce and explain what is to be taught may help to influence the attitudes of the pupils involved.

A second dimension is the consequences of the message itself. Messages which arouse fear in the audience have been shown to alter attitudes (for example, towards Communist China, atom bomb testing and capital punishment — see Leventhal's review of 1970), although this is not the case in all experiments (see Janis & Feshbach (1953) on dental hygiene). Positive attitudes can conversely be encouraged by making an audience believe that something will be useful to them (see Carlson, 1956). Clearly in a liberal pedagogical climate, methods involving threats or fear-creating situations are unacceptable, although undoubtedly the commanding presence of some teachers can still exert this kind of influence on some pupils. Utility on the other hand is readily welcomed. In a foreign language context in Britain for example, cultural understanding and linguistic competence could be shown to have an instrumental purpose in terms of career prospects in an extended European market. Work on the influence of 'integrative' and 'instrumental' factors in language learning has been carried out, linking achievement with such factors (McDonough, 1981; Ansubal, 1968; Hermann, 1990) but, as McDonough points out, the link between the two can be somewhat ambivalent: '[such motivation] could have been the result and not the cause of successful progress' (McDonough, 1981: 153; this point is dealt with in more detail below).

Experiments which enhance the presentation of the environment, in which communication takes place with, for example, the use of humour and even refreshment showed an increased likelihood of changing attitudes (see Windes (1961) on forms of presidential campaigns and Janis, Kaye & Kirschner (1965) on the beneficial effects of eating and drinking while trying to bring about attitude change). Recent teaching methods such as Suggestopedia would endorse these notions of influential atmospheric factors, although teachers may experience some institutional resistance to the actualisation of the 'circle of upholstered armchairs...light comfortable room…tastefully furnished…and…famous cup of coffee' recommended by Leontiev (1981: 122). There is, however, some sense in which the teaching of, for example, French culture, can be enhanced by an appropriate background atmosphere in the classroom (Byram, Esarte-Sarries & Taylor, 1991: 35ff). There are also opportunities for cross-curricular links when language teachers join forces, for example, with Home Economics teachers to give learners the chance to cook and eat food from the country in question.

It is clear then that many of the strategies suggested by psychologists as influential in inducing attitude change are already present in the canon of language teaching methodology, and experience shows that attention to details of presentation usually reaps considerable rewards in terms of audience reaction. However, the general impression created by the findings of these experiments may seem quite alien to the kinds of norms generally accepted in education, indeed the term 'persuasion' which features frequently in these psychological studies, encapsulates the ethical problems which are apparent here. Clearly, encouraging positive attitudes can be seen as desirable, but when this is interpreted as a kind of brainwashing or indoctrination by covert means, then this seems difficult to accept. The focus in the majority of these factors is not on what is being said, which could be seen as the cognitive component of the teaching, but rather on the more generalised ambience of the classroom, relating to the affective response of the pupils. It is perhaps when the focus is exclusively on the affective that teachers will experience unease.

This emphasis on persuasion raises the underlying issue, usually left undebated among language teachers: the ethics of positing an educational purpose of 'encouraging positive attitudes'. It is usually taken for granted that this is an acceptable purpose, perhaps because 'positive attitudes' are so self-evidently good and because 'encourage' does not necessarily imply that attitudes should be changed. It can simply mean that existing positive attitudes are further nurtured in and through language and culture learning. It is likely, however, that many teachers do hope that neutral and negative attitudes will be changed, although they perhaps see this as a corollary of language learning rather than an effect they can bring about by direct influence. Indeed the factors we have analysed so far are likely to have an indirect influence.

The question nonetheless arises as to whether teachers of language and culture do wish to have a direct influence. If so, it is through the cognitive dimension that they have greatest control over the 'message' they wish to convey. As pointed out already, the relationship between the cognitive and the affective is a complex one when measured in terms of outcomes.

In terms of 'input' Petty & Cacioppo point to another important aspect of attitude change, namely the level of involvement of the participant, and draw a useful distinction between different types of communication: the 'central route' and the 'peripheral route'. Two important factors are identified here: firstly, that the information being transmitted is seen differently in each case, and secondly, that this relates to the involvement of the listener. The central route involves attention and cognitive commitment: 'a person's careful and thoughtful consideration of the merits of the information'; the peripheral route is more likely to appeal to the affective and to the inattentive: 'some simple cue in the persuasion context (e.g. an attractive source) that induced change without necessitating scrutiny of the merits of the information presented' (1986: 125).

As we saw earlier, the presentation of information in a particular way has certain effects on a listener's affective response. If the formal aspect of the *message itself* is considered, then we have a cognitive rather than an emotional response. Experiments carried out by Hovland and others looked at the effectiveness of different kinds of argument to persuade troops to continue fighting. They differentiated between one-sided arguments, where only positive facts were presented, and two-sided arguments where opposing facts were also included (Hovland, Lumsdaine & Sheffield, 1949). Results showed that the influence of the different kinds of argument depended on the educational level of the listener: the more educated were influenced by two-sided messages, the less educated by one-sided messages.

Expectations of the shape or division of information can also be influential. Research into political speeches shows that information divided into three parts tends to receive applause (Howitt, 1989 and Jefferson, 1989). Order of presentation can also be influential so that conclusions or important factors are presented first in the interests of clarity (McGuire, 1968). Earlier in his analysis on attitude change McGuire identifies comprehension as a vital early step in the five behavioural stages necessary for attitude change: 'attention, comprehension, yielding, retention and action' (1968: 173), endorsing the importance of early orientation.

Other experiments have shown that the number of arguments which are presented can also be influential. In an experiment with presenting prosecution and defence arguments, it was shown that the more arguments presented for a particular side, the greater the agreement that was created. The differentiations here are interesting with the strongest influence operating for the first seven arguments, with a minimal additional influence from seven to ten, and thereafter little noticeable change (Calder, Insko & Yandell, 1974).

Language and range of arguments can be a further contributive factor. Billig is particularly illuminating on the subject of skilful argumentation (which he terms 'witcraft', implying the using of one's 'wits') and eloquence (1987: 104–5). Zimbardo *et al.*'s review of the work done by the Hovland research group comments on findings that complex or subtle messages tend to produce a longer lasting change in attitudes as do repetition and active participation (1969: 100).

Changes in attitude may vary in durability so that short-term and long-term effects need to be taken into consideration. It seems that both cognitive and affective forms may be instrumental here. Zimbardo *et al.*'s findings suggest that information which requires more processing may have a more long-term effect; similarly the 'sleeper effect' of the low-credibility presenter mentioned above may also be more influential in the final analysis. The conclusion here then seems to be that the easy message, positively presented may only have a short-term impact, particularly where there is no reinforcement through repetition.

However skilled a presenter a teacher may be though, in terms of producing elegantly structured material and a skilfully created positive atmosphere, using such strategies as those suggested above, there is still a sense in which the *content* of the language classroom will still override any formal virtuosity. In any kind of communicative process, whether it be in the classroom or in a more general context, one of the most important conditions for effectiveness is to achieve a common point of departure with an audience. In pedagogical terms it is vital to identify the levels of knowledge and attitudes of pupils, a point endorsed in the National Curriculum proposals:

> One of the benefits of a good modern languages course is that it enables learners to stand back from their preconceptions as well as to learn about another way of life. Ways to promote this and ways to avoid simply passing on clichés include: starting from learners' own knowledge of the topic. (1990: 61)

Two particular theories are of interest here: Festinger's 'cognitive dissonance' and Heider's 'balance theory'.

Festinger (1957) argues that holding ideas in one's head which are consistent with one another induces a feeling of well-being, and that, conversely, internalised ideas which are inconsistent with each other produce discomfort. He suggests that people actively seek to reduce dissonance or inconsistency. Perhaps most interesting for language teachers in terms of resolving dissonance are the experiments carried out with role-playing, where it was revealed that playing out a role, provided that coercion was not employed, encouraged people to shift their attitudes to accommodate the new stance (Janis & King, 1954; Culbertson, 1957). Active participation helps to focus attention and the dissonance experienced internally may be accommodated by change in attitude. Melde, as we saw earlier, might describe this change in terms of confrontation and decentering, through learners being obliged to take the foreign interlocutor's perspective.

Heider's theory of balance focuses similarly on notions of consonance and dissonance, but here the emphasis is on interaction with others and relies more on the affective dimension. His analysis rests on the premise that we expect preferred associates to share our own preferred ideas and behaviour patterns, thus creating a sense of 'balance'. Where unacceptable ideas are professed by those we like, a variety of strategies can be used to correct the sensation of 'imbalance' (1958). Avoidance, repression and distortion, strategies suggested by Sampson (1971) in his review of Heider's theory, are unlikely to be strategies of interest to the teacher, but certain others bear closer examination. Changing one's own attitude, accepting differences in ideas and attempting to change other people's attitudes are further possible strategies and perhaps correspond to the positive, neutral and negative audience positions on the affective scale.

Of particular interest in terms of teaching language and culture is the option of 'cognitive differentiation'. Sampson suggests that one method of establishing 'balance' is to recognise that the point of focus may have subtle differences within itself and that the complexity of a subject may mean that different aspects are being referred to within the one focus (1971: 104). For language teachers this means above all the presentation of a differentiated and multi-perspective account of the foreign culture (Fritzsche, 1993). If then some affective bond can be established within a language context (between teacher or pupil or between people from different cultures), so that the 'balance theory' can be operative, it seems likely that the necessary cognitive (and affective) changes will arrange themselves.

A third cognitive process influencing attitudes is the operation of pre-existing attitudes in selecting material. Any new information will be processed in the light of other related knowledge already assimilated. Any introduction of new material should be carefully organised in terms of the first item presented since this is likely to affect subsequent attitudes. However, no pupil is a *tabula rasa* and all are likely to have previous preconceptions. These will not only act as an internal processing filter but are also likely to influence the ability to accept incoming information. As Fishbein points out, a person:

> may not believe all the information he is given, and at the same time he may form additional inferential beliefs that can influence his atti-

tude. Thus the salient beliefs that a subject actually comes to hold...may not directly correspond to the information provided. (1975: 253–4)

Inferential beliefs, those beliefs which can be inferred because of what a person has already experienced and what he thus expects, can thus distort incoming information. The result may be that preconceptions and stereotypes are not altered but reinforced, because only confirming information is selected. Certain experiments have shown that exposure to more information can lead to a strengthening of existing attitude where people are on opposite sides of an issue (Lord, Ross & Lepper, 1979). Here the notion suggested above that increasing amounts of information may lead to attitude change is contradicted.

It has thus become evident that the relationship between the cognitive and the affective remains unclear. Specific circumstances may lead to quite opposite effects to what might otherwise have been expected. What is clear, however, is that teachers can have influence over cognitive, affective and moral development, and thereby play a significant role in young people's education in an international world. There are no easy recipes here any more than there are in pedagogical practice in general, but it is evident that teachers of language and culture are not just technicians inculcating the skills of manipulating linguistic structures and of responding appropriately to specific behaviourally-circumscribed social situations. By striving to bring learners from egocentricity to reciprocity, teachers are stimulating their personal growth in an international world.

Conclusion

There has of course always been a sense in which foreign language learning was seen as a preparation for travel to other countries. What has become more evident in recent decades is that language learning is insufficient; it leads to encoding of a message rather than communication and interaction with another person. There can be no negotiation of shared meanings and understanding of the world if interlocutors simply encode their own meaning without seeking to understand its relationship to that of others.

Doyé (1993) suggests that the discussion of the aims of language teaching is now complete:

There exists today a widespread consensus concerning the justification of the demand that foreign language teaching should not just be limited to the mediation of competence in understanding and using other languages, but that, in addition or closely linked to this, foreign language teaching should include the mediation of knowledge about the culture, from which the language arises, and attitudes towards members of the culture. (1993: 19, our translation)

Although he is doubtless right in his estimate of the debate at theoretical levels — and he notes that policy documents in Germany and Britain contain this view — he may be over-optimistic with respect to classroom practice and textbook production.

It has been the purpose of this chapter to consider the psychological implications of the aims Doyé identifies. We have argued that foreign language teachers who take these aims seriously need to consider the relationship of their teaching to theories of cognitive development in general and moral development in particular. It is not self-evident that all learners of school age — even those in post-compulsory schooling — have necessarily reached a point where they are open to new perspectives from a different culture. Language teachers would however be ill-advised to conclude that if a certain stage of development has not been reached then they must either abandon their aims or only begin to teach languages to older learners. Psychological stage theories are contentious and there can be no easy applications to language teaching. It is arguable that language teaching can actively contribute to developing that openness, as has always been the claim. However it is clear that mere exposure to acquisition of the linguistic competence is insufficient. Teachers need to structure their work with an eye to their knowledge of learners' psychological development.

Our investigation has also shown that the assumption that language learning leads to positive attitudes towards other peoples and cultures cannot be held without further reflection. Attitude formation and attitude change are complex processes and mere exposure to language learning and information about other cultures will not necessarily lead to the desired results. There are complex relationships between cognitive and affective components of attitudes towards other peoples, between information and the ways in which it is presented, between general psychological development and specific development of perceptions of foreign and native cultures and countries.

This dimension of language teaching requires as much further research as does our understanding of learners' acquisition of linguistic competence — perhaps more so. It is no different in this from all kinds of teaching and teachers cannot wait for simple recipes. They are in any case unlikely to be forthcoming, since teaching and learning are such complex human phenomena. In the meantime, however, we can take note of the relevance of research on cognitive and affective development and introduce the implications into our methods. It is to these issues that we turn in our next chapter.

2 Methodology and Methods

A rigorous and consistent methodology for teaching language and culture requires a more comprehensive learning theory than we presently have available. We have seen in the previous chapter that general theories of psychological development are relevant to our understanding of learners' acquiring insight into and positive attitudes towards a foreign culture and people, and identifying with the perspectives of people from a different culture. The relationships between the different elements — cognitive, affective, moral — and their realisation in specific social situations remain insufficiently clear for us to draw out methodological consequences without qualification. This is not an unusual situation for most teachers, and occasional mistakes in the past, of clinging too closely to simplified versions of new theories of learning or even to learning theories which turned out to be untenable, have made teachers of languages and other subjects more circumspect. On the other hand, a descent into unprincipled eclecticism and unrestrained intuition can be equally dangerous.

Take, for example, the issue of stereotypes of foreign people. Neither textbook writers nor teachers address the question directly. It seems as if they intuitively avoid bringing learners' existing hetero-stereotypes into the open and hope that the negative overtones of most stereotypes will be quietly counteracted by presenting positive, attractive images of the foreign country and people. This is particularly the case for teachers of German. Although children's views are still strongly influenced by images of Nazi-dominated Germany (Phillips, 1981; Cullingford, 1991), there are very few textbooks in use in Britain which tackle these images; we suspect the same is true of other countries in Europe. (For an interesting approach to this problem, see the discussion of *Deutsch Konkret* by Vanstone & Mennecke, 1993.) Yet stereotypes are tenacious and do not disappear simply as a consequence of exposure to attractive images and the process of language learning (Cain, 1991).

The same point can be made about other people's stereotypes of the country and people to whom learners themselves belong. It is evident that the success of their relationships and communication with others will depend in part on those stereotypes. They need to be aware of the effect of both negative and positive images on their reception when they meet people from other cultures. Since an organised visit is increasingly part of the school curriculum for foreign language teaching, the importance of this issue is also growing, but is again a neglected area. There are some exceptions. In a textbook for teaching English in Germany (*English G...A3*: Schwarz *et al.*, 1987), one chapter deals with mutual impressions and comments by English and German pupils on their respective school systems. As mentioned in the previous chapter, in the work of the Deutsch-Französishes Institut in Ludwigsburg the concern with mutual images has been a *leitmotif* of both theory and practice. The more sensitive issues of negative stereotypes and the pejorative language associated with them — 'les rosbifs', 'the frogs' — are still largely avoided. In some cases, textbooks have deliberately introduced stereotype emblems — a frog in *Action! Graded French* (Buckby, 1980), a German sausage in *Einfach toll* (Smith, 1985) — and it might be argued that these provide opportunities for confrontation of stereotypes, were there not a complete absence of any indication of this in the accompanying teacher's books. (For studies of the cultural contents of textbooks, see Doyé (1991) and Byram (1993).)

In sum, there is sufficient evidence that the lack of a theory-driven methodology, however incomplete, leads to inadequate teaching and poor textbooks. We propose therefore in this chapter to discuss a number of principles which can guide teachers' methods and in a subsequent chapter to provide several case-studies which embody some of those principles.

Comparison

There is a central role for comparative methods in language and culture teaching. Although contrastive analysis in language studies has lost much of its direct influence, it is still a widely-used technique in classrooms, irrespective of its disappearance from textbooks. Much comparison is, we suspect, now incidental and implicit but teachers know that learners do compare and contrast as part of their general strategies of accommodation and assimilation. The same applies to learners' perceptions of foreign cultures, and Lado's essay on contrastive analysis of cultures is still a valuable text (Lado, 1958).

Our own research has shown that language teachers use comparison frequently, especially in talk about the foreign culture. The comparison may not be entirely overt, but based rather on juxtaposition. Take, for example, the following exchange from a French lesson:

T: Qu'est-ce que c'est, saucisson?

P: Sausages.
T: Sausage, yes, what sort? What sort of sausage? Walls?
P: (Silence.)
T: Sort of salami-type of sausage, that sort of sausage.

In this example there is a gradual refinement of the explanation which draws upon pupils' own culture — as it is perceived, at least, by the teacher. The process of comparison in fact involves both implicit contrast — 'not Walls' — and implicit extension of pupils' existing perceptions of 'sausage' — 'sort of salami-type'.[1]

Current practice is, then, not unfamiliar with comparison and contrast as a teaching technique. To what extent is this supported within a broader methodological context? We shall consider this from three angles: learning theory; educational purposes of foreign language teaching; and the relationship of linguistic and cultural learning.

The statement within the English and Welsh National Curriculum that one of the educational purposes of foreign language teaching is 'to develop pupils' understanding of themselves and their own culture' (DES, 1990: 3) is perhaps the most explicit statement available in documents of this kind. It probably expresses a conviction among many language teachers and will become more widely acknowledged as a consequence. The value of language and culture teaching is that it can contribute to this educational purpose, shared with other school subjects, by providing pupils with a perspective on themselves from beyond the normal limits of their experience and perceptions. It can provide them with that Archimedean point from which they can move their whole world.

Learners cannot simply shake off their own culture and step into another. It is not a question of putting down their 'cultural baggage', for their culture is a part of themselves, has formed them and created them as social beings (Byram, 1989: 111–13). Learners are 'committed' to their culture and to deny any part of it is to deny something within their own being. Consequently they will attempt to assimilate, to use a Piagetian term, or 'anchor' it (Moscovici, 1984: 29) within their existing categories. Comparison, and especially contrast, is a means of helping learners to realise that this process will not do justice to the reality lived by other people, to their culture and cultural values and meanings. When they accept that other people have other schemata through which they understand their physical and social world, learners are in a position to take up, cognitively, the perspective that others have on the learners' own socially-determined representations of what might initially seem to be the same social and physical world (see also Ertelt-Vieth, 1990, 1991, for a particular use of comparison to identify *lacunae* within and between cultures).

We saw in the preceding chapter how Melde and others have argued from developmental psychology that comparison, 'confrontation', is a means to shift learners' perspective to encompass that of a foreign culture and society. In this argument, the emphasis is rather upon stimulating learners' moral development as individuals and giving them a means of grasping the foreign social reality as a pre-requisite for intercultural communication. The reflection and critical apprehension of self and one's own society is given less emphasis in terms of educational purpose. Nevertheless the psychological theory points quite clearly to the need for a comparative method: learners need to become aware of their own cultural schemata — and of the affective, attitudinal dimension of those schemata — in order to effect an acknowledgement of those of a different culture. Confrontation with their own culture seen from the perspective of others is an important means of bringing unconscious and 'naturalised' beliefs into consciousness so that their relativity and specificity can be acknowledged.

A third angle on the use of comparison is afforded by an examination of the link between linguistic and cultural learning. Unfortunately, most attention in language teaching is given to methods of teaching and learning grammatical structures and, latterly, linguistic functions. In the former case, vocabulary acquisition is treated as a matter of learning equivalents of lexical items in the first language, whilst avoiding through contrastive analysis the more obvious 'faux amis'. In the era of teaching functions and notions, the concept of an abstract 'notion' realised in the lexis of different languages, suggests that lexical items from one language are to be equated with specific items from another. Even within the European context, however, this runs contrary to our argument that cultures are in many respects unique, that shared cultural schemata are part of individuals' social identity and that those schemata are expressed in unique ways in the language. In the revision of the Council of Europe's Threshold Level, some recognition of the specificity of notions in cultures is afforded through the introduction of the concept of sociocultural competence. This remains however focused on communicative behaviour rather than the underlying concepts, values and beliefs which shape people's social identity (van Ek & Trim, 1991: 102).

We need therefore to give more attention to vocabulary, to semantic structures and fields within which lexical items are interrelated and interdependent. When learners acquire an understanding of the connotations of lexical items in the foreign language and contrast them with connotations of an apparently equivalent item in their own, they begin to gain insight into the schemata and perspectives of the foreign culture. This can and should begin at the earliest stages of language and culture learning. For example, English pupils learning French can investigate the connotations of *'pain'* and *'bread'*. They can first survey among the members of their class *when* and *with what* they eat bread. They will have learnt at an early stage the question-forms and grammar necessary to ask everyone and establish some elementary statistics. It is unlikely that they will find numerous connotations of 'bread' with 'vegetables', or with a warm meal or 'dinner'. The fact that they will find variations and tendencies among their peers is a useful reminder that generalisations have limitations and must be treated with care. This is particularly important at the second stage when they are presented with results from a similar enquiry among a group of French pupils. They can be encouraged, through observation and questioning in the foreign language, to see that there are different connotations and different tendencies amongst their French peers. In doing so they are beginning to break down simplistic equivalences, to resist their tendency to assimilate *'pain'* to 'bread'. There is also an opportunity for them to be introduced to French stereotype opinions about English bread and eating habits: the beginnings of a change in perspective and possibly a re-consideration of their own stereotypes and attitudes (cf. similar exercises on bread in Seelye (1984: 130–32) and on *'fromage'* in Zarate (1986: 139).)

Clearly such an elaborate process of vocabulary learning cannot be applied to all lexis. The example we have given refers to an aspect of culture which is significant and significantly different in the two cultures concerned. In order to identify similar phenomena, Lado proposes the methods of contrastive analysis. He suggests three kinds of contrast:

- 'same form, different meaning' — when a foreign observer attributes a different meaning to a phenomenon to that understood by native-speakers and thereby misunderstands the phenomenon
- 'same meaning, different form' — it is common for people from one culture to assume that their way of doing something, from accepting an invitation to writing an essay, is the same everywhere whereas the underlying meaning or purpose might be the same but the realisation of it different
- 'same form, same meaning, different distribution' — a particular behaviour may have the same meaning but be less general than in the foreign observers' own society, for example in forms of greeting or leave-taking shaking hands is more frequent in some societies than others. (1957: 114ff)

Once significant contrasts have been established, we can make the link with vocabulary acquisition by establishing 'key words' (Williams, 1983). The advantages of key lexical items are various. First, they make evident the link of language and culture, the particular characteristic of language as an indicator of cultural items and concepts and as a carrier of the meanings of those concepts in a complex field of connotations. Williams describes key words as having two important characteristics:

> they are significant, binding words in certain activities and their interpretation; they are significant, indicative words in certain forms of thought. (1983: 15)

Key words also give learners a focus and help them to realise that even between cultures which are in many respects similar, having inherited common origins and traditions — as is the case among European cultures — there are nonetheless significant differences which can be isolated in concrete and particular cases. Thus in teaching about a selected aspect of culture in a 'unit' of work, learners' attention can be drawn to specific key words and learning objectives can be formulated with reference to them.

There are two contrasting processes of vocabulary learning with respect to key words. We saw in the example above that one process involves a dissociation of words which seem to be translation equivalents, an undermining of apparent identity often encouraged in bilingual dictionaries so that learners begin to adjust their existing schemata. This is all the more important if the words, from superficially similar cultures, are of the same historical roots. Thus in two separate units of work for learners in upper secondary we have developed ways of demonstrating that 'family' is not identical with 'famille', and that 'immigré' is not the same as 'immigrant'. Techniques include showing how name-giving traditions vary in France and England, how expectations of what constitutes a 'family gathering' are different. In the second case, the techniques include using statistical data to show the history and origins of immigration, data from questionnaires about English and French people's perceptions of the numbers and geographical origins, contrasted with sociological data revealing actual numbers and origins. At the end of the unit it may be useful to summarise by asking learners to portray in diagrammatic form the contrasting connotations of key words identified by themselves and their teachers during the process of study.

The key-word technique might be all the more important in a second kind of vocabulary learning. Where learners meet cultural phenomena which have not even an apparent equivalent in their own culture, they have to learn vocabulary which is untranslatable in even a minimal sense. A relatively simple case can be found in social institutions where, for example, legal processes are quite different and 'le juge d'instruction' in the French system has no comparable equivalent in English law and legal proceedings. Even here, though explanations of the function can be given, the connotations cannot be easily transferred. Other examples arising from our experimental work have occurred when French pupils in lower secondary have studied how their English peers tend to have spare-time jobs, delivering newspapers in the early morning or baby-sitting in the evenings, or working in a shop or on a market on Saturdays. To understand the concept of 'Saturday job' — which is untranslatable — pupils have learnt how children have been employed since the beginning of the industrial revolution, how contemporary employment is regulated by law, and how their English peers speak about their work in interviews. In terms of contemporary connotations the latter provide a means of analysing why young people have a Saturday job or a spare-time job, what it means to them with respect to financial independence, with respect to the contrast with school work, and so on. The historical dimension on the other hand helps to explain how the phenomenon arose and that it is not some arbitrary and therefore unreasonable peculiarity of the 'other' culture which can be dismissed as bizarre.

At more advanced levels of language and culture learning, for example in higher education, it is possible to link a key word approach on a contemporary level to historical explanation. In *Keywords* (1983), Williams offers very suitable material for teaching in this way. He traces there the history of key words in British culture — including the word 'culture' itself — and shows how their current meanings have grown out of and, for some speakers, still relate to, past usages. He provides 'thick definitions' of the words which give openings into accounts of culture and society in Britain at specific periods of its history.

It is interesting to speculate as to whether students carrying out field-work (see below) might focus on key words as a means of linking their language learning with the 'thick descriptions' (Geertz, 1973) which field-work reports aim to achieve.

The analysis of key words in the foreign culture, whether historically or contemporarily, will lead to the same kind of comparative process at an advanced level as in the examples given for beginners and intermediate learners. The reflection on self and native culture remains fundamental to this approach as to others.

A Body of Knowledge

Although there have been variations in the ways in which language learners have been taught about foreign countries, people and cultures — notably in the rich tradition of *Landeskunde* in Germany — for many teachers the principal purpose has been to provide information to support the learning of the language in early stages, until the language learning became subservient to the study of the literature — and sometimes of the history — of a given country. (For further detailed accounts of the development of cultural studies/*Landeskunde/civilisation* see, for example, Melde, 1987; Byram, 1989; Zarate, 1986). Although criticisms have been levelled at this tradition it would be misguided to assume that learners do not need some 'background' information. Indeed it is misguided to think that such information is mere 'background'. For the link between cultural learning and linguistic learning is indissoluble in principle, even if attempts have been made to reduce and diminish the link in practice.

Our earlier research demonstrated that an unsystematic approach to providing information leaves pupils precisely with unstructured information rather than knowledge (Byram, 1989: 120) and is without effect on pupils' understanding of others in the face of powerful messages from the media and elsewhere (Byram, Esarte-Sarries & Taylor, 1991: 380). It is evident however that any body of knowledge made available to learners has to be a selection. In the time normally available for language and culture learning in schools and other institutions of general and vocational education, it is not possible to provide a comprehensive account of the culture of a community where the language is spoken as a mother tongue. This in turn is to assume that only one such community is chosen even though in many cases the foreign language is native to different countries throughout the world.

Before considering criteria for selection, let us review the kinds of knowledge required by a learner. For it is clear that being native to another culture, being socialised into different values and meanings, the learner cannot be modelled on a native speaker of the language he/she is learning. For the native speaker has knowledge which is internalised and unconscious but which the learner has to know consciously and, in some situations, substitute for his/her own unconscious knowledge. Much of this is 'recipe knowledge' of how to conduct social transactions, from the commonest greetings, through use of public services, to the complexities of 'the silent language' (Hall, 1959) of non-verbal behaviour, and the expectations of conversation turn-taking, rules of politeness (Brown & Levinson, 1978), and the maxims of normal communication (Grice, 1975).

Native speakers also have stores of conscious knowledge acquired through formal education and the many informal channels of media and social interaction. The range and kinds of knowledge vary widely within a speech community, along dimensions of social groups such as class, gender, profession and leisure pursuits. This is the kind of knowledge which is crucial to the understanding of literature, in particular the realist novel, but it is just as significant for successful communication and interaction with native speakers (Risager, 1991). Such knowledge has historical, geographical, sociological dimensions; it is the shared understandings to which speakers allude in conversation — to an historical or contemporary figure, to an architectural or geographical feature of a widely known landscape, to a social institution. Sometimes they check that the allusion is understood, for not all native speakers have the same body of knowledge, but there are many allusions which are taken for granted. Were they all to be explicated, conversation and interaction would break down.

It is this second kind of knowledge which has been most prominent in textbooks and teaching, although the advent of 'communicative language teaching' focused on preparing learners for a visit to a foreign country — particularly influential in Britain — has also introduced learners to the knowledge required for the commonest social transactions a tourist might meet. There is therefore a need to make both kinds of knowledge available to learners in direct ways which meet the constraints of time and the requirement that it be accessible to conscious control, substituting where appropriate for the knowledge learners have acquired unconsciously in their own cultural environment.

The question of selection has two aspects: what selection of factual and other knowledge to make from what social group or speech community; and in what order to present it to learners. The latter could be resolved either by determining an order to be followed sequentially or, more reasonably, by creating a 'spiral curriculum' (Bruner, 1966) which takes account of levels of complexity and abstraction but also of linguistic learning so that cultural learning can be conveyed to a large but not necessarily exclusive extent through the foreign language. Furthermore, selection cannot ulti- mately be separated from teaching methods, particularly from comparison and contrast, and the aim of making learners more conscious of themselves and their own culture.

But before we can begin selection from 'a' culture, we need to define the social group whose culture we are to focus on. Traditionally the social group has been a 'given'. If, for example, German is the language, then 'the Germans' have been the chosen group, but problems arise with English both in terms of selecting America, Australia, Canada, Britain and, in the latter case at least, in terms of choosing 'the English' as opposed to 'the Scots' or others. In the preface to Levine & Adelman's textbook for teaching culture this problem is acknowledged with the hope that 'the ESL teachers and students will augment our descriptions with examples of cultural diversity' (1982: x). The problem is partly overcome by ensuring that no monolithic, homogenising image is presented of whichever nation is taken — this is a function of the comparative method described above. The selection of 'the Germans' or 'the French' is however also a function of learners' common perceptions, of the effect of stereotypes as the first stage

of apprehension of the unknown. Finally, the linguistic and political reality
— seen from the learner's initial outsider viewpoint — is reflected in the
association of 'the' language with 'the' people of a particular nation state.
Learners identify 'the Germans' or 'the English' as those who belong to a
nation state and some of the characteristics which constitute 'being
German' are embodied in the practices and social institutions of the German
state — and are recognised as such by Germans and non-Germans alike.

One aspect of the question of order of presentation is related to this
association of language, people, state and stereotype. Social groups maintain their identity by emphasising some of their own characteristics in
contrast with those of other groups with which they have contact, to mark
the boundaries between them (Barth, 1969). Auto-stereotypes of what it is
to be 'English' are in implicit contrast with English views of what it is to be
'German' or 'French' or 'American', being three of the best-known contigu-
ous groups for which the English have detailed hetero-stereotypes. These
boundary-marking features are, however, a simplification and ignore both
the mundane cultural practices and routine behaviour of taken-for-granted
living, and the complex cultural beliefs and shared values and meanings of
a given society (cf. Byram, 1989: 87ff).

These reflections and our discussion of learning theories in the preceding
chapter lead to the following guidelines to the general nature of a course of
language and culture:

- learners need to engage actively with alternative interpretations of the
  world, meeting phenomena which express some of the shared meanings of the foreign culture and which they can compare and contrast
  with their own;
- a selection, particularly in the early stages, should be partly determined by auto- and hetero-stereotypes in the foreign group and in the
  learners' own national social group;
- both taken-for-granted, routine knowledge and conscious knowledge
  of the shared cultural world held by the foreign group has to be made
  accessible to learners so that they can adjust to routine behaviour and
  allusive communication;
- learners need to have access to and analyse the complex values and
  meanings of a national culture and other cultures existing within
  national and state boundaries, some of which are manifest in cultural
  institutions and artefacts — for example, literature, film, history,
  political parties, social welfare, education — others being ephemeral
  and in the process of becoming part of a shared reality.

These guidelines embody a degree of progression: from confrontation
with stereotypes to engagement with the most complex cultural phenom-

ena of literature and other artefacts. At the same time, a spiral curriculum will bring learners into contact at an early stage with such artefacts — which they will 'read' superficially — to return to them later for more complex analysis. Similarly, advanced learners can return to analysis of routine behaviours — the rules of verbal and non-verbal interaction, rules of 'politeness' for example — which they will have met and acquired with only superficial comparison and reflection at an early stage.

As for the content of cultural learning, presented either as structured information or integrated into linguistic learning, we propose the following analytical categories as a first stage of selection and with no concern for order of presentation or progression:

Minimum content: Areas of study

- *social identity and social groups*: groups within the nation-state which are the basis for other than national identity, including social class, regional identity, ethnic minority, professional identity, and which illustrate the complexity of individuals' social identities and of a national society (NB the issue of national identity is dealt with under 'stereotypes');
- *social interaction*: conventions of verbal and non-verbal behaviour in social interaction at differing levels of familiarity, as outsider and insider within social groups;
- *belief and behaviour*: routine and taken-for-granted actions within a social group — national or sub-national — and the moral and religious beliefs which are embodied within them; secondly, routines of behaviour taken from daily life which are not seen as significant markers of the identity of the group;
- *socio-political institutions*: institutions of the state — and the values and meanings they embody — which characterise the state and its citizens and which constitute a framework for ordinary, routine life within the national and sub-national groups; provision for health-care, for law and order, for social security, for local government, etc.;
- *socialisation and the life-cycle*: institutions of socialisation — families, schools, employment, religion, military service — and the ceremonies which mark passage through stages of social life; representation of divergent practices in different social groups as well as national auto-stereotypes of expectations and shared interpretations;
- *national history*: periods and events, historical and contemporary, which are significant in the constitution of the nation and its identity — both actually significant and, not necessarily identical, perceived as such by its members;

- *national geography*: geographical factors within the national boundaries which are significant in members' perceptions of their country; other factors which are information (known but not significant to members) essential to outsiders in intercultural communication (NB national boundaries, and changes in them, are part of 'national history');
- *national cultural heritage*: cultural artefacts perceived to be emblems and embodiments of national culture from past and present; in particular those which are 'known' to members of the nation — e.g. Shakespeare in Britain, the Impressionists in France, Wagner in Germany — through their inclusion in curricula of formal education; and also contemporary classics, not all of which have reached the school curriculum and some of which may be transient but significant, created by television and other media — e.g. Truffaut's films in France, Agatha Christie in Britain, Biermann's songs in Germany;
- *stereotypes and national identity*: for example, German and English notions of what is 'typically' German and English national identity; the origins of these notions — historical and contemporary — and comparisons among them; symbols of national identities and stereotypes and their meanings, e.g. famous monuments and people.

There are two complementary principles underpinning these proposals. Learners are outsiders to a group and need the knowledge and behaviour which will allow them to interact successfully with insiders, becoming to varying degrees, but only rarely totally, insiders; their existing perceptions and their own culture are part of the content. Secondly, it is the perceptions and knowledge of insiders about their own culture which frame the selection and the perspective from which content is presented; geographical knowledge is selected according to insider perspectives of what is significant in topography, for example, rather than from the viewpoint of a dispassionate geographer. The history of Britain would be presented to learners of English in terms of the knowledge acquired by British people through formal and informal education, caricatured and thus clarified in *1066 and All That* (Sellar & Yeatman, 1930).

At early and intermediate stages of language and culture learning — approximately, as reached in secondary education in many countries — the aim is to provide learners with 'beacons' by which they can orientate to the behaviour, talk and texts they meet in the foreign environment. We are not proposing that language and culture courses should be history, sociology or geography courses. We want them rather to give an understanding of the significance of particular periods of history or social institutions or geographical facts in the understanding the foreign group has of itself and its identity. These can then be compared and contrasted with learners' own national views of themselves and their identity and, through confrontation, a process of shift in perspective begun. Zarate has demonstrated the practice of this process by contrasting three synchronic accounts of Jeanne d'Arc in French history texts, each with a different emphasis: nationalistic heroine, political catalyst or martyr-victim (1986: 51–54). Warner also offers an analysis of differing attitudes to Joan of Arc in different countries demonstrating an equivalent diachronic perspective (1981).

As well as this process at work in historical studies, Zarate (1991) also offers an example from the domain of geography. Learners in the northern hemisphere are confronted with maps of the world where Australia is at the centre and Europe 'upside-down' at the bottom. At advanced levels of learning — in late secondary and tertiary education — we would expect students to investigate in more detail and more analytically the nature of national perceptions of history or cultural artefacts or religious institutions and beliefs. They would draw upon a range of disciplines, but principally on anthropology and ethnography, and would study ethnographic analyses of the culture and society in question.

The specific realisations of these categories will depend not only upon the level reached by learners but on the culture and society they are studying. An example of a subsequent level of more concrete proposals is provided below. This served originally as a check-list for the evaluation of courses for teaching German in Britain at lower secondary level. As such it reflects what is possible despite what might appear to be too demanding. All the suggestions were to be found in at least one course-book, indicating in principle the feasibility of introducing beginners to all the categories, except 'national cultural heritage'. In fact, even this might have been included, since one of the courses included an introduction to the legend of Siegfried (Byram & Baumgardt, 1993). The proposals are included here as an indication of how our general categories can be made more concrete; a full realisation as a course of study would require an integration of this list with a linguistic syllabus.

Minimum content: Themes and topics in German

Social identity and social groups:
- groups by social stratification
- occupational groupings
- regional identity (including language and dialect, and East-West identities)
- sub-culture identities (especially young people's)
- ethnic and cultural minorities (*Gastarbeiter*, Linguistic Minority Groups, *Aussiedler*, asylum seekers)

Social interaction:

- greetings at different levels of formality, verbal and non-verbal
- levels of formality in language, especially DU/SIE
- behaviour at meals and explanation of food
- gender relationships
- taboos

Belief and behaviour:

- teaching procedures to make learners aware of the taken-for-granted nature of certain actions and their meanings (some of which are moral and religious), e.g. 'going to school', 'going to church', 'home', some foods such as 'bread', concepts of the state and authorities, especially law and order, 'asking a policeman', fashion and consumer values
- teaching procedures to introduce students to routine/'recipe' knowledge, e.g. how to use public transport, appropriate behaviour in a restaurant

Socio-political institutions:

- government (Federal and state/*Land*) and elections
- European organisation
- health-care
- law and order and state security
- trade-unions
- the arts

Socialisation and the life-cycle:

- schools and education as a means of socialisation
- apprenticeships and vocational training
- the family and education/socialisation within the family
- leisure and work/school
- media/advertising as socialisation
- the life-cycle, especially age and relationships between generations
- ceremonies, especially those marking significant moments in the life-cycle

National history:

- division and re-unification
- the period of National Socialism
- Weimar Republic
- unification of Germany (1870–1918)

National geography:

- distribution of population and areas of industrialisation
- neighbouring countries and the lack of national boundaries

- topography: the North/South difference
- climate and vegetation, and the natural environment

National cultural heritage

- contemporary artists widely known in Germany
- classical authors and the 'stories' of their most widely known works, read for example in German schools (e.g. Goethe and *Die Leiden des jungen Werthers*, Schiller and *Die Räuber*)
- classical musicians and painters (e.g. Wagner and the story of the 'Ring')

Stereotypes and national identity:

- explanation of stereotypes and the stereotyping process
- information on German auto-stereotypes
- raising awareness of English/British auto-stereotypes
- symbols of national stereotypes and their meanings
- indication of phenomena in a common heritage

Our final principle in determining a body of knowledge and the content of a language and culture course is expressed in the phrase 'multi-perspectival realism'. By this we mean that the image of a particular society and culture must be founded in the reality of contemporary life. The techniques of presentation may be both 'realistic' and 'fantastic'; images and 'stories' may be of actual people and places or may be caricatures or fiction, but they must always refer to reality. It is however important that learners should not have the impression that a specific image can be generalised to the whole society and culture in question. There has to be a variety of perspectives, a 'multi-perspectivity' (Fritzsche, 1993), from inside and outside the culture on whatever topic or theme is in focus at any given moment. In terms of teaching materials, for example, this means ensuring that a range of representations of any of the topics mentioned above has to be provided. This would have to be complemented by a methodology which emphasises differentiation in the data presented from a culture. In terms of assessment, to which we shall return in a later chapter, it would mean expecting a multi-perspectival dimension to learners' responses to and accounts of the foreign culture, and an avoidance of generalisation.

Fieldwork

In our ideal model of cultural studies and language learning (Byram, 1989, 1991), we distinguish between 'cultural awareness', based in the classroom, and 'cultural experience', based mainly in residence in the foreign country. Residence which is so structured that learners acquire insight into the foreign culture through direct experience coupled with reflection — related to the tradition of 'participant-observation' in ethnography — we call 'fieldwork'. There are limits to what can be achieved in the classroom and through the use of textbooks (Mennecke, 1993), although the classroom is also a privileged place in which to prepare for and reflect upon fieldwork and experiential learning.

In our discussion of psychological theories, we examined the concept of 'empathy' as pursued in the classroom in teaching history. The empathy of cultural experience claimed for fieldwork and participant-observation is described by Clifford, drawing on Dilthey:

> In the influential view of Dilthey understanding others arises initially from the sheer fact of coexistence in a shared world; but this experiential world, an intersubjective ground for objective forms of knowledge, is precisely what is missing or problematic for an ethnographer entering an alien culture. Thus, during the early months in the field (and indeed throughout the research), what is going on is language learning in the broadest sense. Dilthey's 'common sphere' must be established and re-established, building up a shared experiential world in relation to which all 'facts', 'texts', 'events', and their interpretations will be constructed. (1988: 35)

Clifford points to the advantages and problems of fieldwork: there can be no substitution in the classroom for experience, but valid experience is not simply an immediate consequence of immersion in a foreign culture. As Clifford points out, ethnographers are trained observers with a theory-driven purpose to their observations and experience. Language learners, except possibly at university level (as we shall see in a later chapter), do not have the theoretical training of professional ethnographers. On the other hand, when Clifford describes the process of fieldwork as 'language learning in the broadest sense', he brings ethnography and language and culture learning into close proximity.

It is one of the much debated aspects of traditional ethnographic fieldwork, that it is assumed that ethnographers do not need a thorough knowledge of the language, since they can acquire the specific information they require for their focused investigation through a working knowledge of the language and the help of interpreters. As Clifford suggests, this has serious consequences for the authority of ethnographic texts (1988: 41ff). For the teacher and learner of language and culture, however, the centrality of linguistic learning to 'language learning in the broadest sense' is undisputed. Indeed a typical experience of language and culture learning will consist of a long preparation for fieldwork, a relatively short period of residence, and a long period for reflection and analysis. In our model of learning it is in the interdependence of cultural awareness and language awareness with cultural experience that the preparation and analysis are located.

The degree of similarity between fieldwork in ethnography and in language and culture learning varies according to the level of learning reached and the experiential opportunities learners may have for residence in the foreign country. At one extreme, early learners may have just a few days organised visit to the country, with minimal opportunity to experience and observe (Byram & Esarte-Sarries, 1991: 190). At another extreme university students may spend as long in the country as many ethnographers do (in Britain most students are required to reside in the country for 8–12 months).

But what of those learners who have no opportunity for fieldwork in the foreign country? There is no doubt that they cannot have access to the experiential learning of co-existing within a shared world. On the other hand, the language learner — different from the ethnographer — is learning about his/her own culture too. Some of the techniques which can be employed in fieldwork in the foreign country — surveys, observations of behaviour, ethnographic interviews (Spradley, 1979) — can be brought into play in learners' own environment (see Chapter 4, Case Study 5).

Zarate and colleagues (Zarate & Troutot, 1990 — see Chapter 4, Case Study 4) have also devised ways in which learners can be given access to a highly focused aspect of the foreign culture. They provide, as it were, the fieldnotes and recordings which an ethnographer might have made about the perceptions of the inhabitants of a particular *quartier* of Paris. Learners are to interpret. They do not enjoy the process of experience, of participation, but they do have the opportunity for interpretation of the observations. This approach could be extended into the principle of the 'section bilingue' and bilingual–bicultural education.

The main principles of bilingual education are well-known, particularly from the Canadian system (Swain & Lapkin, 1982): the use of the foreign language as a medium of teaching other subjects, sometimes and particularly for older learners in secondary 'sections bilingues', with supporting language-as-subject lessons. There are also experiments which attempt to provide not just a linguistic competence but also support for bicultural identity among children of immigrant parents (Byram & Leman, 1990). In these cases one of the significant factors is the social identity of the teachers who are native-speakers and usually have been born and educated in the country of origin. They are therefore 'carriers' of the culture and realisations of the cultural identity to which learners aspire.

'Sections bilingues' in secondary schooling may have similar characteristics to those in 'international schools'. In monolingual schools, they are less ambitious with respect to cultural learning and use the language as a medium for teaching the 'normal' geography or history etc., much as they would be taught in the learners' mother tongue. Experiments of this kind have existed in Britain in individual schools for many years. In Germany, there has recently been introduced a more systematic approach with the use of several languages (French, English, Italian, Spanish, Russian) to teach Geography, the Social Sciences, History and Biology (Otten, 1992). Since they do not attempt to convey the foreign culture's values and meanings — not even by giving the foreign national perception of national and international geography, for example — these programmes are using the foreign language as a code rather than as a language in its own right. The results are encouraging in terms of learners' linguistic learning and their mastery of the grammar, functions and lexis of the foreign language. They cannot, however, be said to acquire cultural learning and the vocabulary — with its connotations and semantic fields — of the foreign language.

Our proposal would be different, and an extension of the 'cultural awareness' and 'cultural experience' dimensions of our model. We proposed already in that model (Byram, 1989: 145–46) that the 'cultural experience' element should take as its subject matter the culture of the foreign country and become a 'section biculturelle'. The material proposed by Zarate and colleagues suggests that not only geography, but also history and other school subjects can be taught in the foreign language from the perspective of the foreign culture. For the introduction of data 'from the field' gives new possibilities which bring intermediate learners much closer to experiential learning. Similar proposals and materials have come from the team working in Ludwigsburg.

Here two projects running from 1978 focused on the gathering of teaching material from France and the trialling of this in a variety of schools in Germany. The material 'from the field' included interviews from a number of French people involved in the two target areas (the education system, and regional identity and industry), and the making of a video film. Baumgratz *et al.* in their overview of the projects point particularly to the value of simulation exercises with native speakers that can function as preparatory orientation strategies:

> Nonetheless they [the simulations] represent a conception of situations — in our case transnational communication situations — which can serve as orientation for the individual. (1988: 20, our translation)

Our own research, to be reported in more detail below, suggests that more advanced learners — and perhaps those at intermediate levels too — can be introduced to some fieldwork techniques applicable in their own environment. By carrying out investigations among people of their own culture, they supply the data which serves the comparative method funda-mental to culture learning. These data, gathered in the first language but reported and interpreted in the foreign language, give learners a more conscious understanding of their own culture and can also serve as raw data for parallel classes in the foreign country. Each serves as 'fieldworker' and 'informant' for the other.

At an advanced level — in upper secondary and higher education — it may be possible to separate the formal study of language and culture. In the English and Welsh education system, students may study 'English Language' and 'English Literature' as independent subjects. In the former, the focus is on linguistic analysis and the acquisition of an understanding of the English language, with Linguistic Science as the parent discipline. A similar separation could lead to a course in 'French Language' and 'French Cultural Studies'. The former would aim to develop students' linguistic skills as well as their understanding of the French language as an object of study. The sociological dimension of the linguistic study — the socio-linguistics of French — would also place emphasis on the cultural meanings embodied in the French language and in its vocabulary in particular. This would provide a link to a course in 'French Cultural Studies' in which the 'cultural experience' work of our model for lower secondary would be the subject-matter and French would simply be the language of instruction. Attention would be paid to language as such only when difficulties arose, as is done in bilingual education; there would be no overt teaching of language and no evaluation of linguistic skills informally or in formal assessment.

Such a course would have to include fieldwork. Students would be trained in fieldwork techniques and introduced to anthropological and ethnographic concepts. The teaching of anthropology in the International Baccalauréat serves as a useful guide and demonstrates the feasibility of our proposals.

The aims of the syllabus are stated as follows:

(a) to develop in the student the means whereby s/he can come to a better understanding both of other societies and of her/his own;
(b) to familiarise the student with the methods by which social anthro-pologists attempt to understand the structure of society and the nature of social assumptions and beliefs;
(c) to lead the student to a greater awareness of the theoretical implications of the discipline. (RAI, 1990: 7)

The first aim is clearly shared with all language teaching and the second has been introduced into experimental courses for upper secondary and university students of languages. The third aim is also part of the experimental course for university students (cf. case studies in Chapter 4) and approached indirectly through the course at upper secondary level. This is clearly an opportunity for inter-disciplinary work with anthropologists and sociologists at both levels of education.

Conclusion

In our discussion of attitude formation and attitude change in Chapter 1, we suggested that many of the techniques for influencing attitudes discovered in experimental psychology are already part of teachers' professional craft. Bringing them into relationship with research findings helps teachers to exploit them more consciously and be aware of the ethical issues involved. In this chapter, too, we have discussed methods and methodological issues which are part of many teachers' armoury but we have attempted to clarify the implications and purposes as well as suggest how they might be more consciously developed within an overall framework of language and culture teaching. Comparison, provision of information about a foreign country and giving learners the opportunity to visit the country are all common phenomena in foreign language teaching.

On the other hand these methods are usually part of teachers' professional intuitions, their acquired craft knowledge. They are scarcely ever the focus of training courses, either before or after teachers take up their professional duties. Consequently, they are not central to professional discourse and there is little consideration of their rationale, of how they are practised systematically and what purposes they fulfil — or whether they are successful. In discussing them at some length, we hope to have placed them nearer to the focus of teachers' formal agenda and to raise questions which will take the discussion further. In Chapter 4, we offer some descriptions of specific cases where these methods — and others — are being put into operation in a systematic and conscious way. In Chapter 3, we consider how teacher education might better contribute to preparing teachers for the methods we have discussed here and the kinds of curriculum development illustrated in our case studies.

Notes

1. This example was collected and analysed by Susan Taylor (cf. Byram, Esarte-Sarries & Taylor, 1991: Chapter 5).

3 Teachers for Language-and-Culture

Most foreign language teachers in Western European education systems — and doubtless in many other countries too — receive both academic and pedagogical education, though the former usually dominates and sometimes almost excludes the latter. Their academic studies are dominated in turn by the study of literature in the foreign language. In some countries — for example France and Germany — literary studies are complemented by study of the country and its institutions (*Landeskunde* and *civilisation*) but there has been a tendency to afford it only low status and reduced time allocation, even though there are indications of change (Campos *et al.*, 1988). Although courses of other kinds exist and are increasing in popularity — for example, *Langues Etrangères Appliquées* in France and European Studies in Britain — graduates of such courses do not usually become teachers.

The consequence is that most established and many new teachers have been formed mainly in the mould of literary studies and criticism. Their knowledge and skill in a foreign language may be sound but their study of the language and of language as a phenomenon has been largely within the framework of traditional grammar rather than modern linguistics. Similarly their knowledge of the culture and society pertaining to the foreign language may be adequate to support their literary competence but their study of the culture and society will be at best incidental and based on limited personal, experiential learning rather than systematic description and analysis.

It is their experience of the foreign country which is likely to have been the prime source of their knowledge of culture and society and, furthermore, the means by which they have acquired linguistic fluency and a better understanding of language and culture as an integrated whole. Such experience is however very variable from individual to individual and from one education system to another. In Britain, most teachers — and all new teachers — will have spent one year of their academic course in the foreign country. In Denmark, language teachers have other subjects to teach too, and are not obliged to spend any period abroad. In France and Germany, language teachers are specialised in training and outlook and many will have spent a year during or after their academic course in the foreign country, but there is no obligation to do so and not everyone does. Despite these patterns of study and residence in the foreign country, the latter does not of itself guarantee acquisition of cultural knowledge and understanding (Alred, Byram, Esarte-Sarries & Ruane, 1992).

It is thus evident that in some education systems the introduction of a social studies dimension into language teaching — particularly in upper secondary courses — creates a disjunction between training for teaching and teaching itself. The implications of our proposals in earlier chapters could make the situation worse, and this is one of the reasons why we address the question of teacher education in this chapter. There is a broader issue too. Although our earlier chapters have been mainly couched in terms applicable to language learners in secondary education, they apply *mutandis mutatis* to learners in higher education, both those specialising in foreign language studies and others for whom language learning is ancillary. The latter include that growing number of students who are being encouraged to take parts of their courses in other countries within the European Community, through mobility programmes such as ERASMUS and LINGUA. Whatever their principal professional interest, all such students need an intercultural communicative competence and can benefit from an education through language and culture learning.

Courses in language and society already exist, as we have said. Yet, in addition to the fact that graduates from them rarely become teachers, their status as new courses is still much debated and their methods and contents much discussed. In Britain, one survey of first degree courses identified under the title of 'European Studies' only 15 and under 'International Relations/Studies' a further 6 (King, 1990: 113–17). Another survey found many more with 'European' within the title of the degree and it is such courses which can roughly be described as specialising in language and society. Ager (1992: 5) provides a summary (from Evans, 1990) which, as he says, has to be treated cautiously since it is based on self-report and possibly idiosyncratic definitions.

Ager also points out that only 6,000 students are involved of 'the more than 120,000 students of Language, Social Sciences, Law and Business in the Universities alone' (Ager, 1992), i.e. excluding polytechnics and other higher education institutions (Table 3.1).

This analysis suggests therefore that those just entering a career in language teaching with an adequate knowledge of the culture and society of their language are a small minority. If we turn to the alternative source of development, in-service teacher education, we find courses which offer

Table 3.1 Disciplines offered within 'European Studies' and related programmes at first degree level

Subject	Number of institutions offering (total: 58)		
	of which:	Univs (33)	Polys(25)
French	58	33	25
German	58	33	25
Spanish	37	18	19
Italian	18	13	5
Russian	12	9	3
Politics	37	24	13
Economics/business studies	32	13	19
History	20	14	6
Law	18	17	1
Society	11	6	5
Geography	4	4	0
Literature	3	2	1
Options available	18	11	7

(Ager, 1992: 5, Table 1. Source: Evans, 1990)

teachers opportunities for study-visits to the country — often provided or supported by the cultural institutes of the country in question — and secondly, courses held in the home country by the usual providers of in-service education. The former are on the whole experiential in their methodology and are seen as an opportunity to gather 'authentic material'. In a survey of several Western European countries, Edelhoff concludes that, insofar as cultural studies/*Landeskunde* is mentioned at all in in-service education, it is focused on factual information and realia, renewing teachers' out-dated knowledge of country and people (1987: 134). We have argued earlier that a body of knowledge is certainly required but that intercultural communicative competence depends on other kinds of learning. Even with respect to acquisition of knowledge however, the hamster-like collection of facts and realia is not an adequate basis for understanding. Cultural studies needs a disciplinary framework for teaching and learning about a particular country and society. This may not have to be explicit to learners in secondary education but should be part of the academic and pedagogical knowledge of their teachers.

The Need for Theory

The debate over a disciplinary framework is not easy. Since future and practising teachers are expected to study the whole way of life of at least one country where the foreign language is spoken natively, it might seem that they are being required to become historians, sociologists, economists, political scientists and so on. Furthermore, there arises the question as to whether they are expected to study the society and culture according to the traditions of those disciplines as they are established within the society itself. Or should they be taking an external perspective, drawing on the different disciplinary traditions of their own society? Or should they be making an explicitly comparative study?

It is clearly absurd to believe that students can be educated in such a range of disciplines without superficiality. An alternative is to define the discipline of cultural studies for language learners in terms of the object of study. The conclusion of one survey carried out on behalf of teachers of French *civilisation* in Europe is to focus on the question of the identity of a country and people both as it is created within the society and as seen from the outside:

> To identify as the central principle of the discipline 'civilisation' the study of the formation and the dynamics of this notion of collective identity is to establish a solid basis for the development of a programme which will offer students an in-depth understanding of contemporary France and, by extension, a more developed understanding of the factors which have shaped their own collective identity, regional or national. (Campos *et al.*, 1988: 184, our translation)

This proposal is attractive because it allows for comparative methodology and a reflection on the native culture and society which are fundamental to teaching and learning in secondary education. Teachers and future teachers are thus involved in the same process as those they teach. The focus on the self-image of a culture and society also allows a close link with linguistic learning — through the concept of key words, for example — which we believe is necessary at all levels of learning, although some institutions surveyed by the authors practise a separation of language and cultural studies.

There is a second area in which theoretical work is still underdeveloped. To suggest that teachers and future teachers — in university studies or in-service education — should experience the same kind of learning as those they teach raises a question seldom if ever addressed in the pedagogical theory of studies at this level: the question of a theory of learning. We argued in an earlier chapter for the development of a theory of cultural learning which takes into account the cognitive and moral development of learners. There is an equal need in university and in-service teaching. Here too learners are exposed to experience which requires a capacity for decentring, for understanding another's viewpoint and experience which is no less demanding than for pupils in secondary education. Yet the question of a cultural learning theory to underpin the teaching of cultural studies in universities does not appear in the literature.

The discussion of French *civilisation* by Campos *et al.* postulates three levels of learning. The first is to correspond to the '*niveau seuil*' defined by the Council of Europe group; this is seen as providing information about the semantic field of vocabulary. The second is seen in terms of information 'not specifically linguistic', which allows for an understanding of texts which 'give an opening onto the *civilisation* of the country studied'. The third is characterised by 'a critical dimension', and is said therefore to be the preserve of the university. It is unclear whether this implies a psychological development in learners or a definition of university study by its function, but the latter appears to be the main concern of these authors, who do not address psychological, learning theory issues elsewhere in their discussion either.

In his excellent account of how students and teachers become 'Language People', Evans is mainly concerned with personality theory and considers how university students can be perceived as progressing through a 'life cycle' of which language study is part. He suggests that 'development of an ethical system' is part of language studies and reviews a number of theories which might help to clarify the stages students reach. It is a matter of concern that he concludes that 'modern languages students are not greatly involved in this particular developmental task,' and that 'it is not at all sure that they are autonomous and individualistic in Kohlberg's sense' (1990: 61). If this is the case then some of the intentions of cultural studies teaching are unlikely to be fulfilled.

A more particular aspect of learning at university which equally calls for a well-developed learning theory is residence in the foreign country. Although this is not a universal requirement, as we pointed out above, where it does exist there are significant psychological issues involved. The literature on cross-cultural adaptation and 'culture shock' (e.g. Kim, 1988; Furnham & Bochner, 1986) clearly shows that the experience of residence in a foreign country makes major demands. As Kim points out, theorising about 'sojourner adaptation' has largely been formulated in terms of problems and difficulties to be surmounted, but it is possible to see 'culture shock' as a necessary and inevitable part of intercultural learning and growth. There have been a number of models of adaptation developed which suggest stages of personality change,such as the following account of 'trans-formation' in an intercultural situation:

- a first stage, the reduction of the other to one's own code: an ethnocentric — or, better, culture-centric — position;
- a second stage, the entry into the cultural code of the other: the implication being to become the other;
- decentring in relationship to cultural codes, one's own and that of the other; awareness of their culturally relative character;
- the search for or the creation of mediations, of unifying symbols which will permit the learner to move into one code and into the other and, on the basis of the establishment of an intermediate space which becomes an anchor point, to situate him/herself in relationship to these codes (Clanet, 1990: 123, our translation)

As Clanet suggests, however, progress through these stages can be delayed or even halted, can take a longer or shorter period. The determining factors are complex but such a theoretical model needs to be related at least to theories of cognitive and moral development.

The case of foreign language learners choosing to go to a foreign country for a long period of residence is not dealt with specifically in this literature. They are however different from those who migrate for economic reasons, who are sent abroad for business reasons, who volunteer for Peace Corps work for ideological reasons and so on. For the latter kind of sojourner, learning another language and culture conditions the success of their sojourn but is not its primary aim. University language students on the other hand spending perhaps a year in the foreign country have as their first purpose learning language and culture, and seek an employment or a place of study in order to do this. Residence is thus a substantial period of 'fieldwork', as discussed in an earlier chapter. They are already well acquainted with language and culture and are developing a professional identity which involves them not only in seeking a means of mediation for themselves, 'an intermediate space' as Clanet calls it, but also in becoming an agent of mediation for those they teach (cf. also Kramsch's notion of a 'third place', 1993: 233).

There can be no doubt about the magnitude of the experience of living abroad. Evans (1990: 48) argues that it involves basic issues of identity and describes the effect in the following terms:

What these students have in common and what distinguishes them from other students of other disciplines is a distance from their own culture, a capacity to see the world from another's point of view, to find it strange and yet not to reject it, to be happy (1990: 48)

In a more wide-ranging study of the Year Abroad including French students living in Britain and English students living in France, we identified a number of dimensions of change: stages of adaptation to the culture, changes in identity and effect on the process of maturation. The changes are evident to students themselves and they see themselves as more 'open', 'mature'. Some underwent significant changes in identity, with some English students feeling 'more French', others feeling more aware of their English culture and identity and yet others feeling 'more European' and less insular in outlook on other cultures in general (Alred, Byram, Esarte-Sarries & Ruane, 1992). It is clearly necessary for this kind of experience to be an integral part of a theory of learning in higher education and of a model of teacher education.

Developing a Model of Teacher Education

In a comprehensive attempt to define 'Attainment Targets for Foreign Language Teacher Education in Europe', Willems identifies the following four main headings for describing the knowledge and skill which might be expected of a language teacher:

- language acquisition theory and principles of learner autonomy as elements in language teacher education;
- the European dimension in the education and training of teachers;
- the foreign language teachers' communicative competence in the target language and their meta-linguistic and meta-communicative knowledge;
- the language teacher's classroom skills (Willems, 1992).

It is under the second heading that he suggests teachers need 'knowledge, insights and skills with respect to culture and society'. The 'knowledge' category includes knowledge first about Europe, its history, languages, environmental problems etc., second about the target language community and third about aspects of cultural theory. Knowledge about Europe is required to be 'elementary' in order to facilitate co-operation with colleagues in social sciences. This betrays a certain unease with a model which requires an encyclopaedic approach, a recognition that teachers need a disciplinary basis and yet that in-depth study is beyond practical possibilities. Under the notion of 'insights', Willems includes 'empathy with the cultural norms of the target language community' and 'an increased awareness of one's own 'cultural logic' in relation to others'. Here as elsewhere the developmental psychological implications of a requirement of 'empathy' are not considered. There is however a very useful consequence of attempting such a specification, in that it reveals the range of qualifications and experiences required of a language teacher and the content of knowledge and skills — language learning theory, linguistic and cultural competence, classroom performance — within which cultural learning has to be seen. It makes clear that pre-service academic and pedagogic education and training cannot suffice. It is equally clear that neither theory nor practice are sufficiently developed in language teacher education to provide a basis for detailed models. Willems' listing of knowledge and skills is a useful starting point but does not contain the principles on which courses can be planned.

We can offer here a tentative model, based on a number of research projects, which places the academic element of teacher education in a wider context of language teaching in higher education. The model draws first upon research into ways of integrating residence abroad into a language course and, secondly, on research focused on the cultural content of language learning. A description of the former is included in Chapter 4 (Case Study 6). Its essential innovation is to draw upon anthropology and ethnography as a means of structuring the fieldwork/residence part of language courses. Students are prepared for the fieldwork by a course in ethnography; they then write an ethnographic dissertation during the fieldwork and introduce this into their course on return to their university. Secondly, our proposals for cultural content in language courses arise from the analysis of textbooks used in secondary education described in Chapter 2, but the areas of study proposed should be pursued at different levels of abstraction.

Our proposal puts courses for future language teachers in the broader context of language learning for all students. The different specialisations of students will require particular emphasis: linguistics for languages students, literary criticism for language and literature students, language for specific (engineering, legal, historical etc.) purposes for engineers, lawyers, historians. That part of their languages course which is concerned with intercultural communicative competence, however, has the same basic requirements whatever their specialism. Furthermore, the concept of a residential period in a foreign country as part of the course is not confined to language specialists at least as far as Europe is concerned. ERASMUS has created opportunities for engineers, lawyers and so on to study in other European countries. Engineers need to understand the culture of engineering in other countries. They also need a means of exploring the broader culture to develop their general intercultural competence, in addition to their special interest.

This suggests that there is a common ground of practical needs and general educational purpose in higher education just as there is in secondary schooling. Let us call this a course in foreign language-and-culture.

Ideally such a course would be co-ordinated through secondary and into higher education. There would be an agreed curriculum content and co-operation on treatment of it. Insofar as such content as we shall propose can be treated at a number of levels of detail and increasing conceptual abstraction, the 'same' content would need to be dealt with on several occasions in a spiral curriculum, at secondary and higher education level, depending on the point at which learners begin their language-and-culture course. Contrary to the proposals of Campos *et al.* cited earlier, there would be no separation of language and culture even at university level, and there would be a systematic methodology even at the earliest stages. This methodology would ensure that learners perceive relationships between information associated with the language they are learning, that they begin to acquire a knowledge of the foreign culture and not simply an accumulation of disparate items of information.

What should the content be? It should provide learners with the content knowledge and linguistic and cultural skills which they need to communicate successfully with someone of equivalent background and education in the foreign country. They need to understand cultural allusions — conscious and unconscious on the part of the foreign native-speaker — and to be able to adapt their behaviour — verbal and non-verbal — appropriately. A proposal for a 'minimum content' was introduced in Chapter 2. The order in which this content might be treated, and the methodology to be used, will depend on the level of learning. Some aspects might be treated only briefly and descriptively at an early level and treated in much greater depth and more analytically at an advanced level. The methodology should however be comparative whatever the level. An account of a course for advanced learners in upper secondary, developing a comparative methodology is described in Chapter 4 (Case Study 5) and could be adapted to higher education. There should be comparison, analysis of the native-speaker perspective and acquisition of techniques for ethnographic investigations.

Where students are to spend a period in the foreign country — and this need not be more than a term or preferably a semester — a course in ethnography should be introduced. This would complement the course on content knowledge and allow advanced students to use in their language-and-culture course the analytical anthropological concepts they acquire in the Introduction to Ethnography (see Chapter 4, Case Study 6). For example, topics such as 'Language and identity' or 'National identity and personal boundaries' studied in an ethnography course provide concepts to support the study of a particular language-and-culture under themes such as 'national history' or 'social identity and social groups', from our proposal for a 'minimum content'.

The parent discipline for the language-and-culture course should be anthropology and ethnography. The course should take as its focus the experience of the individual — rather than the sociological study of social institutions, for example — and should relate that experience to the language being learnt. Students can study in the language and they can also study how the language embodies the concepts and values which they find in their analysis of the culture.

We suggested already in Chapter 2 a 'Minimum Content' in terms of areas of study. This should be the framework for the kind of course we are proposing here. Although the specific realisation for the teaching of German was prepared with beginner and intermediate learners in mind, many of the topics and themes would also be appropriate in higher education. The difference would be in degree of detail and of conceptual analysis. For example at an early level, 'formality in language' might focus only on the use of *du* and *Sie* — without mentioning the finer points of sociolinguistic analysis. At higher education level *du* and *Sie* is only part of the detailed socio-linguistic analysis which learners should undertake.

Finally, we should remember the significance of post-residence courses. Our study of residence abroad among university learners of French (Alred, Byram, Esarte-Sarries & Ruane, 1992) showed that students need the opportunity to reflect on their experience. It is at this point that the course in language and culture can be linked with the follow-up to the 'Introduction to Ethnography'. Here students can develop further their understanding of specific aspects of language and culture by reflecting on their general experience and by referring to their own ethnographic report on their fieldwork during residence.

Summary

To summarise, the model can be represented diagrammatically. The proportions of each section will depend on learners' particular specialism but the pattern is general enough to provide a framework (see Figure 3.1).

Students who intend to become language teachers would take, as their Main Study, the language and society option in language studies. Like all other students they would concurrently take a language and culture course and an ethnography course. During residence abroad they would be encouraged to seek an occupation within the education system but carry out an ethnographic study which takes them into another social domain.

There needs to be added to this model of undergraduate academic studies a professional component on language teaching methodology. In some education systems this begins concurrently with academic studies

	Main study	'Language & Culture'	Ethnography	Residence
'Years' 1&2	Non-language studies. Language studies: - language & linguistics - language & literature - language & society	Subsidiary course for *all* students (using approach from upper secondary experiment with more themes) in foreign language.	'Introduction to Ethnography' for *all* students preparing for residence in L1.	
'Year' 3				Study of main subject. Ethnographic fieldwork and report.
'Year' 4	Continuation of main study.	Combined course: - reporting on fieldwork - relating fieldwork to 'themes' - reflecting on experience (of 'culture shock') in FL		

Figure 3.1

and in others it is consecutive to it and may be carried out in a separate institution. Wherever placed, such a course needs to include:

- cultural learning theory with specific reference to younger learners, including a knowledge of theories of 'culture shock' and experiential learning during learners' residence or visits to the foreign country for which they may be responsible;
- methodology of language and culture teaching;
- practical experience of language and culture teaching in the classroom and in the field.

It is essential that, wherever practical, fieldwork should be integral to language and culture learning and therefore part of the professional component (cf. Byram & Esarte-Sarries, 1991: 186–96). This entails that cultural learning theory should include both classroom learning and learning in the field with respect to young learners. Here language teacher education will need to search widely for sound theory since particular studies of young people experiencing 'culture shock' are difficult to find.

Some indication of how young people react can be gleaned from the following quotations from interviews with a group of 13–14 year olds. In the first, a male informant describes his feelings on a visit to France:

- You thought you were alone and things — like, couldn't get to know things — you thought someone was talking about things you couldn't understand — just, like, wondering what they were talking about.

The second expresses fear of others more explicitly, when describing his failure to understand the foreign language

- I was scared — they were saying all these things and I didn't know what to do…

A third makes clear the significance of linguistic competence in experience of the foreign country:

- It felt good. Like, when you talk to them and you actually thought to yourself 'I talked to a French person' — and you get back home — 'Mam, I talked to some French people' — It was good fun talking to them.

It is clearly important that the psychology of such reactions be understood by teachers, just as much as the methodology of the teaching of grammar, pronunciation and other aspects of language teaching.

Conclusion

Writing in 1993, the symbol of European integration, we are only too aware of the changing role and the shift in the significance of foreign language teaching. The opening of frontiers within a part of Europe is a confirmation of the trend to mobility and migration which has been present for at least half a century. Although the differences between rich and poor, between North and South, and between Europe and America, the Pacific Rim and other parts of the world, are not to be underestimated, it is clear that people from different cultures will find themselves living side by side. If they are to understand each other — and not simply communicate information — language-and-culture learning has to be more complex and rich than the emphasis on technical communication has hitherto suggested (Hunfeld, 1992).

It follows that teachers of language-and-culture need a more complex and enriching education. Our suggestions in this chapter have emphasised that teacher education, in both its academic and its pedagogic dimensions, needs to provide opportunities for learning which is both cognitive and experiential. Foreign language teachers are among the most important mediators. They need to experience a foreign culture as well as analyse it. They need to reflect upon their experience as well as carry out comparative analysis of their own and the foreign culture. And they need to understand the implications of cultural learning, both cognitive and affective, for their practices in the classroom as well as for their teaching 'in the field'. The responsibilities of the foreign language teacher for introducing learners, whether young or old, to learning which challenges and modifies their perspective on the world and their cultural identity as members of a given social and national group, are enormous. Teacher education has to face the implications and provide them with the practical and theoretical support for those responsibilities.

4 Principles in Practice: Illustrative Case Studies

The purpose of this chapter is to provide some concrete illustrations of principles enunciated in earlier chapters. It is inevitable at this stage of the development of cultural studies and cultural learning that examples will be incomplete. Some will illustrate proposals for courses and syllabuses; others will describe the detail of particular classroom processes; others will suggest what might be done but has not yet been realised. We have looked for examples from different stages of learning, including courses for teachers. They are not all directly connected with the philosophy of this present volume but all nonetheless closely enough related to help our readers to realise the practices we envisage. We have not, therefore, attempted to link each case-study to our theoretical chapters. Readers will, we hope, make such links — and links with their own practices — for themselves. We have chosen a simple order, which follows the stages of language learning, starting with proposals for beginners and young learners.

(The appendices for Case Study 9 are to be found at the end of the study in question. All other appendices are to be found at the end of the book.)

Case 1: 'Cultural Awareness' and the National Curriculum for England and Wales

The National Curriculum for England and Wales is part of a major Education Reform Act passed in 1988. It specifies, for subjects considered to be essential for all pupils, levels of attainment in the subjects — 10 levels in all, usually covering compulsory education from 5–16, but for foreign languages covering only the 11–16 age-range. Each subject is specified in terms of 'attainment targets', which for languages are the four skills of listening, reading, writing and speaking, each skill being further specified in terms of ten levels.

The curriculum for languages, as for other subjects, arose from a process of creating a working group, consulting on their recommendations and ultimately making the modified recommendations law, in the shape of 'statutory orders'. The report of the working group provides the rationale for the statutory orders which contain only the bare recommendations. We need therefore to consider both documents.

The major innovation of the national curriculum is the introduction of the concept of 'cultural awareness' and recommendations for a comparative methodology. The working group added to an established list of educational purposes in language teaching the following statement: that one purpose of language teaching is 'to develop pupils' understanding of themselves and their own culture' (DES, 1990: 3). They go on to introduce the phrase 'cultural awareness' which they define as 'the promotion of understanding of and respect for other cultures (...) one of the most important aims of modern language studies.' This is then to be used 'to develop a more objective view of their own customs and ways of thinking' (DES, 1990: 36). As a third stage, they describe the relationship between cultural awareness and linguistic learning in a way which corresponds with our proposals in earlier chapters:

> A growing awareness of the culture of the people who speak the language of study is intrinsic to the learning of it and it is in this context that the areas of experience have been defined in the second part of the programmes of study. Without the cultural dimension, successful communication is often difficult...comparison between the learner's own way of life and that of the other language community are an essential means to better understanding of both. (DES, 1990: 37)

The 'programmes of study' and 'areas of experience' to which this extract refers are the recommendations and statutory orders which describe the means by which the attainment targets of the four skills shall be reached. The 'areas of experience' are an attempt to specify themes and topics which the working group believes are essential for language and culture learning in lower secondary education. By implication they constitute a 'minimum content'. Each area is introduced with the following formulation: 'During each key stage, pupils should have regular opportunities to explore in the target language topics which...'. 'Key stage' refers to the years 7–9 and 10–11 of compulsory education. The areas are as follows:

Area A. Everyday Activities

> During each key stage, pupils should have regular opportunities to explore in the target language topics which deal with activities they are likely to engage in at home and at school. This should include the language of the classroom.

> Examples of topics: home life, (...) shopping, (...) going out, leisure activities and sports, (...) school life (...)

Area B. Personal and Social Life

...topics which deal with aspects of their personal lives; relationships with family, friends and others; social attitudes, customs and institutions which are relevant to them.

Examples of topics: self, family and friends (...), health and fitness (...), major institutions (schools, hospitals, clubs, etc.) (...), personal, teenage and social attitudes towards religion, politics and society (including stereotyping and equal opportunities).

C. The World Around Us

...topics which deal with the physical environment including their own home, home town or region and environmental themes at home and abroad.

Examples of topics: (...), home town and region (...), weather and climate (...), the man-made environment (...), home region compared with a region abroad.

D. The World of Education, Training and Work

...topics which deal with education, training, employment and careers; the world of business and industry.

Examples of topics: school subjects,courses and further study or training (...), personal experience of the world of work (...), personal finance (...), unemployment (...).

E. The World of Communications

...topics which deal with the various means of communication, including the use of information technology and the media.

Examples of topics: writing and sending letters (informal and formal) including the use of electronic mail/fax (...), radio, television and satellite TV (...), computers and IT at home, school and work, advertising.

F. The International World

...topics which deal with experiences of travelling or staying abroad; contact with speakers of the foreign language; wider international issues.

Examples of topics: (...), school visits and exchanges (...), national stereotypes (...), the foreign language in use in different countries or regions of the world

G. *The World of Imagination and Creativity*

...topics which deal with imaginative and creative activities of all kinds; hobbies and interests; the creative arts in one's own and other cultures.

Examples of topics: designing and making (...), fashion and make-up (...), TV, cinema, theatre and other entertainments (...), making a class cassette, magazine or video. (DES, 1991: 27–9)

Turning to methodology, the working group and the statutory orders make a number of proposals which include comparison:

Learners should therefore have frequent opportunities to (...) appreciate the similarities and differences between their own and cultures of the communities/countries where the target language is spoken. (DES, 1990: 36)

They also present an implicit psychological theory, that learners can be led to a shift of perspective, to decentre and to reflect critically on their own culture, thus relativising their previous taken-for-granted view of themselves and their culture:

Learners should therefore have frequent opportunities to (...) identify with the experience and perspective of people in the countries and communities where the target language is spoken [and] use this knowledge to develop a more objective view of their own customs and ways of thinking. (DES, 1990: 36)

By introducing the phrase 'identify with the experience', the working group open the way for teachers to encourage learners to empathise with people of other cultures, at least in a cognitive sense.

Finally the working group argue that foreign language teaching has a particular role to play with respect to combating prejudice against minority groups within learners' own society:

One of the most potent agents in combating prejudice is the appreciation and enjoyment of diversity. This is particularly true of cultural and ethnic diversity. Of all the subjects in the National Curriculum, the study of a foreign language most directly addresses the existence of other cultures, opening up areas of knowledge and understanding which extend far beyond the way in which the language is spoken and written. Language teachers are therefore frequently involved in presenting and interpreting the experiences and identities of people in other communities. In doing so they inevitably find themselves dealing with questions such as:

- does the depiction of different ethnic groups faithfully present their perspective and their voice?

- do all pupils, as a natural part of their language course, learn about the culture and experience of groups other than their own?

Schools which have pupils from a diversity of backgrounds will have no difficulty in recognising the importance of these questions. Pupils in schools without this advantage have an even greater need to be made aware of the rich cultural diversity which is a part of all modern societies. (DES, 1990: 81–2)

The working group have thus placed foreign language teaching firmly in the centre of liberal education. They have a vision of cultural awareness which opens opportunities to language teachers never previously made explicit. It remains to be seen whether the opportunities will be seized.

Case 2: 'Fachdidaktische Kriterien zur Integration von Landeskunde und Kommunikation'

Although a full understanding of Melde's (1987) proposals can only be acquired from the rationale she develops in great detail in her book, the conclusions she draws in her final chapter are an important example of the proper integration of linguistic and cultural learning. Moreover, as they may not be accessible to all English-speakers, we hope that this overview will function as a temporary substitute until a translation is available.

Melde's work takes as its starting point the teaching of French in Germany. She provides a detailed psychological and sociological rationale for a methodology which will allow learners to acquire an understanding of the French perspective on everyday life and society. The principles of her methodology include a comparative approach, through integration of cultural and linguistic learning, to achieve a 'co-ordination' of French and German perspectives which facilitates intercultural communication and encourages learners' moral development. Her book deals almost exclusively with the theoretical underpinning of her position, which has been realised in teaching materials published separately but as part of an overarching project.

Melde proposes three identifiable but overlapping stages in her methodology, which represent a progression in both linguistic (*kommunikative*) and cultural (*landeskundliche*) domains:

I   Comprehension of the French cultural world through partner-oriented everyday (*Lebenswelt*) communication in the private domain.
II   Comprehension of French society through the media-oriented communication of political and cultural public life.
III   Introduction of the observer perspective of the social sciences.

She then summarises the content of each stage under three headings: methods/materials, cognition/cultural studies, and communication/language acquisition. Each of the three stages is further broken down into three steps and for each she gives detailed explanations of the methodological, cognitive and communicative processes which should be pursued. In her commentary on the summary she refers to two units of work developed for the teaching of French in Germany, aimed at learners in upper secondary: *L'école en France* (Melde, 1987) and *Le Languedoc-Roussillon, une région face à l'Europe* (Melde *et al.*, 1987). Her proposals do not include decisions or criteria for selecting a specific domain of French life or a particular range of topics. She suggests implicitly that the methodology is all-important and can be adapted to whatever topic is chosen.

In order to provide an overview of the methodology, we reproduce the three steps of each major stage under the three dimensions; detailed suggestions of the kinds of materials and techniques to be used are not included:

Stage I: Comprehension of the French cultural world through partner-oriented everyday (*Lebenswelt*) communication in the private domain

Step 1:

Methods/materials — reconstruction of the theme/problem from the insider perspective of members of French culture by means of conversations, interviews, reports, stories (authentic recordings).

Cognition/cultural studies — empathising into French culture through appropriation (*Nachvollziehen*) of everyday knowledge and the perspective of its members.

Communication/language acquisition — receptive comprehension of interviews, reports, etc. through excerpts from the French cultural world.

Step 2:

Methods/materials — constructive confrontation with the described perspectives on specific problems/themes.

Cognition/cultural studies — developmental work in appropriation of the described perspectives on specific problems/themes (shift of perspective).

Communication/language acquisition — analysis, interpretation and evaluation of the described perspectives on specific problems/themes.

Step 3:

Methods/materials — comparative approach, comparison with learners' own cultural world.

Cognition/cultural studies — distancing from and relativisation of learners' own perspective through comparison ('co-ordination of perspectives').

Communication/language acquisition — make comparisons to learners' own world (reporting on one's own experience, comparing French and own world etc.).

Stage II: Comprehension of French society through the media-oriented communication of political and cultural public life

Step 1:

Methods/materials — reconstruction of the theme on the basis of the process of public self-presentation (Selbstverständigung) of French society.

Cognition/cultural studies — appropriation of the process of self-presentation of French society through the processing of the chosen theme / problem in political-cultural public life.

Communication/language acquisition — receptive comprehension and analysis of extracts from regional and trans-regional newspapers, the means of communication used by associations and societies, parties, the government, administration etc.

Step 2:

Methods/materials — constructive confrontation with the perspectives and problems as represented in communications and mass media.

Cognition/cultural studies — appropriation and comprehension of positions and perspectives articulated in the media, from the internal French, societal context (taking over another perspective).

Communication/language acquisition — analysis interpretation and evaluation of the articulated positions and perspectives for specific excerpts from French reality.

Step 3:

Methods/materials — comparative approach, comparison with learners' own society.

Cognition/cultural studies — distancing from and relativisation of learners' own (national) perspective by comparison ('co-ordination of perspectives').

Communication/language acquisition — drawing comparisons with the treatment of the theme in German public life.

Stage III: Introduction of the observer perspective of the social sciences

Step 1:

Methods/materials — introduction of the observer perspective of the social sciences to throw a systematic light on selected aspects and structures of French cultural life and the French system from within internal French developments and conditions.

Cognition/cultural studies — comprehension of the French cultural world and the French system from within internal French conditions and developments (acquisition of French perspectives).

Communication/language acquisition — reporting, summarising, commenting and interpreting diagrams, statistics, text extracts which describe and explain aspects and structures of the French cultural world and the French system.

Step 2:

Methods/materials — introduction of the social science observer perspective to promote understanding of similarities and differences which hinder or promote Franco-German understanding concerning the securing of the future and of self-determination in Europe.

Cognition/cultural studies — comprehension of Franco-German commonalities and differences as a pre-condition for Franco-German understanding concerning the securing of the future and of self-determination in Europe ('co-ordination of perspectives').

Communication/language acquisition — reporting, summarising, commenting, interpreting diagrams, statistics, text extracts which allow a comparison of selected aspects and structures of German and French society.

Step 3:

Methods/materials — introduction of the social science observer perspective in order to emphasise the threat to the communicatively structured cultural world in France and Germany.

Cognition/cultural studies — comprehension of the necessity of defending and broadening the communicatively structured cultural world which guarantees self-determination through communicative understanding and the construction of political will in France and Germany (criticism of society).

Communication/language acquisition — reporting, summarising, commenting, interpreting diagrams, statistics, text extracts which confront the threat to the communicatively structured cultural world in France and Germany.

Melde's argument for progression is to take learners into the individual, private world of the foreign culture and thereafter into the world of public life and socio-political struggles as they are mediated through newspapers and other mass media. Learners shall, in both cases, be led to appropriate the insider perspective and then, by comparative techniques which relativise the learner's own cultural perspective, to grasp the potential of a 'co-ordination of perspectives' for developing proper communication. Melde argues however that a third dimension — that of the social science observer perspective — is required in order to acquaint learners with the taken-for-granted knowledge which is not explicit in the texts etc. of the foreign culture and, secondly, to provide information on learners' own society which will facilitate comparison.

This third dimension — which will be brought into the first two stages wherever necessary — will also provide the means for reflecting upon the need to defend and promote Franco-German efforts in securing self-determination for the individual within his/her cultural world. This stage, says Melde, is more likely to be reached with learners in the 16–19 age group. It is also the aspect which will be most difficult to realise, given the lack of appropriate training for teachers. The use of texts etc. to introduce learners to the French perspective, to compare and relativise their own individual and national perspectives and to establish a co-ordination of perspectives, calls upon teaching techniques which are already familiar. The social critical dimension on the other hand requires teachers and students to grasp the historically-determined nature of individual and national perspectives: the relationship between people's statements and the particular socio-historical context in which they find themselves. Melde is here drawing upon the work of Habermas and Bourdieu which is unlikely to be familiar to many language teachers.

As indicated above, Melde's proposals can be seen in practice in two course units published by the team in which she worked.

Case 3: 'Understanding Politics and Political Institutions in Britain'

This work was carried out by the lower secondary team of the Institut National de Recherche Pédagogique[1] in the context of the research entitled 'L'enseignement de la civilisation en classe de langues vivantes en France et en Grande-Bretagne' under the scientific responsibility of Albane Cain.

The unit to be described here is an attempt to introduce the teaching of 'civilisation'/cultural studies in a systematic way into lower secondary foreign language teaching in France. It aims to make learners aware of selected aspects of political life in Britain and comparable institutions and practices in France. The pupils concerned have been learning French for almost three years and are aged approximately 14; the classes contain a wide range of motivations and abilities and are in no sense 'selected'. We have decided to describe two specific lessons in two different schools which deal with the early stages of the unit. It will be clear that teachers and classes differ and, consequently, different techniques are used. In both cases this is the first time the unit and materials have been used. Nonetheless there are clear indications of a common purpose and a strong comparative methodology.

Lesson 1:

The class is a group of 25 children in 4e (third year of lower secondary) in a *collège* in rural France. They are nearing the end of their third year of learning English and today is their first lesson of a series devoted to politics in Britain.

The aims of the unit are to introduce pupils to a factual knowledge of selected aspects of British political life, to compare with and induce reflection on similar aspects of French politics and to bring them to understand the significance of some British political institutions from a British perspective.

Although today's is the first lesson, they have completed a one-page informal questionnaire for their teacher on their existing knowledge of what will be the principal facts and concepts of the unit. They know they are going to start something new and that they have a visitor who has come to see what is happening. The classroom is ready: slide-projector, overhead projector and audio-cassette player are set up and the slides etc. inserted. Pupils come in, sit down and two of them draw the curtains.

The first slide is a picture of English banknotes and coins, with the Queen's head visible. 'What is this?', 'Who can you see?'; 'The Queen!' reply several pupils.

The second slide follows quickly: postage stamps, including one Christmas stamp with just a silhouette of the Queen's head. 'Who can you see?', 'What has she got on her head?' The answers come quickly.

The third slide shows a close-up of a policeman with 'E II R' clearly visible. 'Where's the Queen?', 'What does "E" mean?', '"R" does not mean "reine" but "regina" in Latin — the Queen'; 'Why is there a "2" between "E" and "R"?'; 'Yes, she is the second, we don't say "Elizabeth Two", but "Elizabeth the second".'

It is easy to see where the teacher is taking the lesson so far; the pupils reply easily, mainly in single words and, apart from the linguistic remark in the last statement, the focus has been clearly on the pictures and the recurrence of the Queen. There will be other moments in the lesson when the teacher corrects a linguistic error, or asks a pupil to correct the error him/herself. The main focus is however clearly on content not medium, and pupils manage to respond adequately throughout the lesson in spoken or written form.

The lesson continues. The next slide shows a post-box and again the symbol 'E II R', and the teacher introduces the words 'symbol' and 'monarchy', which are similar to cognate French words and cause no comprehension problems.

The fifth slide shows the front page of a newspaper of 1952 with the headline 'King dies in his sleep' and with photographs of King George and Princess Elizabeth. By question and answer — 'What happened when he died?', 'Was the Queen elected?', 'It's hereditary — "héréditaire"' — the process of accession to the throne is clarified.

The next slide shows Buckingham Palace and after establishing what it is and who lives there, the teacher moves to saying 'What about France? If we compare, who is Head of State? Where does he live?' and shows a picture of the Palais de l'Elysée. 'France is not a monarchy. How did M. Mitterand become president?', 'Is it hereditary?', 'How long do presidents remain?', 'After seven years, what happens?', 'What is the symbol of our republic?', 'So Marianne is a symbol of what?', 'Yes, of the French *republic*; because France is a republic.'

At this point the teacher puts an overhead projector slide on the screen with a grid which pupils copy and complete:

	Britain	France
Regime		
Head of State		
Accession		
Official residence		
Effigy (= head) on stamps		

After a few minutes the teacher asks what they have written and, as pupils answer, he writes their responses onto the grid:

monarchy	republic
queen/king	president
hereditary	elections/vote
Buckingham Palace	Palais de l'Elysée
Queen	Marianne

He adds the phonetic script for the first two words and emphasises which syllable is stressed. In asking them about accession — 'Who is her eldest son?' — he discovered they have heard of 'Lady Di' but not Prince Charles.

The next stage is to listen to an abridged version of the Queen's Christmas broadcast; the pupils have a transcript and after they have listened, including the national anthem at the end, they carry out short exercises which ask them when she was speaking; the words she uses to characterise her role; what she says she expects from the British people; and the words referring to religion. The text they hear and read is as follows:

> In 1952, when I first broadcast to you at Christmas,the world was a very different place to the one we live in today. Only seven years had passed since the end of one of the most destructive wars in the history of mankind.

> Next February will see the 40th anniversary of my father's death and of my accession. Over the years I have tried to follow my father's example and to serve you as best as I can. You have given me in return your loyalty and your understanding, and for that, I give you my heartfelt thanks. I feel the same obligation to you that I felt in 1952. With your prayers and your help, and with the love and support of my family, I shall try to serve you in the years to come.

> May God bless you and bring you a happy Christmas.

In asking them which words they underlined to explain what the Queen's role is and what she expects of the British people, the teacher identifies 'serve' and 'loyalty, understanding, prayers'. The last word leads to other words they have identified referring to religion: Christmas, prayers, God. The teacher then introduces comparison again: 'Does M. Mitterrand use words like that? Does he say "May God bless you"? Why not? (Silence.) Perhaps you don't know. In France we have a separation between state and religion. In Britain, there's no separation. In many English schools, pupils sing religious hymns, the headteacher says prayers.'

More slides are introduced as the lesson moves to the last ten minutes of a fifty-minute period. First a picture of the Queen making her first Christmas broadcast in 1952. Next a picture of the British coat of arms: 'Is there anything surprising? Yes, it's in French, "Dieu et mon droit", and again there is a religious word.' He moves briefly into French: 'Ce n'est pas un état laïque, en France le chef d'état n'a rien à faire avec la religion' [It is not a secular state, in France the head of state has nothing to do with religion]. He then draws attention to the lion and the unicorn and elicits the symbolic significance of the former — 'Think of La Fontaine!' — and tells them that the unicorn symbolises purity and strength — 'An imaginary animal.'

As the lesson draws to a close, pupils are told to look again at the grid they completed when they are at home, in preparation for the next lesson. The lesson ends; one pupils asks the teacher if they are going to do more of this next lesson — he sounds interested and enthusiastic — he wants to know what they will be doing next. The teacher says it will be a surprise. The last pupils leave the class and the lesson is over.

The second lesson of the series is in another school, with a different teacher and a different class. These are children from an urban setting, living in a 'new town' designated as an educational priority area.

Much the same content — but not identical progress — has been covered in the first lesson as we had seen in the rural school. The pupils had been given homework and after they had quickly settled into their seats — on a hot, late afternoon — the teacher begins to ask the homework questions:

'When did Elizabeth become Queen?'

'After the death of her father.'

'What was the date of the speech?'

'Christmas.'

And so on, establishing the year, the words she uses to characterise her function, the words referring to religion, what she expects from the British people and from her own family.

The second stage is entered as the teacher says 'Now I want you to sum up the Queen's role. What did we say about the pictures, where did we see the Queen's effigy?' The notion of symbol is not entirely elicited but the pupils remember the principal facts.

The teacher now points to the grid familiar from the first lesson but apparently not done by this class. They copy it from the board onto a new page, because the teacher says they will have further things to add to it later. As they complete the grid, first individually and then as a class, they do first the French side, which in this version is on the left, and then the British side — marked 'United Kingdom'. The teacher explains they are going to write 'monarchy and parliament' opposite 'republic' for the UK. She also writes House of Commons and House of Lords and explains they will do these later. One pupils says something, inaudible to the observer, but the teacher's reply refers to 'what you've done in history', to which some pupils say they have not yet done this in history. The opportunities for cross-curricular links are making themselves evident.

Completing the rest of the grid is quick and seems to cause the pupils no problems. Occasionally the teacher draws attention to the pronunciation of particular words — the place of stress in 'republic', the pronunciation of 'Buckingham Palace'.

The next part of the lesson brings in new material. The teacher shows a colour photograph and gives each pupil a photocopy of it with a date and origin on it: 'Nouvelle République du Centre Ouest — 18.7.91'. The picture shows Mitterrand, Major, Kohl and Bush. The teacher asks what the date is, who they can see. They quickly identify Mitterrand and Bush. 'What is Bush?' and one pupil says 'President of the United States.' They cannot identify John Major, after the teacher has said, in French, that the photograph was taken at the international summit of the seven main industrialised countries. Eventually someone suggests Major and the teacher can go on to ask 'Is the Queen there?' — 'No.' The teacher then explains and writes on the board 'The Prime Minister represents the United Kingdom at important international meetings' which they copy onto their photocopy and underline 'represents'. They are clearly used to having photocopies to stick in their exercise books. By a similar process, using a photograph, taken from the television screen, of the Queen and Mitterrand together at a dinner reception, the teacher makes the point that the Queen *entertains* in the evening and has a different function. They write on their photocopy 'Buckingham Palace in the evening.'

In the last twenty minutes of the lesson the class listens to an interview. The teacher introduces it in French by saying that it is to help them understand the function of the Queen and the prime minister. She then explains in English that the interview took place soon after the elections of April 1992 with a man called Keith who is a fireman; each document is carefully contextualised. The teacher then uncovers a number of questions on the board and gives pupils some essential words. She distinguishes between those which are 'transparent' and others, for which she adds a French translation. She also underlines those which she wants them to note, leaving them to decide for themselves which others they want to note:

(Transparent)	(Others)
post	the *Conservatives*
role	*power*
to gain = to win	to *choose* = choisir
replacement	
majority	

The questions about the text are on the board with an account of the interviewee: 'The person who is interviewed is called Keith; his profession is fireman'.

Tasks:

(1) find out the new Prime Minister's name
(2) reasons why he became Prime Minister (three)

(3) the Prime Minister's role according to Keith
(4) who chooses him? who nominates him?

They listen to the interview after the teacher has explained that Keith is from Wales and the accent is different, 'so you have to be careful.' The recording does indeed prove difficult for this class but the accent is only part of the trouble.

Nonetheless the teacher establishes with them, and writes on the board, the key points:

(1) John Major
(2) leader of the Conservative party, elections, nominated by the Queen
(3) like a headmaster, he listens to ministers and decides
(4) his party, the Queen

Just before the 60-minute lesson draws to a close, the pupils receive a final photocopy of a picture of John Major standing outside No. 10 Downing Street: 'Where does the French Prime Minister live?' — 'Matignon.' — 'Where does the English Prime Minister live?' — 'At 10 Downing Street.' These facts appear to be well-known.

For homework the pupils receive a printed list of 'The New Cabinet' of John Major and four questions to work on:

(1) French equivalent of 'the Cabinet'
(2) Tick equivalent Ministries in France and the UK
(3) Who presides over the Cabinet in France? in the UK?
(4) Which are the important Ministers for *you*?

Following lessons will introduce the role of the Prime Minister, compared with the French President, will explain how Members of Parliament are elected, how the Lords are selected, how in the Commons government and opposition parties sit on opposite sides of the House; and there will be constant comparison and contrast with French institutions. At the end of the unit pupils will have acquired some factual knowledge and begun to understand the words 'monarchy', 'republic', 'democracy', by associating them with concrete examples — including pictures, ballot papers, aural and written texts — and hopefully they will have developed a clearer grasp of these words and the concepts — and relationships between concepts — which are established in the British way of thinking, British culture.

Case 4: *Ma Ville et Celle des Autres*

This three-part teaching pack (teacher's book, student book and cassette) was produced in 1990 by BELC (Le Bureau pour l'enseignement de la langue et la civilisation française à l'étranger) in Paris for the teaching of

French as a foreign language. The aims are to bring students to an understanding of the subjectivity of perceptions of and the range of reactions to an urban space. Here the emphasis is as much intra-cultural as inter-cultural, since students are directed to the very different frames of reference of the different interviewees, all of whom are French, rather than emphasising differences in perceptions between cultures. This intra-cultural awareness-raising can be seen as a first step towards inter-cultural understanding and relativising.

Michelle Troutot and Geneviève Zarate are co-authors and were assisted by four other members of the BELC team in carrying out the interviews on the cassette. There are 12 'intercultural' exercises in the pack, designed to raise students' awareness of their perceptions of space and in particular of an urban environment. The suggested length of classroom time varies between 30 and 90 minutes for each exercise. Virtually all the photographs are of the small area of Paris (the *Marais*) which constitutes the main focus of the pack. Two large street maps are included in the student book so that students have the opportunity to build up some knowledge or 'feel' for the area as they progress through the activities. The cassette contains very short extracts from interviews with 11 different inhabitants of the *Marais* (five male; six female); mostly middle-aged (eight aged between 35 and 55), two older (67 and 82) and one younger (20). Transcripts of the interview extracts are given in the student handbook. The extracts are interspersed with a repeated catchy tune which encourages the students to be alert and yet provides a kind of stable point of return in a series of exercises designed to de-stabilise and problematise students' own preconceptions of what constitutes 'space'.

The teacher's book provides suggestions for implementing the material and background information on the interviews and, most importantly, the educational objectives for each exercise. The teacher's book is not simply a useful adjunct to the teaching material but seeks to explain and broaden the teacher's frames of understanding as well as the pupils'. In Activity 4, for example, where an interviewee's perceptions of the *Marais* unusually coincide with officially designated zones, a variety of contributory factors and interpretations are provided which may help to explain this perception (he walks a lot so he knows an extended area, his former work delivering goods was linked to administrative boundaries, he wants to upgrade where he lives, he adopts an impersonal approach because the interviewer is not known to him, compared to a later interview with a known interviewer). Not only is the pupil required to challenge his own preconceptions, but the teacher is asked to do the same.

The activities in the student book are designed in three stages. Firstly, students are asked to construct their own mental maps of their town (including personal responses to different loci and routes that they may take). An example is given in the student book. These different constructs are then brought together in group work with joint group maps being produced. Even at this first stage the students have the opportunity to discuss their own differences in perception and to be thus prepared for the variety of mental maps they will encounter later. These group maps form a point of comparison, a point of return for later activities in the pack, and it is suggested that they may be displayed in the classroom.

The second activity in this first stage is a comparison of 'official maps' (obtained by the teacher from tourist boards or hotels) with the students' own maps. Students are able to see the differences in priority between the two kinds of maps without either map being valued more highly than the other. Official maps may provide information, for example of administrative boundaries, street names and public buildings, of which some inhabitants themselves may be unaware. Personal maps can include affective factors (odours, visual impressions etc.) totally missing from official publications.

The next stage is a series of exercises based on extracts from the interviews with different inhabitants of the *Marais*. As an introduction to the change in focus from the students' own town to Paris, a transitional familiarisation exercise is included. Here students are asked to match eight sounds (heard on the cassette) to eight photographs of the *Marais*. This exercise fulfils several functions: students are drawn further into an affective dimension, already anticipated in the personal responses in map-making in the first stage; they encounter the district which will form the focus of their study as they might first encounter it themselves through sight and sound, although of course without the tactile and olfactory dimensions; some visual clues are provided to anchor later descriptions (virtually all the photographs are of buildings or streets mentioned by interviewees) and students are encouraged to be 'detectives', to correlate and deduce information, a skill developed extensively throughout the exercises.

The eight interviews provide eight different possibilities of perceiving the *Marais* and one or more extracts are given at each stage to illustrate these views. Students are encouraged to relativise personal viewpoints either by comparing the mental constructs offered with official street maps or by looking at the processes they used in constructing their own maps.

The next four activities explore the notion of which students have already become aware, namely that space is perceived through visual

markers. The markers offered are: those which coincide with official desig-
nations — administrative districts, well-known public buildings; natural
boundaries — the river, an arterial road, the Rue de Rivoli; shops and
friends' houses which delimit a small area; and a series of places which
serve as thresholds of entry to the *Marais*. Thus students are made aware of
physical boundaries and markers which are imposed on the surrounding
urban space by people's varying mental maps.

Activity 8 offers a more affective approach to personal environment with
an extract describing routes through the *Marais* chosen according to the
protection they afford from wind, cold and heat. This is followed by an
exercise encouraging students to identify locations associated with particular sensations in their own town. The affective dimension is underpinned
by the work that some students will have done in preparing their own
personal maps and by the series of photos in the student book which
prompt reflection on contact with different surfaces: a child faltering on
paving stones, bare feet on grass, obstructed pavements, and high-heeled
shoes passing over a grating. A final stage of this activity provides two
different interview extracts describing opposing olfactory experiences of
the same spot (*rue des Rosiers*): one positive with the fragrance of herbs for
sale and the other negative with fumes from exhaust and street pollution.

Activity 9 moves onto a different plane, focusing on human relationships. Two people's constructs of the *Marais* are offered based on the
location of friends' dwellings. One of these comes from the interviewee in
Activity 6 and shows that constructs on different bases can produce mental
maps of different sizes: in the earlier extract the interviewee delimits a space
of seven or eight roads in his construct of the local area according to shops
and neighbours; in the later extract this is extended to a larger area, as he is
thinking of where close friends live. Students are also asked to consider the
different kinds of networks that form personal relationships. The young
man in the two extracts had himself used two different human networks,
one incorporating shops and local friends/neighbours and one of close
friends. These two networks belong to two different mental maps. The
second extract describes a much smaller personal space delimited by
friends who live close to the interviewee's workplace (a bookshop).

Activity 10 relates again to personal relationships but here on a business
level. The interviewee sees the *Marais* in terms of his clientele. He draws on
a specialised market because of the location of his shop, the art-lovers who
may patronise his picture-framing business. The economic advantage of the
area depends for him on the up-market clientele; this clientele is seen in a
second interview extract to disadvantage another interviewee who finds
the resulting street market prices far too high. In this activity, as in Activity

8, the same few roads are seen in two quite different ways by different interviewees. This duality is carried further by exercises focusing on different names for the same place which relate in turn to different frames of reference. Thus 'Beaubourg' which is mentioned by both interviewees relates to the street in which the building is situated, a more locally-centred frame, and the 'Centre National d'Art Moderne de Georges Pompidou' belongs to a more institutional and national 'frame'.

In the last activity in this second central section of the pack students are encouraged to recognise what is ignored in an urban environment and also asked to consider cultural boundaries. A single extract is used which links back to an earlier interview extract. M. Dangouet who is the interviewee in both cases reveals an interesting additional construct in his later interview. His first interview points to a mental map congruent with an official, public construct, that of the 3rd and 4th *arrondissements*. When asked in the second interview about a street which lies in close proximity to his own, M. Dangouet replies 'Je vais jamais par là' ['I never go that way']. This area is not one he recognises since it is ethnically marked: 'ça doit être le quartier juif' ['that must be the Jewish district']. Students are thus alerted to three crucial factors: first, that spatial proximity does not necessarily signal personal proximity (the interviewee chooses two *arrondissements* as his own area and not a neighbouring street); second, that parts of an urban space can be ignored out of existence if they represent issues people are unwilling to acknowledge or engage in; and, third, that in addition to other boundaries determined by personal relationships (friends and business contacts), there are also culturally/ethnically determined boundaries. Students are encouraged to reflect both on the relationship of the two interview extracts and on their experiences in their own towns in terms of areas they may ignore.

Throughout the introductory exercises and the main body of listening exercises students have been encouraged to relativise the information they encounter, setting it against counter-interpretations both from other interviewees and from differing accounts from the same interviewee. They have been encouraged to compare the experiences of the interviewees with their own experiences. Here some opportunity is afforded for intercultural comparison, but there is equal if not greater emphasis on the diversity of perceptions amongst the French interviewees. A further important pedagogical benefit of the activities is the structuring of the exercises to develop the students' deductive and analytical powers. Information is withheld so that students take responsibility for their own learning and deduce autonomously. In the later extracts, for example, students are asked to identify the voices of interviewees or information about them. In Activity 10, students are asked to study the information given by one of the interviewees and to deduce further information. Mme Rosenberg describes the market near the Beaubourg, which she dislikes because it is expensive, and two other markets which are 'très comme avant' ['very much what they were like before'] and 'très, très spécial, très coloré' ['very very special, very colourful'], which she likes. The implication here then is that these markets are favoured because they are cheaper but students are asked to deduce this information rather than it being given.

The final stage of the teaching pack consists of five different exercises which will allow students to evaluate how their skills and knowledge have developed in the course of using the teaching materials. Students have had the opportunity to absorb information about the *Marais* both directly and indirectly through interviews, photographs and by consulting the maps. The first exercise in this activity questions students on what they have learnt, thus making them aware of this information absorption. A second exercise allows students to evaluate their deductive powers by spotting likely assumptions that could be made from two interviewee extracts (describing changes in attitudes towards the area, one positive, one negative). These two exercises offer multiple-choice answers. The next two exercises are more open and ask students to evaluate their own reactions. In Exercise 3 they are asked whether they have altered their responses to urban space in any way (by noticing new things or changing their usual route). In Exercise 4 a series of multiple-choice statements allows students to assess their possible reactions in an unknown town, the extent to which they would either act autonomously or as a tourist. The last exercise carries this idea further by providing some introductory material on St Nazaire (two maps) and asking students to analyse information and imagine how they might react if they were staying in this town for the first time. Interestingly the lack of extra visual material or personal statements from the residents in this last exercise points up the difficulty of understanding or engagement in a 'flat' textual presentation and to the superior route to understanding provided by the previous eleven activities.

The exercises in the pack cover a range of affective and cognitive domains. In secondary literature on intercultural learning, time and space are both highlighted as useful areas on which to focus in culture teaching and learning. Brown for example mentions the particular perceptions of time used by the Hopi tribe (1987: 139). The two dimensions, territoriality and temporality, in Hall's 10-part primary message system (1959: 222–3) are mentioned by both Hughes in his overview of suitable cultural topics (1986: 164–5) and Pfister & Poser (1987: 51–7). The latter also refer to Tinsley & Woloshin's (1974) analysis of 'deep culture' with its five areas of orientation in human behaviour which include time and space.

Time-line exercises such as those used in a lesson in Case Study 5 below and these activities on spatial awareness from Troutot and Zarate provide a foundation for such intercultural comparison. By focusing on different interpretations which exist *within* a culture students will be prepared for differences that exist *between* cultures.

Case 5: Cultural Studies/'Civilisation' for Advanced Language Learners

The work described here is part of a joint research project of the School of Education, University of Durham and the Institut National de Recherche Pédagogique in Paris, part of which is described in Case 3. The work is incomplete at the time of writing. The research is supported by the Leverhulme Trust.

Courses for advanced learners in upper secondary education in England are usually one of only three subjects studied by learners at this level. Until relatively recently, this has meant in-depth study of the language and of selected works from the literary canon. For a decade or more students have been offered the opportunity to substitute social and contemporary studies for literature study, although there is still only a small percentage who choose to do so: 10% in the statistics for the University of London Examinations Board, the only board to publish these separately. This may reflect teachers' rather than students' preferences.

The project presented here attempts to improve on the social or contemporary studies options by providing a systematic theoretical and methodological basis. Hitherto, approaches to social studies have been ad hoc and largely atheoretical. The project has been realised in terms of a pilot course devised by teachers and researchers. The course is in tune with existing examinations, to ensure that the pupils involved do not feel that valuable time is being wasted. It also draws on existing teaching materials and techniques. The major innovation is in drawing upon social anthropology and ethnography to create a new theory and methodology which places students' own experience as the starting point for their work and as a basis for comparison with their study of other cultures; the pilot course is focused on France and French society.

The course is summarised in the following statement of the fundamental principles and in the subsequent description of aims and pilot units of work.

Overview of the pilot course:

The fundamental principles of the course can be summarised as follows:

- the study of language is inseparable from the study of culture, by which we mean the way of thinking and acting in a social group; language embodies many of these social actions and expresses the underlying values and beliefs;
- by 'culture' we refer to what a person needs to know in order to be part of a social group: ways of thinking and valuing, ways of behaving, shared knowledge of the world;
- the acquisition of a foreign language involves acquiring some of the culture it embodies, through learning modes which include 'study' and 'practice' of language and culture;
- the course of study shall be structured by principles of progression: in the nature of the content, in the difficulty of conceptual learning, in techniques of teaching and learning;
- study of one language and culture shall prepare students for study of others and therefore includes acquisition of techniques for study of other languages and cultures in the future.

The purpose of the pilot course is to illustrate how these principles can be put into operation, to propose specific topics and their associated learning aims, and to demonstrate techniques of teaching and assessment. The course includes teaching material used in piloting the ideas and principles but the material is only illustrative; we are not writing a new textbook but rather proposing new principles and methods. The teaching materials can easily be replaced by other materials to suit other teachers and students, and to keep the course up to date.

The aims of the course

The course is intended to introduce students to five specific aspects of French culture, i.e. the knowledge and feelings French people share about specific areas of their way of life as a national group. Students are to acquire an understanding of the knowledge and feelings by analysis and experience of illustrative primary texts and exercises, and an ability to use the associated language for communication with French people. In communication on the five topics, they will have an understanding of the associated and connotated meanings of the language and be able thereby not only to exchange information but also to establish a relationship with their interlocutors.

The second main aim of the course is to introduce students to methods of study of other cultures which they can use whenever they meet other languages and cultures in the future. Here our dominant model is that of the ethnographer and some of our techniques which students shall acquire are taken from ethnography, i.e. the investigation and interpretation of the culture of a foreign community and people.

There are therefore general aims for the course and more specific aims and objectives for each unit. The general aims underpin each unit but are not repeated at the beginning of each unit. They are formulated as follows:

Introductory statement of general aims

The aims of the course are:

- empathy with French people and some feeling of what it is like to be French;
- a body of knowledge about key aspects of French culture;
- ethnographic techniques with which to approach other cultures and the curiosity, openness and independence to do so;
- a perspective on students' own culture, allowing them to relativise or 'denaturalise' it and see it as specific to time and place rather than assuming it is the norm;
- some understanding of the link between language and culture and an understanding of culture-specific verbal and non-verbal behaviour, and the ability to use these in a culturally appropriate way;
- positive attitudes towards and interest in French people and speakers of other languages.

Overview of the pilot units

Each unit contains:

- a statement of aims;
- a number of 'stages' of work, each with its statement of learning objectives;
- material for use in each stage;
- a 'fieldwork option' of work to be carried out during a visit to France.

The five units

In each case attitudes and concepts which are both underlying and contained in statements from and behaviour of native speakers are analysed as well as a basic framework of knowledge being taught.

- *Family* (name-giving, ceremonies, meal-times, differing household structures and links with relatives).
- *Education* (education system, historical context, social context).
- *Work* (patterns of employment, prestige of jobs, mobility, nature of work in relation to leisure, and remuneration).

- *Regional Identity* (nature of regional identity in Britain and France, regional identity as part of social identity).
- *Politics* (power structures in social groups, both private and public).

In order to illustrate the detail of the course, we include the following description of two lessons, one part of the *Education* unit and the other part of the *Work* unit.

Lesson 1

The class is of nine Lower Sixth pupils in a single-sex comprehensive. The boys sit in rows and are mostly co-operative if rather reticent at times (perhaps because of the presence of a visitor). They are in the third term of their 'A' level course but this is only the second term of working with the project syllabus. They are half-way through the second unit (Education) and have previously studied the implicit values of school systems (from both pupils' and teachers' points of view) and the structure of French schools. In the previous week, working with a native French speaker, students had discussed a series of questions on school which they would prepare individually, try out on their peer group in English and then present the findings in the following lesson. This 90-minute lesson focuses on the handling of pupil dissatisfaction with school and uses a variety of methods to do so (listening comprehension, discussion and role-play). The lesson consists of nine short stages ranging between five and 15 minutes, all focused on a comparison of English and French attitudes and forms of protest in a school context. French is spoken throughout virtually the whole lesson.

Before starting on the lesson proper, the teacher checks that the students understand what will happen in the following lesson (that they will be presenting in French the findings of their surveys). She then explains that 'On va regarder ce qui se passe quand il y a des problèmes dans les lycées' ['We will look at what happens when there are problems in post-16 schools']. The first activity consists of pupils discussing in pairs (in French) possible courses of action when students are dissatisfied with school — examples are given of a shortage of books or teachers — and they are given two minutes to discuss. The boys talk easily and fluently with each other and take the task seriously. They are used to gathering ideas autonomously and producing them in French. The teacher circulates and listens to the boys, helping them with vocabulary where desired.

Although the task has been explained clearly, they seem mostly to talk about what problems might exist rather than solutions. When asked for their ideas, the groups demonstrate this interpretation by producing their list of problems: lack of money for books and for sports equipment, and discipline, for example. The pupils become quite frivolous when asked about solutions and suggest jokingly 'death'. This process of questioning allows the pupils to recognise the *lack* of a tradition of protest in British schools and the strangeness of the idea of thinking that change is possible. Another pupil voices his dissatisfaction at not being able to leave school: 'Je voudrais partir [quitter] l'école quand je n'ai pas le [de] cours' ['I would like to leave the schools premises when I don't have a lesson']; asking the headmaster to change this regulation is suggested as a possible solution to this problem. A strike is also suggested but this also meets with embarrassed low-key laughter. In experiencing their reactions affectively and at first-hand the pupils have something concrete against which to set the later information they encounter. This stage lasts approximately 15 minutes.

In the next stage (15 minutes) students are asked to think in more general terms about the key words 'strike' and 'demonstration' ('grève' and 'manifestation') which are written on the board. Firstly the meaning is checked of both words and the students are asked if they have ever taken part in either. Then they are asked to find a piece of paper and quickly write down four or five French words or phrases which they associate with 'grève' and 'manifestation'. They work individually on this task for five minutes. This task allows teacher and students to understand the students' preconceptions. Associated vocabulary is then written on the blackboard in the equivalent French for 'strike', 'money' 'police', 'military attacks', 'anger', 'not working', 'taxes'. For 'demonstration' the French equivalents of 'lots of people', 'lots of noise', 'horses', 'dogs', 'fighting'. The teacher also introduces the word 'revendication' [demand] which relates to the topic and will be relevant later. Pupils are then asked to think about these words globally: 'Est-ce que tous les mots-là sont quelque chose d'intéressant, de positif, ou quelque chose de négatif, qui vous fait peur?' ['Are all those words something interesting or positive or something negative which makes you frightened?'] Students are then asked to vote on whether they think the words are positive or negative by raising their hands.

The next stage is the first of two listening comprehension exercises. The students have a written transcript of the recording with words blanked out which they have to fill in. This is part of a worksheet containing other exercises related to the tape (Appendix I). The recording is part of an interview with a 17-year-old French exchange student (Stéphane) from Brive, which was taped particularly for the project. In the hour-long interview he talks about his own experiences and feelings and in this section describes the student demonstrations that took place in Paris in 1990 and the history of student demonstrations (1968, 1981). (Elsewhere he describes in more detail the student demonstrations in Brive in which he participated.)

The teacher explains the context of the extract and asks the students to read the introduction to the exercises which provides the same information (Stéphane's age, name, his involvement with the protests and how the protests started). The teacher also reads out the introduction to make sure that students are fully aware of the context. The words 'déclic' [trigger] and 'viol' [rape] are translated as they are key words in the exercise. The meaning of 'surveillant' [supervisor] is checked (students had already encountered this while watching a previous video.) The teacher explains the format of the exercise (listening to some short extracts and filling in the gaps, each extract to be played twice with the tape being stopped in appropriate places the second time).

The pupils are then questioned about the missing words, which are supplied orally and written on the board. Pupils are asked if there are vocabulary problems ('rassister' is a problem word). The teacher then pinpoints particular vocabulary herself, explaining in English 'co-ordinations lycéennes' [student committees] and 'voyous' [louts]. These explanations are also amplified in French.

The second extract is played to the pupils in the same way. In going through the missing words the meaning of these is checked and explained in English and French where there might be problems ('la rentrée', 'locaux', 'serait'). The two exercises take 15 minutes altogether. The words blanked out on the exercise are key words for comprehension interspersed with words which could cause aural difficulties.

This stage is followed by two five-minute activities to consolidate the information heard in the extracts. Firstly the students are asked to recall certain vocabulary items — they are given the English equivalents. Secondly, they talk together for two minutes in French about the content of the two extracts using the first three questions given on the worksheet under *Parlez* ('Qu'est-ce qui a déclenché les manifestations à Paris? Quels étaient les problèmes dans les lycées? Comment est-ce que les lycéens ont réagi?'['What triggered off the demonstrations in Paris? What were the problems in the schools? How did the pupils react?]) (see Appendix I). The teacher circulates checking that pupils are discussing the right topics. The questions are then discussed in the whole group, each question being further amplified by reformulation to allow for maximum opportunities of answering. Pupils are also given the opportunity to answer in English (to the third question) and, when no answers are forthcoming, by the teacher re-formulating the question into English. The pupils then in fact answer in French. The students are asked in English if there are any problems and the content of the first extract is summarised quickly in English.

The next stage is a third listening exercise of a similar gap-filling kind, following the format of the two previous listening comprehension exercises (played twice, checked and vocabulary discussed). This takes approximately five minutes and is followed by a longer 10-minute development of the content, starting with a few minutes' explanation in French of the historical background (May '68). Students are then asked to read through the passage and are questioned in English about its content, concentrating on student attitudes to strikes in France and the contrast with attitudes in England. (Students are more prepared to demonstrate in France, there is a tradition of demonstrating in France). The teacher then demonstrates to the pupils how this information links back to their own reactions as to how to register dissatisfaction: 'Au début de la classe je vous ai demandé comment vous pouvez changer des choses au lycée et Simon a dit 'faire la grève' et vous avez ri. Vous n'avez pas pris ça au sérieux, tandis qu'ici vous voyez que pour Stéphane il y a toute une histoire de grèves d'étudiants' ['At the beginning of the class I asked you how you can change things at school and Simon said 'Go on strike' and you laughed. You didn't take it seriously, whereas here you see that for Stéphane there is a whole history of student strikes'].

This difference in attitudes is given an experiential, affective dimension in the final stage of the lesson: a role-play with Stéphane explaining why the students have demonstrated and an English student who reacts with amazement. Students are asked to spend a few minutes deciding on their role, and thinking about what they will say. The teacher also gives a possible outline: Stéphane will talk about the problems in school, what triggered the demonstration, the history of demonstrations/strikes. The English friend could give his own reactions and ask Stéphane questions. Students are asked to stand up and separate out in the classroom. Role-plays are familiar to them and these are often done with pupils standing up to encourage them to be dynamic and alert. After five minutes the boys are asked to change roles and change partners. The last five minutes are spent in collecting in homework and making arrangements for the following lesson.

Lesson 2

The class consists of five Lower Sixth pupils (4 female, 1 male) in a different comprehensive school. The class have completed almost two terms of their 'A' level course during which they have studied three units from the project (Family, Education and Work). This lesson represents a summing-up of the ideas in the unit on Work, before a final presentation by students of case-studies they have made of individual jobs (postman, dentist, social worker, chef). The lesson lasts an hour and is divided into three main activities: a general discussion with students on the meaning and nature of 'work', students working on their own looking at their own patterns of work and rest, and looking at a television programme of a bus-driver/conductor to identify his patterns of work. French is used throughout the lesson. They have been observed by researchers from the project before and some of them were interviewed at the beginning of the autumn term before the project work had started.

The first stage of the lesson lasts about 20 minutes and consists of the teacher asking pupils a variety of questions on the topic of work. The students in general speak easily and fluently and are relaxed and co-operative. This discussion represents a summarising of ground already covered in this unit. Students are encouraged to think about the nature of work: 'Est-ce que c'est quelque chose payé ou non-payé? Quelle est la différence entre le travail et les loisirs?' ['Is it something paid or not paid? What is the difference between work and leisure?'] Students readily provide examples of work which is not paid but which could still be considered as 'work': household chores, schoolwork, voluntary work in hospitals and charity shops.

Students are then questioned individually about the work they do during their free time. Only one student does no work at all. Those who have jobs are also questioned about where they work, what hours they do and why they choose to work. One student works in the holidays in a hotel, waiting and washing-up with very long hours (9.00am-1.00am, with only an hour's break). She does this primarily for money for clothes, but also to meet people. Another student works in a local supermarket during the holidays and also gives 'earning money' and 'meeting people' as his main reasons. His day is shorter (10.00-6.30). Another student does occasional baby-sitting and the fourth student has worked in Woolworths for three months but had been given the sack. Students here were given the opportunity to think about what jobs are available to their age-range and the differences in people's working days. Further questions about parents' attitudes to their working show them to be encouraging, since children then earned their own money for entertainment or clothes, although there had also been some worries about schoolwork being affected. There are implicit questions raised here then as to the long-term and the short-term value of different kinds of 'work'.

The second stage of the lesson consists of students working on their own, writing two time-lines in French, one of a week-day and one of a day at the weekend, outlining periods of work and rest and what these consist of and how long they last. One student asks the reason for doing time-lines, although the activity itself was familiar (Students had previously done a time-line recording family celebrations throughout the year and looked at similar time-lines done by French students. An example of a French time-line is given in Appendix II.) The identification of differences between work and non-work provides an answer to the questions asked at the beginning of the lesson. Students spend about 10 minutes on this exercise, whispering to each other in English and occasionally asking for vocabulary.

When the students have finished they are asked to compare the hours of 'work' on a week-day and at a weekend. Generally work on a week-day is found to take up more time (since homework is included). One student comments 'mais c'est mieux au weekend parce que c'est payé!' ['but it's better at the weekend because it's paid!'] Activities considered as 'rest' include watching television, listening to music and going out with friends. Activities which are more active are seen differently: one student sees walking the dog as a relaxation, while another student, who belongs to a school team and has to train, sees her rowing as 'work'. Students are thus encouraged to become conscious of the significance of whether an activity is voluntary or obligatory 'work' and of different people's perceptions and attitudes in determining whether an activity counts as 'work'.

In a final stage of the discussion, lasting five minutes, students are then asked about what kind of job they would choose and what criteria are important. Students offer the following: good holidays and time off, job satisfaction, good pay, excitement, interesting work. Each student can see that within their own classroom there is a diversity of motives. The teacher is also asked in a good-humoured way why she chose her job and she gives 'enjoyment of French' and 'meeting people' as her reasons. Students are thus encouraged to use their own experiences to challenge familiar con-structs.

The final stage of the lesson is visual with students watching a pro-gramme on a day in the life of a rural bus-driver/conductor, M. Filatre. (A transcript of the programme can be found in Appendix III.) The three-min-ute extract is played twice and students are asked to answer three questions: 'Est-ce qu'il travaille toute la journée?, Qui emmène-t-il dans son bus?, Quand est-ce qu'il commence et finit sa journée?' ['Does he work all day? Who does he take in his bus? When does he start and finish his day?'] Although M. Filatre has a long day — 6.00 am to 7.00 pm — he has two long breaks of two hours and three hours. This day applies if he takes children to school with journeys to school in the morning, home and back at midday and home in the evenings. He also has a different timetable on the days when he transports factory workers, starting then at 3.30 am and finishing at 2.30–3.00 pm, also with breaks in the day. The 'time-line' of M. Filatre's work-day thus furnishes an interesting alternative to those experienced by the pupils in school and in other work-places that they have encountered.

Students had also watched a similar programme on the daily routine of a farmer and had worked individually on self-study packs including interviews with people in different professions discussing their duties and a typical working day.

The unit on Work, following Family and Education, brings pupils to the study of a third stage of socialisation into a society's values and routines. It produces fewer opportunities for contrasting French and English culture because, against a common Western European stage of industrial development, the similarities are more marked than the differences. Nonetheless, the focus on both French and English patterns of work and perceptions of 'work' and 'leisure' provide young people who are themselves in the process of experiencing this stage of socialisation with the opportunity to reflect on that experience by studying its significance in another society.

Learning ethnographic techniques

One of the principles of the course is to teach students techniques with which they can carry out independent study, either of other aspects of French life and society, or of other countries and cultures. These techniques are modelled on those used by ethnographers during their, usually, long-term studies of a community. We have attempted to introduce these techniques into the classroom, first by providing students with data gathered by such techniques and second by asking them to use the techniques to gather their own data. This usually takes place in their own environment and provides data for comparative study as was the case in the preparation of questions to ask their friends in the unit on Education, mentioned above. It may also take place during a period of residence in the foreign country. Such residence will normally be of short duration: a visit organised by the school or college, a holiday with parents or friends. Nonetheless we encourage students to treat such visits as occasions for fieldwork, and to put into operation their acquired techniques to study in the field one or more of the themes studied in the classroom.

The acquisition of techniques takes place in the classroom and home environment. This can be augmented by a 'training' session where students concentrate on the techniques *per se*. One such day for our project included sessions in which students discussed observation techniques and fieldnotes — using a video-recording and sample notes from one student's fieldwork during a work-placement in France; design and analysis of questionnaires — comparing a poorly-designed questionnaire with a good one and designing their own on a different topic; informal interviewing — discussing interview techniques, drawing up an interview schedule and carrying out an interview with a French person. At the end of the day the students designed a schedule of work that they would carry out in the field to investigate a selected theme. Teaching material for this training day is given in Appendix IV.

Case 6: Preparing University Students for Residence Abroad

This project is incomplete at the time of writing. The project is directed at the Thames Valley University by Celia Roberts and by Michael Byram of the University of Durham, and funded by the Economic and Social Research Council. This description was co-authored by all members of the research team (see Preface).

The project focuses on preparation for the residence in the foreign language community which is part of undergraduate language studies in all institutions of higher education in the United Kingdom. It is during this time that learners may acquire an insider's experience of social and cultural practices and thereby a fuller understanding of the beliefs and values expressed through and constructed in the foreign language. The project takes as its model the approaches and techniques of the ethnographer, who is traditionally a researcher attempting to understand and interpret the cultural world of a social group by living within it, as a participant in its daily life, for a substantial period of time. As language students also become participants in a foreign language community, the model seemed appropriate and was developed with the help of a professional anthropologist, Brian Street, of the University of Sussex. The project consists of the development and trialling of a course in ethnography for undergraduates in the year before their residence abroad; the supervision of students during residence abroad when they write an ethnographic study; and the integration of the preparatory course and ethnographic study into the students' whole course of language studies.

It is however also one of the aims of the project that such a course should be taught by language teachers who are themselves not specialists in ethnography. In this way the project can, we hope, become a normal part of any undergraduate course. The two teachers who volunteered to join the team had therefore to be both teachers on the course and themselves learners studying the concepts and techniques of ethnography. Constraints of space do not allow us to describe the whole process and we have decided to concentrate on specific issues we consider of general interest.

From a group of 10 volunteer students, we choose Gary for a case study. Such a brief case study can provide only a glimpse of the experiences and changes perceived by both students and teachers involved but in the ethnographic spirit of the whole project, it can illuminate the particular orientation of one student in his own context. Gary was an 'average' student, neither the keenest nor the most reluctant. He, like the others, showed initial resistance to what were, in his words, 'mindboggling ideas' when we discussed, for instance, what gift-giving or the construction and maintenance of social boundaries can tell us about a particular set of cultural practices. Yet, within a relatively short time, he came to grips with several concepts and techniques for approaching a community 'from within', using the vehicle of ethnography.

We adopted a two-fold approach on the course, involving on the one hand discussion of key concepts drawn from social anthropology and sociolinguistics; and providing, on the other hand, opportunities to practise ethnographic methods of data collection, namely fieldwork, participant observation and interviewing. These two strands fuse in the simultaneous development of reflexivity and awareness of methodological issues.

Towards the end of the course, students were asked to do what we called a 'home ethnography'. This involved doing fieldwork on the students' home ground, during the Easter holidays. Gary decided to study a group of close, mainly male, friends who also work for his father, who runs a small welding business in Bradford. His primary interest was in exploring the social roles and cultural models of this particular group of working class males and how they include and exclude others.

Though this was a project of modest scope and dimensions (a 3000 word essay done over the Easter vacation) he began to look in a more analytical way at the dominant discourses and interactional styles of his social circle, and started to categorise them according to how they perceived their social worlds. He also related them to broader anthropological concepts e.g. the social construction of cultural values, focusing on what it means to be a 'hard man', how solidarity is managed, and what all this might suggest about what it means to be a 'northern working class male'. Obviously his work raised many more questions than could ever be discussed in such a short time. Perhaps the most valuable lessons learned by Gary and the other students were about asking good questions, eliciting good quality data, and using anthropological concepts in order to unravel the cultural meanings. Thus Gary learned to rely more on his own observation of reality rather than on unmediated or perceived knowledge and in the process he became aware of at least some of the stereotypes which had previously conditioned some of his perceptions and responses.

What relation does this bear to the experience of residence abroad? The way we see it is that by studying interactions and the value systems constructed out of them that Gary had previously taken for granted, he developed skills and an awareness of cultural processes which he can use and develop further when abroad. By using them to carry out an ethnographic study in Spain he would be motivated to develop his linguistic and intercultural competence.

Such enhanced awareness and sensitivity would help maximise his perception of what is culturally specific and also minimise 'culture shock' (Furnham & Bochner, 1986). Gary found it useful to get hands-on experience in his own environment, albeit in a modest way, before going abroad. The practice of 'making strange' in order to make the strange familiar, of really trying to 'get inside the heads' of people, was an essential part of his development. The following extract from his essay illustrates some of the cognitive and affective effects of this process — a personal and intellectual challenge whether at home or in a different cultural setting.

> After a failed attempt at my original title, I was rather stuck for some other topic on which to base my study. The ideal was to choose a group of people to which I had unlimited access and which I could observe without being conspicuous or influencing their behaviour. The obvious solution was to observe my friends. Although rather reluctant at first, as I thought nothing ever happens, after three weeks of 'making strange', close observation and many a drunken night out running off to the toilets to scribble down notes on beer mats, I eventually learnt that there was much more happening than what met the eye, and that I did not know these people as well as I thought.

> This paper is mainly centred around the way in which people organise themselves into groups. By groups I mean to say a collection of people who are drawn together due to their common factors, such as interests, obligations, aims etc., and which are characterised by their own image, values, attitudes, vocabulary and codes of behaviour.

> Detaching myself from the normal routine has definitely changed my outlook. I have realised that we are not, as I thought, simply just one group of friends and acquaintances, but that we are all divided into groups and furthermore into sub-groups, each one endowing a member with an image to project, a role to perform and a code of behaviour.

Gary found that taking less for granted and developing a more critical and systematic approach, generated an unexpected amount of data for analysis. It is then problematised and related to broader anthropological themes. The student, in effect, is developing intercultural competence in a way that is meaningful to him. Seeing a cultural group from the inside necessarily entails close observation of the fine-grained detail which usually remains invisible. One source of misunderstanding, confusion and conflict was the misuse of roles, which is an example of group behaviour exercised out of context, that is to say, two members belonging to the same groups do not interact with the same group code of behaviour, when one carries out his role as a member of another group whilst the other fails to realise. On one occasion, Andrew was not very pleased when Lorraine spoke of something she was supposed to know nothing about as it was told in confidence to Derek, by Andrew.

'How the xxxx does she know that. It must be Derek. I'm not telling him anything again'.

Another such example is that when wanting to get in touch with me by telephone, Andrew would ring someone else to relay the message to me. All this simply to avoid ringing my house and running the risk of having to speak to my father, who Andrew can only see as having one role i.e. 'boss'. Having to speak to my father on the telephone would mean a complete reversal of roles, 'boss' would become 'friend's dad' and 'employee/welder' would become 'son's friend'. Andrew would therefore prefer to keep everybody's role separate in order to avoid the distress which occurs when roles are misused — as this leads to a breakdown of group membership, of image, and consequently a loss of identity.

Several of the issues related to cultural identity and touched on in Gary's home ethnography were analysed in more depth during his 6-month stay in Sevilla, Spain. He narrowed down his research questions to an exploration of Sevillano aggression and community among two specific groups in Sevilla. He was also deeply involved in the ongoing process of analysing his own roles and relationships as a participant observer. Like the other group members working on ethnographic projects in Andalucia, the initial encounter with 'the other' provoked feelings of disorientation followed by a rapid process of acceptance, and thereby a more critical awareness. As one of the students commented, the whole process was noticeably accelerated in comparison with the experiences of other students spending a year abroad, partly because they had already discussed these aspects before their departure and in a sense anticipated them. Although the initial bewilderment was thus greatly lessened the 'honeymoon period' was also short. As one student put it, 'The rose-tinted glasses fall off very quickly'.

During their stay, the students were visited twice by a lecturer, as part of the research. On one visit, Gary made the following comments 'We're living this ethnography project 24 hours a day, so we couldn't stop if we wanted to,... it's made me much more aware of not just *what* people are saying, but also of how they're saying it'. Also 'I've been casting my net wide to get a feeling for what I want to look at, which has made me do a lot more, talk to people a lot more and go to places I would never have gone to otherwise'.

Looking for cultural patterns beneath the surface took Gary and his group beyond the stereotyping and negative comparisons with Britain and also made them less romantic about the host society. The cultural learning developed through ethnography (formulating analytical questions; not accepting things at face value; a new focus for language development and a more critical awareness of their own roles and relationships) helped them to live more intensely within the new community, to feel close to it and so more able to develop a critical appreciation of it.

In sum, the programme provides a framework, through exercises such as the home ethnography, which students can use to unravel the strands of the shared cultural knowledge which inform their lives. This same framework, strengthened by the process of self-knowledge, can then be applied to less familiar social and cultural contexts during fieldwork. This also gives an added dimension to the skill-based focus of many degree courses, enabling students to move beyond technical competency to a fuller linguistic and cultural fluency. In a relatively short time, students like Gary can hone their observation skills and become more confident analysts of the cultural meanings to be discerned from ethnographic observation. They are learning to make sense of what is involved in approaching one's own, or another culture in a more positive and sensitive way.

The following two extracts (written by Ana Barro and Celia Roberts) are brief descriptions of two sessions of the introduction to ethnography course which runs through the year prior to residence in the foreign country. The first example concerns learning about ethnographic method. The second is a session developing further some of the anthropological concepts introduced in the first part of the course.

Example 1: Participant observation

The session on participant observation came about a third of the way through the ethnography course and was the first methods session. The rationale for introducing participant observation (PO) at this point was to focus systematically on methods after the students had already attempted some observation tasks. PO was also introduced only after the students were already familiar with some of the conceptual frameworks of social anthropology. In this way, ethnographic methods were developed as a means of illuminating theories of social life and cultural practice and not simply as a tool kit of techniques.

Participant observation is the major fieldwork method in ethnography and in much other qualitative research. To the student new to ethnography it is, simultaneously,both readily understandable and elusive. It is easy to grasp in the sense that it is part of our commonsense way of living in events

— we are both participants and observers. But it is also fraught with practical and ethical difficulties because it means living a paradox: it requires us to participate, to be involved and at the same time to stand back and observe.

The work on PO throughout the course, and introduced specifically in this session, is to introduce students to the notion and discuss and work on these practical and ethical difficulties. The session, therefore, opened with a discussion on the task which they had been set. In this short assignment, they had been asked to observe themselves and to observe others, hanging around in a pub. Typical issues raised were: difficulties with observing the all-too-familiar, practical difficulties of noise and note-taking, issues of identity and ethics — who are you when you stand back from the event you are in — and theoretical issues of what to record or focus on (Spradley, 1980). This type of discussion also raised the notion of reflexivity (Hammersley & Atkinson, 1983) — that we are part of the social world we study and have to be explicit both about the meanings we bring to our observations and about acknowledging that our data-gathering techniques themselves affect the world we are observing. The notion of reflexivity is a difficult one but central to language students who are developing cultural understandings since it helps to problematise the idea that there are fixed social facts about other cultural groups. Students were then introduced to the different degrees of 'participant' and 'observer' implied in the 'participant observer' term and the advantages and disadvantages of each (see Handout One).

Some of the questions arising from the discussion were:

- Relationship between observer and observed? Degree of involvement?
- How much is your being there affecting things?
- How far is observation/analysis affected by personal relationships?
- How far should you try to merge with your surroundings?
- How far will your personal characteristics (e.g. age, gender, ethnicity) affect your research?
- Problem of 'using' only people you like?
- Making friends and then 'using' them — telling them or not?
- Anxiety about having to hold back from a relationship — playing two roles and feeling guilty about deceiving people
- Validity of data
- Which role to adopt, depending on research aims and setting?
- Using different roles to get access to different data.
- Importance of building up trust/rapport.
- Ethical issues about taping, 'eavesdropping'.

HANDOUT ONE	
1. COMPLETE PARTICIPATION (total immersion/holiday job/classroom/friendship group)	
For	*Against*
As if ordinary member (spying/deception?) of the group. No problem with access. No observer paradox (i.e. no effect on observed).	Ethical problem. Restrictions on data collected/note taking. Difficult to ask questions (blowing cover). Difficult to observe/to get distance. Too busy participating.
2. PARTICIPANT AS OBSERVER (hanging around with a particular group/at work studying a group of whom you are not a member). Researched on are aware of researcher's role	
Both involved in group and a stranger.	More difficult to gain access. Possibility of over-identification with the researched. May change behaviour/data.
3. OBSERVER AS PARTICIPANT (classroom recording/observing on the underground)	
Less likely to 'go native'. More distant and formal.	Only brief relationship established. Less detailed/more limited data.
4. COMPLETE OBSERVER (no contact with observed/one-way mirror — video/audio recording of event)	
Naturally occurring material accurately recorded. Minimises reactivity	No interaction with informants, i.e. no questions can be asked. Limits of what can be observed.

Students were then given different examples of pieces of data collected by students both from the previous year of this course and from other courses where students learn about ethnographic methods. They were asked to consider the data in relation to the categories and questions on the PO handout. One example was *The Working Lives of SMAs* (School Meals Assistants) (unpublished MA paper, Thames Valley University). This data was collected by a teacher in the secondary school where she worked (see Handout Two).

Students were asked to discuss in groups the following questions:

(i)   What kind of Participant Observation is this?
(ii) What kind of access would you need to get this kind of data?
(iii) What sort of relationships (if any) would you be likely to have with the people you are observing?
(iv) How could the type of data be collected/recorded?

Not surprisingly, students' reactions to other students' data and analysis were mixed, ranging from admiration that it could be done at all to discomfort at the thought of 'spying' on others. These heterogeneous views

---

HANDOUT TWO

Example: *Following Instructions*

This incident was overheard. The SMA was speaking to the Head of Year about an incident with a student that had just taken place. The student involved and the black supervisor were also present.

SMA: Five boys sitting on the radiators…told them it dangerous…and to go outside…four boys go outside…the other boy stay on the radiator…told him to come down…he start to jump on the radiator…told him to come down…it dangerous…he told me to f*** *** you black bitch…I hold his hands and he come down…and take him to Headmaster…he told me to f*** *** you black bitch…don't touch me…tell my dad to beat you up.

Student: (interrupts) She scratched my hand…look…she dragged me…my dad will beat her up…

Head of Year: You don't talk to dinner lady like that…

Student: Why shouldn't I?

Head of Year: Don't talk to me like that…go and sit by the Head's office (the student leaves)…he will be sent home…

I spoke to the Head of Year the following day about the incident. The student was 'seen' by a Deputy Head, 'he was not sent home but a letter was sent home'. The Head of Year spoke to Ms J., the white supervisor about the incident… 'It was a dicey situation…she is a stormy dinner lady…bizarre situation'. I also spoke to the SMA: 'The boy not sent home …saw him just now running about'.

---

are the fabric of a non-consensus problematising and developmental ethnography which encourages students to find honest solutions to their own problems rather than seek authority from the canons of anthropology and sociology.

Participant observation, therefore, is introduced in an experiential way but with a guiding framework which is designed to help students make informed decisions about how to gain access, make contact and sustain involvement with individuals from the cultural group they are studying. In doing so, it also raises wider questions about preparation for, and effective use of, the period abroad since as participant observers students have a role and a purpose which encourages and structures the social interactions so essential for making the period worthwhile.

Example 2: Belief and action: Categorisations and rituals. Eating habits: taste or symbol?

Introduction

This session is the first of two offering a more in-depth approach to some of the anthropological material on people and the meanings they construct, exploring some of the symbolic meanings that underpin social behaviour, such as what people eat and meal-time rituals.

It has been placed near the end of the course, as part of the second group of concept-based sessions, because it is perhaps more demanding in terms of anthropological ideas and because it gives students a further opportunity to gain experience of data analysis (making connections between raw data and broader anthropological concepts).

The principal aim is for students to reflect upon the relationship, in general terms, between social behaviour and the symbolic patterns and meanings which inform it in particular cultural practices but which are not immediately obvious; in other words, to look for the significance to be found in material and social life beyond its surface realisation, to see that the apparently functional reasons for everyday behaviour are also open to cultural interpretation.

One very accessible way of approaching this complex area is to focus on the ritual and meanings surrounding food in students' own cultural environment. Everyone thinks of food and eating habits when they think of culture — but tend to do so in a superficial way which does not consider the contested nature of food and eating, subculturally, and which does not go beyond description, to explore symbolic interpretations.

Students were given some reading prior to the session, 'Taking the Biscuit' by Mary Douglas (1974), and they carried out a pre-session task. The task involved interviewing friends or family about the kinds of foods they would and would not eat, and their reasons. This allowed them to put their data collection skills into practice and to use their own data, based on their findings, as the basic material for the session (see Assignment sheet).

Concepts behind the task

(1) Society is constructed out of feelings of affinity and estrangement (Lincoln, 1986).
(2) 'It is culture which constitutes utility' (Sahlins, 1976) and not the other way round. In other words, we don't do things for practical reasons and then find a meaning for them. The symbolic meaning is what underpins our practical endeavours.
(3) The rituals around food and the discourses of food help to construct the 'borders, structures and hierarchic relations that constitute society itself' (Lincoln, 1986).

Another important aspect of this session consisted of discussing and reflecting on ways of categorising this data in a meaningful way, i.e. relating it to concepts such as ritual and food, as important expressions or manifestations of one's cultural identity (we may speak of 'eating communities'). This is why the first part of the session, when students worked in groups

---

ASSIGNMENT

Belief and Action (1): Categorisations and Rituals. Eating Habits: Taste or Symbol?

(1) Over the weeks try to engage as many of your friends/contacts/teachers/family members etc. in an ethnographic conversation about their eating habits.

(2) Don't elicit information in an interview — but try to work the conversation around to eating habits. Ideally, they should not feel they have been specifically questioned. But if you prefer to make your interest explicit, then mention that this is a subject you are looking at as part of your course. You may find talking about your own eating habits is a good way to get other people talking.

(3) Elicit as much as you can about:

 - what animals they consider edible

 - what parts of animals they are happy to eat, would never eat (e.g. liver, lungs, tongue,etc.)

 - what meat they would consider eating, if their normal food was not available (zebra, dog, sparrow, etc.)

 - what vegetables they would never eat

 - their feelings if someone sitting next to them was eating a food they would never eat

 - other interesting perceptions that emerge within all these questions, elicit as much as you can about their reasons for eating/not eating certain foods.

(4) Try to construct some 'value' patterns or classifications from the data you have collected. You might be asked to draw up a chart or a diagram.

---

to find structural relations or patterns which were then presented to the group for feedback, was particularly useful.

The key points emerging from this discussion were:

- the rituals and discourses around food are culturally determined;
- there are ways of analysing them and making sense of them by looking, for example, at structural relations (see Douglas, 1974; Sahlins, 1976) or meal-time behaviour;
- cultural and social groups can be constructed and maintained in part by a shared food culture;
- food rituals and practices create order, and also boundaries;
- the whole area of food can be a good way into a culture when students find themselves in a different cultural environment.

The following is a lesson description:

(1) Introduction of topic: the difference between functional and symbolic meaning. Here it was useful to give a couple of examples of symbolic meaning implicit yet shared in attitudes and behaviour, e.g. clothes and the meanings they signal, or someone eating in a restaurant and a home. In the restaurant we would not expect the waiter to put his fingers in the soup, because of 'germs', whereas if it happens at home we don't really mind: it is no longer as 'dirty'. ('Excuse fingers', we say.) What

we consider dirty or polluted in some way depends on the symbolic significance as much as on a functional explanation based on notions of hygiene, purity, or what is 'natural'.

(2) Feedback on the article by Mary Douglas. This is quite a difficult account of the structure of British meals among four working-class families. Douglas suggests an intricate structuring to the food system of these families, moving through lunch to the early evening meal and finally a late-night minor meal of a hot drink and biscuits. As the day progresses one of the obvious changes is from wet to dry food, from gravy and custard to the dry, sweet biscuit:

> Our analysis is beginning to reveal in the dietary system, with undeniable economy of means, the mimetic and rhythmic qualities of other symbolic systems. The capacity to recall the whole by the structure of the parts is a basic technique in music and poetry for arousing attention and sustaining interest.

> The same recurring theme is visible in the sequence from thick gravy to thicker custard to solid icing sugar. One of the structuring rules of this food system is progressive desiccation and geometrification of forms through the day. The first course of the main meal is presented in what appears to the uninitiated as a slushy indistinguishable mixture, in which it is difficult to distinguish the trimmings and solid dressings from the meat and potatoes under their lavish coat of rich brown gravy. The second course, though still wet and viscous, has an undeniable sculptural form, whether it be the sphere of the Christmas pudding, or the trifle decorated with fruit.

The article provoked a number of strong reactions. Some students appreciated the methodology and the structuring principle that emerged. Others found it inaccessible and an over-interpretation of a set of simple practices. This type of discussion was precisely what the article and assignment were designed to provoke: to find the strange and the structured in what appears routine and familiar and to raise issues of description and interpretation.

(3) Assignment feedback preceded by a discussion on the topic of food. One student commented after the session: 'One example that was extremely helpful for me was the reason for not eating dogs or human flesh. I wouldn't eat them, but I have never tasted them and cannot say that they are harmful. If I don't eat them it is because there are some "laws" that tell me not to do it, but these laws have been created by "us". There is not one reality. We create that reality and there are as many realities as different people' (class diary).

For the feedback, students worked in groups and were given about half an hour to discuss their findings, to see if any patterns emerge and then to try and illustrate them in diagram form on an OHP transparency.

(4) Each group presented their chart/diagram on the OHP to the whole class and discussed them. Plenty of time was allowed for this as students discussed not only the findings that emerged but also the different ways of presenting the information in ways that made sense to the group.

(5) The group discussion was then related to an extract from the Sahlins article (see below: 'Food as symbolic code'), which discusses reactions in the USA during the Depression to government suggestions that people could economise by eating horsemeat which 'made Marie-Antoinette seem a model of compassion'.

> Edibility is inversely related to humanity. The same holds in the preferences and common designations applied to edible portions of the animal. Americans frame a categorical distinction between the 'inner' and 'outer' parts which represents to them the same principle of relation to humanity, metaphorically extended. The organic nature of the flesh (muscle and fat) is at once disguised and its preferability indicated by the general term 'meat', and again by particular conventions such as 'roast', 'steak', 'chops', or 'chuck'; whereas the internal organs are frankly known as such (or as 'innards'), and more specifically as 'heart', 'tongue', 'kidney', and so on — except as they are euphemistically transformed by the process of preparation into such products as 'sweetbreads'. The internal and external parts, in other words, are respectively assimilated to and distinguished from parts of the human body — on the same model as we conceive our 'innermost selves' as our 'true selves' — and the two categories are accordingly ranked as more or less fit for human consumption. The distinction between 'inner' and 'outer' thus duplicates within the animal the differentiation drawn between edible and tabu species, the whole making up a single logic on two planes with the consistent implication of a prohibition on cannibalism.

> It is this symbolic logic which organises demand. The social value of steak or roast, as compared with tripe or tongue, is what underlies the difference in economic value. From the nutritional point of view, such a notion of 'better' and 'inferior' cuts would be difficult to defend. Moreover, steak remains the most expensive meat even though its absolute supply is much greater than that of tongue; there is much more steak to the cow than there is tongue. But more, the symbolic scheme of edibility joins with that organising the relations of production to precipitate, through income distribution and

demand, an entire totemic order, uniting in a parallel series of differences the status of persons and what they eat.

These two examples give a flavour of the ethnography course with its mix of conceptual and methodological development. The pedagogy of the course also tried to reflect and illuminate the best of ethnographic practice. This meant respecting and learning from the students' experiences, careful observation of the social patterns underlying group work and class discussion and supporting students in the continuing dialectic between observation/experience and analysis in a relaxed and friendly classroom.

Evaluative comments at the end of the course suggested that these objectives were, in the main, fulfilled. A quote from one student's evaluation sheet sums this up. She said she liked the course because of 'having to look at things, listen to people...an excuse to analyse things you talked about casually already and I found there was some depth behind nearly everything that is going on...it seemed to bring out something in us all — a creativity'.

Case 7: In-service Teacher Education: British Studies in English Language Teaching[2]

Intended mainly for teachers, teacher trainers and inspectors engaged in teaching English as a foreign language, this course combines study of contemporary British culture with reflection on the pedagogy of language and culture and the preparation of materials based on teachers' academic study. It is a 'short-course' of ten weeks with three major dimensions: an introduction to British Studies, investigation of a specific topic, and consideration of teaching, focused on the data collected during the investigation (Woods, 1993).

The introduction consists of lectures and seminars on such topics as 'Popular culture since 1960', 'the Multicultural Society', 'Youth Culture', 'the British Political System' and 'Education'. This is accompanied already in the first weeks by work on language teaching theory.

One of the most interesting dimensions in relation to the focus of this book is however the preparation and execution of an investigation by individual students. The topic is chosen with a view both to its intrinsic interest and to its potential for teaching. The topics chosen during the first run of the course were:

- the reporting of crime in the local newspaper;
- the system of child-adoption;
- the production of newspaper advertisements;
- student life and student organisations in a British university;

- multicultural society in contemporary Britain;

Preparation for the investigation concentrated especially on techniques of interviewing key informants, since methods of collecting and analysing other kinds of data — official documents, media documents and academic sources — were already familiar to students. The kinds of data collected can be illustrated from one investigation.

The student investigating adoption had chosen the topic because it reached into politics and legislation, morality, gender and ethnic minority–majority issues; and also because it is a topic not often dealt with in the more usual sources of information and teaching material. The data collected included:

- interview with a social worker, focused on the legal dimension;
- interview with an adoptive family on their personal experience and feelings;
- interview with a member of staff in a children's home;
- official leaflets and other documentation;
- newspaper articles;
- documents on proposals for new legislation.

Interviewing is clearly the most difficult technique but it brought students directly into contact with key informants such as journalists and policemen, student officers in campus organisations, professionals in advertising, teachers and pupils in multicultural schools, and so on.

The investigations are then reported in an assignment which describes the procedures used, the data collected and the connections in the analysis with themes introduced in the first part of the course. A second assignment concentrates on the interpretation of the data collected in the investigation and demonstrates the practical teaching applications.

The students in the first group to do the course were from Poland, Bulgaria and Japan. They said they had profited from this varied background by learning in informal and incidental ways about each other's countries and cultures. Comparison is an inevitable and welcome part of any experience of another culture and is more systematic if this is accompanied by a course of study. As one student put it, 'whenever there is something puzzling in British culture, then you compare' and then 'the more you get to know British culture, the more you know about your own'.

Case 8: *Ab initio* Learners of German at University: Teaching Cultural Competence for the Year Abroad

This case-study was provided by Sheila Watts, Department of Germanic Studies, Trinity College, Dublin. It provides an example of how linguistic and cultural learning can be combined, in particular with reference to issues of sociolinguistic register which can undermine otherwise successful communication.

A number of universities in Ireland and the UK have expanded the student intake to some honours degree programmes in German by admitting *ab initio* learners as well as those with A-level or equivalent qualifications. The presence of these students in third level courses raises questions about appropriate teaching aims, contents and materials which are addressed in this study. The first section examines some of the special needs associated with *ab initio* learners at third level, and particularly the need for cultural competence in the case of students who are required to spend an assessed year at a foreign institution. The adoption of cultural competence as a learning objective has implications for the choice of a textbook which are discussed in the second section, with particular reference to experiences using *Sprachbrücke 1* (Mebus *et al.*, 1987) in one course at Dublin (TCD). The advantages and disadvantages of working with this particular textbook are discussed and finally, conclusions are reached about its success in meeting students' needs.

At TCD the majority of *ab initio* students are admitted to the degree programme in European Studies, where they make up approximately one quarter to one third of the annual intake of 30–35 students. European Studies, a four-year course combining the study of two languages with history, politics and sociology, includes an integral third year at a foreign university participating in an Erasmus scheme. *ab initio* students attend separate language classes in the first year, but sit the same exams as qualified entrants and join them for all courses from the second year onwards.

The German language courses which are offered to European Studies students were originally designed to meet the needs of learners with about five years experience of learning German at school. Developments in the secondary school curriculum in the last decade have meant that pupils primarily acquire skills in spoken German, often at the expense of the written language, so that making up this perceived deficit is a major part of third level language teaching (West, 1992: 32). Students are expected to be able to cope with the basic requirements of a year at a German-speaking university without special preparation, other than that needed for writing the seminar papers (*Referate*) which will subsequently be presented for assessment.

Although *ab initio* learners share the long-term assessment goals of qualified entrants, their short-term needs in the first two years of the course are different in two respects. Firstly, they need to acquire all four skills in a more even distribution than is the case with qualified entrants. However, the emphasis on written German in assessment procedures means that a disproportionate amount of class time is devoted to it, with the result that *ab initio* students tend to be less proficient orally than their qualified peers. Secondly, we have found at TCD that *ab initio* entrants differ from others not only in their lack of knowledge of German, but also in their exposure to and awareness of German culture. Whereas in the 1992 intake eight out of every ten qualified entrants had visited a German-speaking country, on average for two or three months, only half of the *ab initio* entrants had done so, none for longer than two weeks. If, as I believe to be the case, the institution is justified in admitting two groups of students with such different resources and needs to the same course, then it must make it possible for members of both groups to profit in equal measure from the whole course, including the year abroad.

Profiting from the year abroad cannot simply be seen in terms of the academic requirements which the institution makes of students, but must take into account the students' personal expectations. Students overwhelmingly cite 'speaking German' and 'learning about German culture and society' as the most interesting and relevant aspects of their university course, and many see meeting and getting to know native speakers of German as an important part of the year abroad. Indeed, where students travel and share flats together, meeting primarily other anglophones rather than German speakers, they fail to progress as language learners, so that the institutional and personal aims can be seen to be closely connected.

There are many reasons why students have difficulty in making social contact with Germans, including amongst others age differences, different patterns of study and the difficulty of breaking into established social networks. However, students themselves often refer to the stereotypical view of Germans as being cold and unfriendly, and complain of their rudeness. In a small survey I carried out on student attitudes to the politeness of Germans, there were no favourable comments, and the unfavourable ones included a comment that a particular way of behaving might be 'overpolite by German standards but normal enough for us', and the statement that Germans seem 'not to care so much for please and thank you'. These comments show that these students have failed to recognise that there are norms of social interaction which determine how people behave in different cultures, and that Irish norms differ in some cases quite markedly from German ones. Although the students may have acquired linguistic skills, they are deficient in the other components of communicative competence, interaction skills and cultural knowledge (Saville-Troike, 1989: 24). They do not know how concepts like politeness and formality are realised in German culture, and they judge German behaviour in accordance with their own Irish norms, by which standards it is indeed often rude and unfriendly.

Norms of social interaction present learners with a difficulty, because they are not accessible in a codified form in the way linguistic norms are available in dictionaries and grammars. However, students need to learn these norms in order both to be able to interpret the intentions which lie behind what German speakers say to them, and to be able to modify their active language use to convey their own intentions appropriately. This observation has implications for language teaching: students can and should be equipped with the necessary cultural knowledge and interaction skills prior to visiting the foreign country for any length of time. This can only be achieved by choosing materials which do not concentrate solely on linguistic skills at the expense of cultural norms.

A textbook for *ab initio* learners at third level must take account of their adult status, and so cannot be one which their qualified peers used at school. Textbooks for adults, however, are rarely aimed at the university market, and they very often thrust the learner into the roles of tourist, traveller and consumer. As a result, while schoolbooks feature characters who chat to their friends about pets, birthdays or school subjects, adults in textbooks use their native speaker interlocuters as sources of information and goods. In courses like *Themen I* (Aufderstraße *et al.*, 1983) and *Sprachkurs Deutsch I* (Häussermann *et al.*, 1991), learners ask for directions, shop, order meals and buy tickets. In a university context interactions of this type are problematical as examples of the foreign language for two reasons. Firstly, they are situations which are very similar in most Western European cultures, and their use in textbooks may suggest an absence of any cultural difference, encouraging learners to imagine that they can transfer their Irish behaviour into precise German equivalents. Secondly, the functions which they illustrate are all of people getting others to do things for them without relating to them at a personal level, discussing common interests, making value judgements or expressing emotions of any kind. Clearly students who are to live abroad for a year will not want solely to transact in this way, but will also want and need to interact with their fellow students inside and outside of the classroom.

At TCD we became aware that our *ab initio* learners needed a textbook which would not be directed at tourists, but which would envisage the possibility of real communication on a personal basis between learners and native speakers. We required of the textbook that it would present interactions between characters of different ages and backgrounds, including students, and that the students' attention would be drawn explicitly to the socio-cultural aspects which characterised these interactions. We believed that students would benefit from being able to place both their own behaviour and that of Germans within a cultural context, and that this would lead to their being readier to integrate into German society during their year abroad. On the basis of this analysis of our requirements, we selected *Sprachbrücke 1* and *2* (Mebus *et al.*, 1987 and 1989: referred to collectively as *Sprachbrücke*), a course which describes its main aim as being 'durch den Fremdsprachenunterricht interkulturelle Kommunikation zu ermöglichen' [to make possible intercultural communication through foreign language teaching] (Rall & Mebus, 1990: 11).

Sprachbrücke meets our requirements in a number of respects. Firstly, there are specific exercises which emphasise register and appropriacy, such as that shown in Figure 4.1.

The instructions for the first task draw students' attention to relevant facts, such as age and professions, to help them make appropriate judgements. The second task deals with the linguistic forms which are the realisation of degrees of politeness and formality in the utterances given. In this way linguistic forms are placed in an explicit cultural context which students can recognise and use to inform their own use of German.

Other exercises offer students the opportunity to discuss and evaluate different kinds of behaviour without having to choose between clear cases of right and wrong (see Figure 4.2).

This exercise is part of a lesson where different attitudes to politeness are thematised: earlier exercises include questions like 'was gilt in Ihrem Land/ in anderen Ländern als höflich?' [what is considered polite in your/other countries] and 'was ist Ihre persönliche Meinung: Lügt und betrügt man, wenn man höflich ist?' [what is your personal opinion: are people lying and deceitful, when they are polite?] (Mebus *et al.*, 1987: 195). Students are encouraged to reflect about their cultural norms and to see them from a foreigner's perspective which will enable them to gauge how Germans may react to their behaviour. Exercises of this type are most successful when taught by native speakers, who present a different viewpoint from that of the students.

As well as the emphasis on politeness and formality, the textbook features a number of informal conversations where the speakers use *du*-forms, as would be the norm between students. The extract in Figure 4.3 shows how a dialogue of this type is didacticised.

Students are required to deduce the implicit intentions of the speakers from what they say and so understand both text and sub-text. The interpretation of speakers' intentions is rarely explicitly taught, despite its primary importance for understanding. *Sprachbrücke* differs from more traditional textbooks in that it does not confine the interpretation of speakers' inten-

Wer spricht wie zu wem?

1. Ordnen Sie bitte zu! Achten Sie dabei bitte auf das Alter und den Beruf der Gesprächspartner und auf die Situation!

A Beim Kaffeetrinken

☐ ⊰ Kannst du mir bitte mal den Zucker geben? - Danke.

a) Ein Bruder zu seiner jüngeren Schwester.

☐ ⊰ Gib mal den Zucker rüber, Kleine!

b) Eine Sekretärin zu ihrer Kollegin.

☐ ⊰ Würden Sie vielleicht so freundlich sein und mir den Zucker reichen? - Herzlichen Dank.

c) Eine alte Dame zu einer anderen alten Dame, die sie kaum kennt.

B Weiderholen des Namens

☐ ⊰ Wie heißt du noch mal?

d) Empfangsdame in einem Hotel zu einem älteren Gast.

☐ ⊰ Wie war noch bitte Ihr Name?

e) Ein Arbeiter zu einem neuen Kollegen.

☐ ⊰ Entschuldigen Sie bitte, wie war Ihr werter Name? Würden Sie ihn bitte noch einmal wiederholen?

f) Am Telefon: Sekretärin zu einem Geschäftsmann.

C Auf einem Fest

☐ ⊰ Herr Peters, gestatten Sie? Frau Peters, darf ich Sie um den nächsten Tanz bitten?

g) Ein vierzehnjähriges Mädchen zu ihrem Freund.

☐ ⊰ Wollen wir tanzen?

h) Ein Student zu einer Studentin.

☐ ⊰ Echt stark die Musik! Komm!

i) Ein älterer Herr (70 Jahre alt) zu dem Ehepaar, das neben ihm sitzt.

2. Wer benutzt den Konjunktiv, „du", „Sie", verkürzte Sätze, Imperative?

Figure 4.1

Höflich?

1. A zeigt B eine Uhr, die er seiner Freundin schenken will.
   A: Wie gefällt dir die Uhr?
   B: Überhaupt nicht.

2. C hat ein neues Kuchenrezept ausprobiert. Er fragt seine Gäste: „Wie schmeckt euch der Kuchen?" Alle finden den Kuchen zu süß. Aber sie antworten:
   D: Ausgezeichnet, wirklich toll!
   E: Mmh, gut, hast du den selbst gebacken?
   F: Ein Bißchen süß, nicht? Hast du eine Stück Brot für mich?
   G: Wie Zucker!
   H: Nicht schlecht, aber ein bißchen süß, oder?
   I: Na ja, fast so gut wie mein Lieblingskuchen.

Wie finden Sie	zu höflich	höflich	unhöflich
die Antworten	zu freundlich	freundlich	unfreundlich
Beispiel:		ehrlich	unehrlich
Ich finde Antwort B...		ironisch	

Figure 4.2

tions to the discussion of literary texts, but recognises that intention is expressed in communication at all levels.

The textbook authors describe their approach to the presentation of German cultural norms in *Sprachbrücke* in the following terms: 'die deutsche Sicht ist […] jeweils nur eine unter mehreren […] und wird nicht als Norm vermittelt' [the German view is…only one among several…and is not taught as the norm] (Rall & Mebus, 1990: 15). This can be difficult for teachers who are not native German speakers, particularly if they come from the same cultural background as a homogeneous group of students, as is usually the case at Irish universities. When the textbook authors deliberately avoid giving guidance on German norms, but suggest that all interpretations are equally valid (as, for instance, is the exercise from p.197, above), the students may succeed in becoming culturally aware in broad terms, but they will fail in their narrower goal of acquiring knowledge specifically about German language culture. This difficulty arises because the authors intend the book to be usable worldwide: this has the effect of making teachers put in a considerable amount of groundwork into more specific comparisons between their own and the target culture.[3]

K: Du Bina, wann gehen wir endlich mal zusammen aus?
B: Ich weiß nicht ... Was schlägst du denn vor, Klaus?
K: Sieh mal hier! Heute abend um halb acht gibt es einen Film. Has du dann Zeit?
B: Was heute? Montag? Montags habe ich immer Sport.
K: Schade! Aber morgen, am Dienstag, da gibt es einen Vortrag.
B: Das geht leider auch nicht. Dienstags gehe ich zum Chor.
K: Hm, und übermorgen, am Mittwoch? Können wir nicht am Mittwochabend ins Theater gehen?
B: Aber mittwochs ich doch Stammtisch!
K: Ach ja! Und am Donnerstag?
B: Da habe ich leider schon eine Verabredung.
K: Am Freitag gibt es ein Konzert. Kannst du dann mitkommen?
B: Ach, wie dumm! Am Freitag habe ich wieder keine Zeit.
K: Das finde ich aber wirklich schade! Und wie ist es am Wochenende?
B: Samstags und Sonntags bin ich nie hier!
K: Na, dann bis zum Sankt Nimmerleinstag!

2. Was ist los?

a) Hat Bina wirklich keine Zeit?
b) Warum sagt sie nicht „nein"?
c) Finden Sie das richtig/falsch/komisch?

d) Versteht Klaus Bina richtig?
e) Warum schlägt er immer wieder eine Veranstaltung vor?
f) Finden Sie das richtig/falsch/komisch?

Figure 4.3

An important question with any textbook is how the learner group reacts to it. *Sprachbrücke* has been criticised for its presentation of German culture through the eyes of the inhabitants of a fictitious country, *Lilaland* (for example in Bosselmann-Cyran & Wigger, 1988: 265). This concentration on culture as communication, to some extent at the expense of material on more concrete details of German life, has led some students to comment that the book teaches more about *Lilaland* than about the German-speaking countries. Lesson nine, for example, begins with the problems a German family experiences on being invited to dinner in *Lilaland*, and the characters discuss a variety of appropriate ways of responding. In discussions with students they complained that they did not want to learn about appropriate behaviour in an imaginary country. In this case it was easy to miss the change of focus in the exercises which followed the introductory text, and which are headed 'was man bei einer deutschen Einladung beachten muß' [what you should think about when you receive a German invitation]

(Mebus *et al.*, 1987: 121). It is questionable whether students will learn what is taught by stealth, and the learning process is clearly impaired if students believe that they are being confronted with unnecessary or irrelevant information.

Sprachbrücke is radically different from other textbooks for adult learners in its omission of almost all the dialogue-types which I earlier characterised as being aimed at tourists. However, students who have spent time abroad report no difficulty in communicating at this level, and most were surprised when it was pointed out to them that they had never specifically learnt appropriate formulas. Thus the omission of the staple material of most textbooks was neither noticed nor felt to be a disadvantage in working with this course.

In its own terms of making students communicatively competent, *Sprachbrücke* is well suited to the requirements of learners at third level. The course enables students to confront the fact that their responses to German culture are the inevitable result of their own cultural characteristics, and that it is not possible to judge German behaviour by Irish norms. Once students have learnt that there is no one-to-one correspondence between German and Irish linguistic behaviour in social situations, it is to be hoped that they will be able to meet Germans without the cultural barriers thrown up by the traditional negative stereotypes. The course is not entirely self-sufficient, but if it is coupled with input on specific cultural contrasts and some additional general *Landeskunde* material, it provides a preparation for the year abroad which is not adequately achieved by any other text book currently on the market.

Case 9: British Cultural Studies in Turkey

This case-study was provided by Laurence Raw of the British Council, Ankara.

The work described here is part of a two-semester course in British Cultural Studies, instituted in 1992 by the British Council in Istanbul in collaboration with the Department of British and Comparative Cultural Studies at the University of Warwick. At the time of writing, only one semester has been completed; hence this description cannot be considered a formal report.

This course is run independently of any Turkish university, and lasts one year. Our group contains only slightly more women than men (which is unusual in Turkey, as most students of the humanities are women), who are drawn from a variety of backgrounds; they include English Literature postgraduates, language teachers, a journalist, a television announcer and professional translators. The teaching of the course is shared between myself (as a British Council-appointed lecturer in Cultural Studies), two Turkish academics from local universities in Istanbul, and lecturers from Warwick who come out regularly to give all-day workshops. Those students who succeed in the examinations will receive a Certificate in British Cultural Studies validated by the University of Warwick, which will be the equivalent of one term's work on their MA course in British Cultural Studies; it is hoped that the brightest students will receive scholarships to be able to complete the course at Warwick.

Hitherto British Studies (and British Cultural Studies) have been virtually neglected both in schools and universities. Most teachers of English — whether Turks or native speakers — perceive cultural study as incidental to the 'real business' of language teaching; they might perhaps allow for some discussion on life in Britain and America, as represented in the course textbooks (and how it differs from life as experienced by Turkish students), but the main aim in class is to train students in using English for the purposes of practical communication. In universities, cultural study is restricted mostly to students in the Departments of English and American Literature, who take one, perhaps two courses (lasting three hours per week each) in British or American 'Life and Institutions'. In the majority of these courses students are given factual information about the history and workings of institutions (the Houses of Parliament and the trade unions are very popular) and are expected to reproduce this information in exams.

The British Council/University of Warwick course came about as a result of dissatisfaction about the low status of British Studies in Turkey, coupled with a desire to introduce new teaching materials and techniques into the education system. The predominant mode of teaching in Turkish universities is the information-loaded lecture: students take notes, and their success in examinations is determined by how successfully they have memorised these notes. The British Council course was designed to place the students' own experience both as a starting-point for their work, and as a basis for intercultural study. Most Turkish universities would have been reluctant to introduce so different a course into their curricula; thus it was necessary for the British Council to organise it themselves.

The collaboration with Warwick University was perceived as beneficial in many ways. It provided a good 'selling-point' for potential students in Istanbul — especially if they wanted to study in England. The collaboration would also provide an opportunity for an exchange of lecturers, with Warwick University staff coming to give seminars and workshops in Istanbul, while the Turkish lecturers could visit Warwick, to see how British Cultural Studies was taught on their MA programme. More importantly, the collaboration was seen as a new departure, both for the British Council and Warwick University; if the Istanbul programme proved successful, it might easily be developed in a modified form by the same institutions in other countries.

The progress of the course so far is summarised in the following statement of its principles, its organisation, and in case-studies of some of the material taught in the seminars.

The fundamental principles of the course can be summarised as follows:

- we believe that 'cultural studies' needs to be introduced in Turkey — to demonstrate how (and why) the study of literature, language and culture are inseparable
- Students should not be exposed to an evaluative notion of 'culture' (which has hitherto been the case in Turkey), where they are led to believe that to learn about British Culture is to be the possessor of superior values. They should be encouraged to compare their own culture with that of Britain: 'culture' in this sense, involves ways of thinking and believing, shared (and differing) knowledges of the world.
- The teaching of the course should concentrate on contemporary Britain and contemporary Turkey, giving students (whose age-range varies from 19–28) the chance to place their own experience at the centre of their work.
- The content of the course should be as varied as possible: we aim to show the diversity of contemporary British culture by examining key texts — written, spoken, musical, and visual.

The course is designed to put these principles into operation. It is taught in a series of weekly seminars lasting three hours, with an additional all-day workshop every month. The seminars are taught jointly by myself in collaboration with the Turkish lecturers; the workshops are run by visiting lecturers from Warwick University.

The course comprises nine units:

(i)   The Country and the City

(ii)   National and Regional Identities

(iii)   Changing Class Attitudes

(iv)   Youth Culture

(v)   Multi-Cultural Britain

(vi)   Re-Thinking the Past

(vii)   Childhood and the Family

(viii) Gender and Sexuality

(ix)   Festivals and Celebrations

It was assumed that while our students, as postgraduates or language teachers, would be competent speakers of English, they might nonetheless possess a limited knowledge of Britain — most of it acquired at school or university, or by watching British programmes either in dubbed form on Turkish television, or on BBC World Service Television. What we tried to do in the first three units was to provide a 'map' — geographical, intellectual, social, political — of contemporary Britain, which would enable the students to relate subsequent units more directly to their own experience. Twenty-two students were accepted for the course this year; only a handful of them had direct experience of Britain (one woman had completed an MA in Media Studies at Strathclyde University; another spent two years working in advertising in London). Thus it would appear that our assumptions were vindicated.

The task of providing what the students needed to know about contemporary Britain could have been achieved through information-loaded lectures. In our course, however, we wanted to introduce task-based and problem-solving approaches to learning. Each weekly seminar contains:

- a specific aim;
- a sequence of 'stages' of work, each with its own learning objective;
- a variety of materials for study, including newspaper articles, video extracts, and fictional texts.

In the second unit ('National and Regional Identities') for instance, we wanted to focus on aspects of 'Scottishness', and how it differed from 'Englishness'. This we considered extremely important, as most Turkish students often equate 'British culture' with 'English culture' (anything to do with Britain is normally translated into Turkish as 'Ingiliz', as in 'Ingiliz Kültür Heyeti' — The British Council). What we also wanted to demonstrate was that there was no easily identifiable 'Scottish' national identity: Scotland is both multicultural and multilinguistic.

This seminar took place in week 4 of our course; by now the students had got to know one another, and had become accustomed to our teaching methods. To prepare for this seminar, they had been given a hand-out composed of short extracts from writers who attempted to explain what 'being Scottish' meant to them. The hand-out included extracts from a recent tourist guide to Scotland (*Scottish Traditions and Festivals* (1991)), poems by Hugh McDiarmid ('The Parrot Cry'), and Jackie Kay ('My Grandmother'), and short passages from William McIlvanney's *Walking Wounded*, and Tom Nairn's *The Break-up of Britain*.

Before starting on the seminar proper, we asked the students two questions — 'What do you know about "Scottishness"?' and 'What do you know about Glasgow?' — and recorded their responses on an OHP transparency.

The students responded easily and fluently; in their opinion 'Scottishness' was something different from 'Britishness': since the Act of Union in 1707, the English had attempted to suppress the Scots, both politically and culturally. This task, however, proved futile: 'Scottishness' could be expressed either in English, Gaelic, or Scots. The students also suggested that while Glasgow was famous for its football teams — Celtic and Rangers (both of whom had been featured on Turkish television) — it was nonetheless a city of great poverty and unemployment. This stage of the seminar lasted approximately five minutes.

There were two main reasons for focusing on Glasgow: it seemed logical to draw upon the experiences of our Strathclyde graduate, while several of the extracts in the hand-out had been written by Glasgow writers ('My Grandmother', *Walking Wounded*).

In the next stage of the seminar (10 minutes), we divided the students into groups of 4 or 5, and distributed two texts — an article from *The Times* of 23 November 1991 ('Should auld acquaintance be forgot?') written by Gavin Stamp about devolution in Scotland, and an edited transcript of a BBC programme 'Ninety Minute Patriots' (broadcast on World Service TV in September 1992), in which several working-class Glaswegians were interviewed about their national identity (Appendix 4.1). At this stage, we did not ask the students to read them; instead we put the titles of each text on an OHP, and asked the students to discuss what they meant. Each group wrote down their findings on the OHP.

Having understood the significance of the title (borrowed from 'Auld Lang Syne'), one group suggested that *The Times* article created a nostalgic view of the past; another wondered whether it was about a new beginning for Scotland, in which one's old acquaintances should be remembered. The second article produced a similar diversity of response: one group believed that it was a diatribe against football hooligans; another realised the significance of 'Ninety Minute[s]', and suggested that the article concerned itself with the kind of patriotism that lasted only as long as a football match. One student pointed out that the article might be critical of the kind of patriotism expressed in words (i.e. by shouting for Scotland at football matches) but not deeds. This was vehemently denied by the Strathclyde graduate. This technique of prediction provided students with something concrete against which they could evaluate the material presented later in the seminar.

In our experience, Turkish students are rarely encouraged to look at the *language* of a text — especially in English Literature seminars. They can readily discuss content, but not form. What we wanted to do was to examine the version of 'Scottishness' represented in the 'Ninety-Minute Patriots' text through the interviewees' responses. As the text was a transcript, rather than a formal article, we explained that it consisted of immediate, first-hand reactions (which might not be articulately expressed); thus in the next stage of the seminar (20 minutes) we divided the text into four equal parts, distributed one part to each group, and invited the students to draw a textual cardiogram, to register the text's 'heartbeat', or emotional content. This required further explanation — as an example, we gave a passage from *Pride and Prejudice* (Appendix 4.2), in which Darcy unexpectedly visits Elizabeth Bennet at home. This extract is full of emotional peaks, troughs and jagged edges, which can be plotted on a line graph, with the vertical axis measuring the emotions of the text — despair, indifference, happiness (Appendix 4.3). The students were also asked to label the most distinctive points on their graphs with appropriate phrases from the text.

The 'Ninety-Minute Patriots' text yielded some remarkably similar cardiograms. Every interviewee expressed conflicting emotions — the joy of seeing Scotland win at football; the despair of unemployment; dislike of the Conservative government; pride in one's country; a desire for independence; a belief that one had to move to England to prosper. Students were asked to identify other linguistic features of the text (10 minutes), which were subsequently written on the OHP — the persistent use of negatives and the nostalgic identification of the past (which in this extract meant pre-Thatcher) as something good compared to the hopeless present.

The next stage of the seminar (20 minutes) focused on *The Times* article 'Should auld acquaintance'. The students began by discussing whether the article was positive, negative or neutral in tone, given that it was written by an Englishman: the consensus of opinion, predictably, inclined towards the negative. We subsequently invited the students to compile textual clines, which were designed to show whether the writer uses a greater proportion of favourable or unfavourable words to describe Scotland. The results served to confirm what the students had predicted: whilst Gavin Stamp certainly likes living in Glasgow, he believes that the Scots suffer from self-hatred, a lack of national identity, and an inferiority complex.

This section of the seminar concluded with the students being asked to compare the versions of 'Scottishness' in the two articles, with their responses to the two questions 'What do you already know about "Scottishness"?' and 'What do you know about Glasgow?', given earlier on. There were clearly some points of similarity; but what emerged was that each group (Turkish students, working-class Glaswegians, the English) had their own version of the Scots' 'national identity'. We endeavoured to demonstrate to the students how this information linked back to their own lives by comparing my reactions to Turkey, as a foreign lecturer coming from a middle-class background, with those of my middle-class Turkish colleague, who has lived all his life in Istanbul.

Nonetheless, it was pointed out by one student that whereas his version of the Scots national identity might be similar to that of the Scots themselves, it did not appear 'valid'; he had had no direct experience of living in or visiting Scotland. This opinion is expressed by many Turkish students — especially in English Literature departments; their courses are meaningless, as English is not their first language, and they have little experience of Britain. This neatly foreshadowed what we had prepared for the final stage of the seminar, where students were invited to watch a short (15 minute) extract from the film *Local Hero* (1983), and subsequently discuss the version of 'Scottishness' it presents. Although the film has a Scottish director (Bill Forsyth), it was financed by an English company (Goldcrest Films) with American money. The cast is mainly Scottish, but two out of the three stars are American (Burt Lancaster, Peter Riegert). Our students readily pointed out that *Local Hero* was designed to appeal to mass audiences; and thus endeavoured to paint an idyllic picture of the Highlands, similar to that of the tourist brochure. The people live modestly yet happily, the sun always sets on a cloudless sky, and American sophistication is eventually forced to accommodate (but not be defeated by) Scottish cunning. It is certainly true that there is no substitute for direct experience of a foreign culture; but what our exercise sought to suggest was that there are versions of the Scots national identity created for the domestic and the foreign filmgoer — indeed many of the students admitted that *Local Hero* (and other films like it such as *Whisky Galore*) provided one of the main sources of knowledge about Scotland). Moreover, *Local Hero* was as much a creation of the media as 'Ninety-Minute Patriots' or *The Times* article — each designed to appeal to a particular audience.

The activities described above only partially fulfilled our original aims: apart from the final activity, little attention was paid to the experiences of those students who had not been in Scotland; and we certainly did not consider any parallels between Scotland and Turkey. But the students' reaction to the first few weeks of the course had shown that they desired to know more about Britain *before* they could be encouraged to make cultural comparisons. Our seminar on Scotland was designed to meet these needs; hence we concentrated almost exclusively on the target culture. The focus has changed in subsequent seminars: in the 'Changing Class Attitudes' unit we have spent a lot of time considering whether Turkey has been more successful than Britain in instigating a 'class-revolution', based on private enterprise and the acquisition of wealth. We need to develop this kind of intercultural comparison further: students should be encouraged to carry out their own research, to lead seminars and take questions. Hopefully they will come to trust more in their own judgement and not rely on the lecturer's word (which is in itself a characteristic of Turkish academic culture).

In Turkish terms, our course represents a radical departure; not only does it adopt a new approach to cultural study in Turkey, but it repudiates the barriers separating literature from sociology, anthropology, media study and so on. This could appear rather frightening to an academic specialising in one of these disciplines; but what we aim to show in our teaching is that British Cultural Studies does not have to taught by a polymath. In this way we hope that the discipline can ultimately become a staple part of both postgraduate and undergraduate course in Turkish universities.

Appendix 4.1

'Ninety-Minute Patriots' — transcript of a BBC TV documentary broadcast on World Service TV, 27 September 1992 — extract:

> Sport is a way in which people can identify themselves. Politically we're nothing. We're governed totally by a London government, who won't even recognise the race, don't even know us; they think we're just fodder there to make use of; their economic servants. The only way we can identify ourselves is through sport... (Terry, manual worker)

> At the end of the day you want to see the boys [footballers] doing their best on their own park, and if they're doing it for Scotland, they're doing it for us, aren't they? Because being Scottish, you think they're a part of us, you know, you get that feeling. They're doing good for you, and you're out there with the players, you know... (Michael, Terry's son)

> At one time people were happy at home — father with his week's wages, and the kids were excited, and mother was getting the dinner ready. You knew it was back to the routine on Monday, but you knew what life was like. Now you wonder will there be a Giro in the morning? Kids don't have any money now, and that's all the fault of the government at Westminster. John Major was for education, and he shut all the schools down. Makes you laugh, doesn't it? He only cares about England, where the money is, not us... (Jessie, housewife)

> If we could get our independence, we could rise and be a nation again. Even if you didn't see it or I didn't see it or my kids — and if it was their kids who saw it, it would be something. Better than the way we're treated now... (Jessie)

Gavin Stamp, 'Should auld acquaintance', *The Times Saturday Review* 23 November 1991, pp.4–6 (extract)

I hate to criticise the great city [Glasgow] that has treated me with such friendliness and tolerance, but some things I must publicly deplore. The average diet is appalling. Junk food flourishes, producing an all-pervasive odour, while the heavy consumption of sugar and fat is alarming. When this diet is combined with heavy smoking — the climate on the top of a Glasgow bus has to be breathed to be believed — it scarcely seems surprising that the average person in the street looks so unhealthy, and that the Scots have one of the highest death rates in western Europe. What Scotland needs is a healthy dose of English middle-class health-conscious environmentalism...

The damage to Glasgow has not only been the result of the usual factors — greed, ignorance, philistinism, indifference — but also of a disturbing lack of self-confidence. This can show itself in an extreme sensitivity to perceived criticism. For instance there is that tiresome business of the Scots objecting to being called Scotch. This has long puzzled me, for, as anyone familiar with books published any time before this century will know, the Scots used to refer to themselves as the Scotch. I do not mind having a surname which is also that of a sticky label on letters; why should the Scottish think the general name of one of the greatest boons that this land has given to civilisation should be something pejorative when applied to themselves?

All too often, the Scots seem diffident about defending what is uniquely valuable and their own, and will only notice when outsiders take an interest. This certainly has been true in Glasgow, with the precious work of Thomson and Mackintosh; it is most depressing. Beneath all this seems to lie a deep-seated national inferiority complex — perhaps the worst legacy of the Union, the tying together of a small nation with a populous one.

Appendix 4.2

Elizabeth...was suddenly roused by the sound of the doorbell, and her spirits were a little fluttered by the idea of its being Colonel Fitzwilliam himself, who had once before called late in the evening, and might now come to enquire particularly after her. But this idea was soon banished, and her spirits were very differently affected, when to her utter amazement, she saw Mr. Darcy walk into the room... Elizabeth was surprised but said not a word. After a silence of several minutes he came towards her in an agitated manner, and thus began, 'In vain have I struggled. It will not do. My feelings will not be repressed. You must allow me to tell you how ardently I admire and love you'.

Elizabeth's astonishment was beyond expression. She started, coloured, doubted, and was silent.

Jane Austen, *Pride and Prejudice* (London, Pan Books Ltd, 1967, p.141).

Appendix 4.3

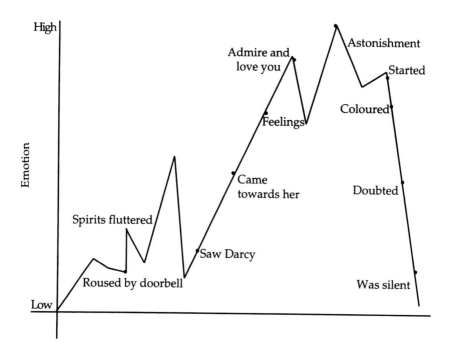

Notes

1: The unit described here was developed by an INRP team consisting of: Anita Baire, Mickaële Guillien, Pierre Heudier, Marie-Jeanne Trividic, Françoise Vigneron, English teachers and Jeanine Lecomte, historian.

2. I am grateful to Edward Woods and Dianne Wall for allowing me to describe their course, and to Yasushi Mano, Zbigniew Mazur, Maria Pipeva, Roumyana Todorova, and Magda Warzecha — the first group of students on the course — for giving me their 'insider' accounts (M. Byram).

3. A more recent textbook addresses this problem by being specifically based on a comparison of German and American cultures and 'mentality' (Behal-Thomsen *et al.*, 1993).

5 Assessing Cultural Learning

Assessment is the aspect of cultural studies and cultural learning which is given least attention. In Valdes's collection of articles, only one article is devoted to assessment (Valette, 1986); Melde (1987) does not address the question at all; Zarate (1986) suggests a number of stages of attainment and gives examples of possible formative assessment but does not deal with this in great detail; Campos *et al.* (1988) also identify three levels of attainment, building on Zarate's proposal; and our own work has only begun to include assessment. A valuable exception is Meyer's research which attempts to establish levels of cultural understanding (Meyer, 1991) and we shall return to this later. Yet it is a truism of educational practice that assessment ensures that teaching and learning are given serious attention and status. One of the reasons why cultural studies has been driven more into the 'background' in Britain than in Germany is the greater attention paid to *Landeskunde* and its assessment, though even so there are many who would say that the situation is unsatisfactory.

In Chapter 2 we discussed the principle of teaching 'a body of knowledge' and suggested a number of categories on which to base a selection. For purposes of assessment, we propose to approach the issue from a different angle. The division we propose here cuts across each of the selection categories and we shall illustrate by drawing on more than one. The chapter will deal first with the kinds of knowledge and behaviours which might be assessed, secondly, with possible techniques of assessment, and thirdly, will describe some experiments in assessment from our own and others' research.

What to Assess

For purposes of assessment, we identify three inter-related areas: 'knowledge', 'attitudes', and 'behaviour'. Our earlier discussions, especially in Chapters 1 and 2, have shown that the relationship is one of interdependence: 'attitudes' have cognitive and affective dimensions, 'knowledge' involves reciprocity and decentring, 'behaviour' depends on identity and empathy. Inevitably, then, our division creates difficulties but will help to clarify what it is we hope students will learn during and by the end of a course of learning language and culture. A further dimension in our own research (see Case 5 in Chapter 4) is the acquisition of ethnographic techniques for independent study of a culture; this could also be assessed separately.

Knowledge

In order to communicate interculturally, students need some factual knowledge. They need to know historical and geographical facts, facts about the society and its institutions, facts about socialisation through formal ceremonies, religious and secular, and so on. This factual knowledge will have been selected according to criteria discussed in an earlier chapter and taught in a variety of ways, but ultimately they will need to know, for example, the date of the French Revolution or of Hitler's accession to power. They will need to know the name of the capital city, and of geographical features. They will need to know what happens at a first communion or how governments are elected. Here already, through giving examples, we have made a selection and by implication suggested these facts are in some sense significant.

We argued in Chapter 2 that the selection should reflect what natives of the culture themselves perceive to be significant, for example in terms of national identity and the maintenance of a national community. It follows that students should not only know the date of the French Revolution but also appreciate its significance for contemporary French culture. This means that students should know what most French people 'know' about the French Revolution. This could be established by sociological investigation or by examining what and how the French Revolution is presented in history books used in French schools. Students should also be able to describe and explain how the significance of the Revolution is embodied in contemporary culture and society: by the symbols in the *Mairie*, by the celebrations of *le 14 juillet*, by the *Tricolore* and the motto *Liberté, Egalité, Fraternité* — what Nora calls 'les lieux de mémoire' (places of memory) (1984).

We have therefore two levels of knowledge, each of which can be sub-divided:

(i/ii)   factual knowledge: divided into minimal objective knowledge of when the Revolution took place and what were the main events; and a more detailed knowledge of causes and effects as presented in *French* textbooks; this would be more clearly significant if we had taken historical events interpreted differently in the learners' own culture, e.g. *Jeanne d'Arc* (see Zarate, 1986: 51–4).

(iii/iv)appreciation of the significance of the facts, divided into: description of their emblematic maintenance in contemporary life; and explanation of how such emblems underpin culturally shared understandings of their importance.

In practice, expectations of what level can be achieved by learners at different ages and stages of learning might suggest that the first two levels, based on factual knowledge, can be attained by initial and intermediate learners in secondary schools. The third and fourth levels pre-suppose capacities for abstraction and analysis — at higher cognitive and moral stages — which perhaps only students in upper secondary and later would normally demonstrate (see the discussion of cognitive and moral development in Chapter 1).

At the fourth level, students would analyse the ways in which the emblems of the historical events are realised in the language they are learning. They would recognise unexplained allusions in texts. They would explain the connotations and semantic fields of key words, revealing cultural schemata or shared meanings (Taylor, 1971) of which native-speakers may not be fully conscious. This would reflect the teaching of vocabulary and key words suggested in Chapter 2 but should go beyond recall of learned analyses — though doubtless this is also worthwhile — to the demonstration of the ability to carry out independent analysis based, for example, on juxtaposed texts.

Attitudes

Since the encouragement of positive attitudes — towards language learning and towards people from other countries and communities — is a tacitly agreed purpose and, in some situations, an explicitly documented aim, there has to be consideration of its assessment. There are a number of difficulties. As we saw earlier, the ways in which attitudes can be changed or encouraged are often indirect: through contexts of presentation of information, through personality, credibility and interpersonal relations. Methods which are more direct and manipulable are often ethically suspect and certainly would not appeal to most teachers. The ethical issues may even cause some doubt about the conscious use of indirect means. All the more problematic are the ethical issues implicit in assessment of attitudes.

For it is important to remember that assessment can take a number of forms and serve a number of functions. It may be possible to measure attitudes in ethically acceptable ways but 'assessment' suggests the measuring of attainments in knowledge and skills which are, in principle, subject to learners' conscious control and deliberate efforts. Furthermore, when assessment functions as examination at the end of a course — as opposed to diagnostic feedback to learners themselves — then it is not used simply to give an account of attainment in the knowledge and skills particular to the subject. Examinations serve as keys to further opportunities of education or vocation, and many teachers would resist using a measure of attitudes as an examination test on which such future opportunities depend.

Can we simply ignore the assessment of attitudes and the educational purpose associated with them? To do so and to remain consistent, we would have to abandon statements which suggest that language and culture teaching is intended to stimulate positive attitudes. We suspect that most teachers would be loath to do so and the widespread acceptance of explicit statements about attitudes in British and other documents is an indication that this is the case. An alternative is to evaluate courses rather than assess individuals. This still involves questions of how to measure attitudes in an acceptable manner (Byram, Esarte-Sarries & Taylor, 1991: 385 and 389; Wiegand, 1992: 55), but they can be resolved.

The assessment of empathy on the other hand, though related to attitudinal issues, has not been considered problematic in ethical terms. The doubts have been, as we saw in Chapter 1, about definitions of empathy, and clarity about what precisely is being measured. Insofar as empathy is a reflection of moral development and reciprocity, it can be argued that this too is beyond learners' conscious control and diligence. Although teachers may accept that they can and should find methods to foster moral development — for which there are clear ethical grounds — they might consider that assessment, even as diagnostic feedback but certainly as examination, might be misguided.

We suggested however that there are both affective and cognitive aspects to empathy. The latter is comparable to the scholarly representation of historical events without distortion from a contemporary perspective. The former involves the ability to decentre, and is dependent on psychological development. If we are prepared to assess only that which is cognitive then we have two options. We can attempt to devise assessment instruments which isolate the cognitive dimension; for example, the use of factual knowledge, the application of the analysis described above as Stages 3 and 4 of knowledge attainment. Or, secondly, we can delay assessment until we can reasonably suppose that learners have reached an appropriate stage of psychological development and that we are assessing its 'application' rather than its 'existence'. This remains problematic insofar as research suggests that not all individuals progress through all the stages (as we saw in Chapter 1) and, moreover, there may still be particular problems of assessment as was noted by Brown in his review of different empathy tests (1987: 108). Brown questions the accuracy of measurement in these tests which identify only extreme cases but do not differentiate among the 'normal' population.

We are left with the professed educational purposes which justify language and culture teaching in terms of the 'insights' it gives into other cultures, the capacity to 'identify' with other perspectives. The alternative, for attitude measurement, of evaluating courses rather than assessing individuals is also available here and some teachers may prefer that programmes be evaluated, rather than individuals assessed. In our own work, we have decided to attempt evaluation and will discuss our experiments below.

Behaviour

Definitions of culture within the context of language teaching usually include some reference to behaviour (e.g. Byram, 1989: 80; Zarate, 1986: 146). Culture defined as the shared knowledge of a given social group is realised in part through behavioural norms and conventions. Goodenough's definition relates knowledge and behaviour through the notion of 'operating acceptably':

> A society's culture consists of whatever it is one has to know or believe in order to operate in a manner acceptable to its members. (1964: 36)

Behaviour in this sense is a very broad term, not limited to notions of politeness, etiquette and social niceties of which members of a culture are aware and might find wanting in a foreigner. It also includes appropriate behavioural response to allusive references to the kinds of knowledge discussed above.

It is nonetheless valuable to identify the kinds of behaviour of which natives of a culture are more or less conscious. Much of this is what we labelled as 'social interaction' in our categories for selecting course content; for example greetings at different levels of formality, gender relationships, taboos. There are two dimensions which can be assessed: knowledge and performance. It is worthwhile to separate these in principle because learners might have cognitive knowledge of aspects of social interaction without necessarily being willing or able to perform or enact the appropriate behaviour. It is also valuable for pragmatic reasons, in that assessment of cognitive knowledge can be more feasible than assessment of performance. Let it be noted in passing that the significance of social interaction, both verbal and non-verbal, has been recognised in research on cross-cultural psychology and in courses of cultural training for people travelling and residing in foreign countries for professional reasons (Seelye, 1974 and 1984; Furnham & Bochner, 1982; Brislin *et al.*, 1986; Condon, 1986; Osterloh, 1986; Levine & Adelman, 1982).

We have then a double distinction between knowledge and performance, and between verbal and non-verbal behaviour. A further distinction can be made between behaviour of which natives of the culture are aware and consciously control and that which is unconscious, although the boundary between them is not clear-cut. Into the former case fall behaviours in which parents deliberately instruct children: greetings, eating manners, and notions of politeness and social hierarchy. Unconscious behaviour includes definitions of personal space, conventions of conversational turn-taking, of eye-contact between interlocutors. Since these unconscious conventions have powerful effects on interpersonal relations, learners need to be made aware of them through deliberate teaching; leaving them to intuit the norms of social behaviour is inadequate. The question of taboos is a particularly good example since taboos, again both verbal and non-verbal, by their nature are avoided by natives of the culture; the learner who notices them only by breaking them is unlikely to 'operate acceptably' from that point on.

How to Assess

Like other aspects of curriculum development, the success of innovation in assessment depends on its relationship with current practices. Proposals must be pragmatic and not too distant from existing practices. In particular, assessment for examination purposes has to link to existing standards in order to ensure continuity of the function of examinations. As a first step, let us consider the case of Advanced level General Certificate of Education practices in England. They raise a number of issues which we suspect are not confined to the English system.

This examination is in the hands of a number of semi-autonomous examination 'boards', most of which are linked to one or more universities, because the dominant purpose of the examination in the past — and still important today — was to select students for university courses. In order to be eligible they have to 'matriculate' by passing, usually, two subjects at 'A' level. In practice they have to get higher than 'pass' grades in more than two subjects, but this need not concern us here, except to say that most students take only three subjects at 'A' level, each in some considerable depth of study.

One of the indications of an increased interest in cultural learning has been the introduction of 'alternative' syllabuses and examinations — alternative to the exclusive study of literature. We shall use the alternative

French syllabuses as examples, but other languages syllabuses are comparable.

There are currently 8 alternative syllabuses available for French 'A' level: Oxford & Cambridge, Oxford, Cambridge, AEB, JMB, London Syllabus A, Syllabus B and Ridgeway.

The general aims of these syllabuses give prominence, as might be expected, to linguistic skills, but in addition more general academic aims are mentioned:

> offer the enjoyment, intellectual stimulation and challenge appropriate to an advanced course of this level...allow candidates to complement their other studies by pursuing selected areas of interest in greater depth and to develop a personal and independent response to them (Oxford);

> the premium on the organisation and practical communication of ideas (London Syllabus B);

> foster the ability to collect, analyse and exchange information, ideas and attitudes through the medium of the foreign language (AEB).

In all the syllabuses, some mention is made of the culture of France as a source of interest.

The aims concerned with culture range from those based on factual knowledge to aims concerned with understanding, sympathy and contact. In London Syllabus A, the aim is: '...to stimulate candidates' interest in aspects of France' (Aim 4) with the objective: 'to test the candidates' knowledge and understanding of the topics they have studied and their ability to show their knowledge and understanding in French' (Assessment Objective for Paper 3 — Topics).

AEB extends the boundaries of demands of candidates' understanding beyond the topic into more general cultural areas: [to] 'encourage an interest in the contemporary culture of the foreign country... (Aim iii) [and to] demonstrate knowledge and insight into aspects of civilisation and culture' (Assessment Objective 5).

AEB also includes French-speaking countries, as opposed to France alone, in two of its topics (A and B) but not specifically in the aims or objectives. This additional broadening of territory is found in all the other syllabuses too, apart from London.

The joint Oxford & Cambridge syllabus introduces an affective dimension into the aims with the notion of sympathy: 'To foster a sympathetic understanding of the culture and civilisation of other relevant countries, including contemporary issues... (Aim 5) [and] to show understanding of texts in the foreign language...and/or to show knowledge and under-standing of aspects of culture and civilisation' (Assessment Objective 6).

Both the London Ridgeway and Cambridge syllabuses promote the notion of contact with the foreign country. The Ridgeway syllabus includes a comparative element and an emphasis on recognising the validity of other points of view: 'To demonstrate knowledge and understanding of aspects of contemporary France... (Assessment Objective 4) to evaluate such issues in particular by comparing the students' own situation with that of young people in France... (Module 1: Jeunes gens d'aujourd'hui [Young people of today]... Aim 2) ... to analyse differences in opinions about these problems in England and France and to evaluate possible solutions... (Module 3: L'Environnement [The Environment], Aim 3) to understand the opinions of others, to summarise and evaluate these opinions' (Module 4: Le Monde du Travail [The World of Work], Aim 2).

The JMB syllabus goes further. It encourages students to reflect on their own culture and comes closest to encouraging an 'insider' view of French culture: '[to develop] awareness and understanding of themselves, of other individuals and of society... (Aim 1d) to encourage first hand contact with the culture and civilisation of France and other French-speaking communi-ties through, for example, a) exchange of letters, cassettes, magazines etc., b) where possible travel and residence... (Aim 4) to further the candidates' appreciation of language by helping them to understand culture and civi-lisation (both British and French) from the viewpoint of the respective peoples... (Aim 5) to foster interest in the views of French-speaking people on current issues' (Aim 6).

The definitions of the cultural component in the different syllabuses also vary from 'aspects of France' to 'contemporary culture', 'civilisation and culture' to 'cultural heritage'. The word 'culture' is interpreted variously in the syllabuses. A traditional interpretation is one where 'culture' is linked to the arts. Thus in London Syllabus B we find that 'aspects culturels' in the topics paper (Paper 2) includes literature, song and film. Where specific guidelines are given for topics, this kind of arts-based 'culture' is included. 'Culture' has thus been re-interpreted from the previously exclusively literary definition, and, where literature is studied, it is in a wider socio-cultural context than in the past.

A second interpretation of 'culture' as 'facts about a country' ('Aspects of France') is certainly well represented in all the specified topics: a region or regions; urban and/or rural issues; the media; agriculture and industry; current affairs; recent history; technological developments; the environ-ment and ecology; and the education system. This focus reflects other interpretations of 'culture' (civilisation, cultural heritage) and offers students the opportunity to understand a country and inhabitants better by understanding the historical, geographical and social context which exists there. The emphasis here then is on students' acquisition of knowledge (for a fuller discussion of definitions, see Byram, 1989).

The widest range of social issues is offered by London in its 3 syllabuses. Syllabus A, for example, offers 'La sociologie des loisirs en France: sport à l'école et après, TV, radio et cinéma, vacances'; 'Le mode de vie des Français: classe sociale et salaire, citadins et paysans, vie quotidienne — famille, cuisine, consommation, cafés, restaurants, supermarchés, hypermarchés, logement' and 'Quelques problèmes contemporains en France: la drogue, la criminalité et le terrorisme, les immigrés et le racisme, le chômage' ['The sociology of leisure in France: sport at school and after, TV, radio and cinema, holidays'; 'The French way of life: social class and income, city- and country-dwellers, daily life — family, food, drink, cafés, restaurants, supermarkets, hypermarkets, accommodation' and 'Some contemporary problems in France: drugs, criminality and terrorism, immigrants and racism, unemployment']. It can be seen that syllabus topics appear to be chosen for their controversiality or visibility, allowing students to marshal arguments for or against a topic more easily.

It is clear then that, in these topic options, social issues are addressed and this would seem fertile ground for preparing students for understanding culture in terms of shared meanings and value systems. Analysing the kinds of examination questions set and the marking systems used will allow us to evaluate the extent to which the criteria for cultural understanding, given in the general aims and assessment objectives of the syllabuses, have been met.

Examination questions fall into two broad categories: either a factual catalogue enquiry or a requirement to discuss a general issue. The latter means that students may use knowledge acquired within their own culture, using current opinions or arguments for and/or against an issue. Thus in AEB we find in 1989, first, the treatment of old age as a general issue:

6 (a) Qu'est-ce que le terme 'troisième âge' suggère pour vous? [What does the term 'senior citizen' suggest to you?]

and then the option of giving an account of knowledge acquired about France in particular:

or (b) Examinez deux actions législatives qui ont visé à améliorer la condition des personnes âgées. [Examine two legal measures aimed at improving conditions for old people.]

The syllabus rubric for the topic specifies study of 'comparaison globale entre les différentes sociétés, attitudes des sociétés européennes envers les vieux, les vieilles personnes au sein de la famille, les vieilles personnes dans la société' [global comparison between different societies, attitudes of European societies towards the old, old people within the family, old people in society]. This rubric implies comparison in terms of a range of possibilities rather than an understanding of attitudes against a background of and contextualised in one particular framework of cultural values and meaning. Students could then explore the different concepts of responsibility towards the elderly in France and Britain, looking at different social class groups and government attitudes as well as varying domiciles.

Students can nonetheless choose an intercultural comparative approach — in fact they would be likely to gain credit for so doing. Examination questions are seemingly left open to allow for a breadth of student response. Examination mark schemes and examiners' comments provide useful indicators of the actual degree of openness.

In current approaches to examinations, linguistic skills are awarded the majority of marks. The notion of a 'section culturelle' and a course in French Cultural Studies independent of language studies is still a long way from this current practice. The 'culture' paper only carries 20% or 25% of the overall grade and, in many of the boards, part of this percentage is awarded for language skills, making the actual 'content' rating even lower. Thus, in London Syllabus A, 15% from 25% is given for content, in Syllabus B, 8% from 20%, in AEB, 12% from 20%.

Consider, then, the criteria and instructions to examiners used in marking examinations. Four main categories emerge: understanding the question and providing relevant answers; structuring and organising the essay competently; displaying a breadth of knowledge; and demonstrating analytical skills and understanding. In the Oxford and Cambridge marking scheme, for example (given in detail so that teachers can assess some of the course-work) the allocations are as follows: content 20%, relevance 8%, use of material, handling/analysing 8%, organisation of argument 8%, expressions of ideas (either French or English) 8%, miscellaneous (insight/originality) 8%. This 60% is reduced to 20% in the overall exam weighting. In the London Syllabus A, the following marking instructions are given:

Candidates are rewarded for:

(i)   The relevance of their answers to the questions set
(ii) Analytical skill
(iii) Fluent and accurate use of language
(iv) Good organisation and control of material
(v)   Good knowledge of the topic

(30 marks for content, 20 for language, the overall 50% reduced to 25% for the final exam weighting.)

Three of these skills reflect general academic training rather than the gaining of specific cultural knowledge and understanding. Students need to understand the implications of academic terminology in questions, to understand the code being used, and their inability to decode questions is often the object of examiners' criticisms:

> despite some good performances even otherwise strong candidates failed to cope adequately with the basic aspect of answering the question…a fair number appeared to ignore words like 'justifiez' [justify], 'expliquez [explain]'. (London, p. 26)

In summary, we can see that, under the 'A'-level system, knowledge of the foreign culture is allocated only a small percentage of the total marks. Moreover, associated with the assessment of cultural knowledge, there is a considerable emphasis on linguistic and academic skills which relativise even more the value given to cultural knowledge. Finally, it is evident that specific criteria concerning the precise nature of that knowledge do not exist.

Other techniques for assessing factual knowledge have been included in the literature on testing. These include 'objective' tests, such as multiple-choice questions, and highly structured question-forms which allow only specific answers by filling gaps or answering short, precise, factual questions. Appendix V gives examples of how such a range of knowledge questions might be structured in a foreign language examination (the chosen focus here is French education). Valette (1986: 182–97) and Seelye (1984: 141–59) also give examples of how cultural knowledge might be tested.

Such tests provide a practical technique which will be efficient in terms of time taken for testing and assessment and also be of maximum reliability. Clearly these are important factors, particularly for examinations leading to qualifications. It can be argued however that reliability has been achieved at too much cost in relation to validity. Short, factual answers susceptible of objective marking are unlikely to reveal students' understanding of the significance of the facts, nor of their degree of cognitive empathy in explaining that significance.

Attempts to improve existing tests have to find ways of giving more emphasis to cultural knowledge, to right the imbalance between linguistic and cultural learning. They have to right a second imbalance, between reliability and validity, and they have to be feasible in normal testing and examining situations. This combination of conditions has led, in other contexts, to the introduction of criterion-referenced tests and examinations.

Our proposals for defining more clearly the kinds of knowledge, empathy and behaviour to be assessed provide a basis for applying criterion-referencing to cultural learning too.

Our proposals can be summarised as follows:

I Knowledge

(a) factual knowledge (of historical, geographical, sociological, etc. phenomena);

(b) explanation of the facts from within the foreign culture perspective (e.g. historical explanations in school textbooks or sociological explanations of contemporary events in the media);

(c) description of the appearance and position of the phenomena in contemporary life (e.g. the 'typical family' used in advertising, or the geographical divisions used in weather-forecasting);

(d) explanation of the significance of the phenomena in shared cultural understandings/meanings (e.g. the belief in a 'North–South divide' within a country's behavioural and social norms, or belief in a country's 'historic mission' in relationship with other countries).

II Empathy

- the degree to which students can explain factual knowledge and its significance — (b) and (d) above — from within the cognitive perspective of the foreign culture;
- the degree to which students recognise the relativity of different cognitive perspectives including their own.

III Behaviour

(a) description and analysis of norms of social interaction in the foreign culture;

(b) performance of social interaction — both verbal and non-verbal — within those norms.

Although the formulation of criteria for assessment purposes is notoriously difficult, it is easier when related to a specific course content. Our proposals for such content — in Chapter 2 — can be related to the three areas suggested for assessment. Any given realisation of the general categories — such as the one suggested for German in Chapter 2 — related to a specific course of study with specific teaching materials, provides a firm basis for describing the 'knowledge' students can be expected to describe and explain. Such knowledge — including that which is called upon to explain behaviour in social interaction — can be tested on paper, in the written mode.

Criteria for the assessment of cognitive empathy have been proposed for the teaching and testing of history (Shemilt, 1984; Fry *et al.*, 1991) and, on a more experimental basis, for testing perceptions of cultural difference by language learners (Meyer, 1991). Both approaches postulate stages on a continuum and are implicitly developmental. Neither of them refers explicitly to developmental psychology, although there are obvious connections with the issues raised in Chapter 1 and in particular with the question of the ethics of testing raised earlier in the present chapter. We shall discuss the detail of the proposals in the following section.

The assessment of knowledge of behaviour in social interaction can also be tested, we suggested earlier, through performance. Such performance — for example, in a conversation with a native-speaker — also draws upon knowledge and empathy. The success of a conversation will depend on at least the following:

- performance within conscious norms of interaction of which native-speakers are conscious, such as greeting, or avoidance of taboos in behaviour or topic of discussion;
- performance within norms of interaction of which native-speakers are not normally conscious, such as turn-taking, proximity in physical space;
- use of knowledge to understand unexplained allusions in the topic of discussion;
- use of empathy to understand the other's cultural perspective and how it might be different from one's own.

In practice, assessment of several dimensions simultaneously requires recording and the opportunity to review the performance several times. The gain in validity is likely to be significant and, if it can be combined with reliable criteria, is an attractive means of combining linguistic and cultural assessment. In the following section we discuss some of our own experiments in this and other techniques of assessment. They are no more than indications of what might be done and remain experimental.

Experiments in Assessment

In an experiment with advanced learners of French in English schools, we were able to trial a variety of methods of assessment in the three different areas that have been noted above: knowledge, attitudes and behaviour. Since one of the declared aims of our work (see Case 5 in Chapter 4) is to provide learners with ethnographic skills to facilitate further study, the trials included attempts to assess these too. Linguistic and presentational skills which form the priorities in existing examinations were taken into account but not assessed separately. Different kinds of task undertaken at the same time allowed us to compare their effectiveness in eliciting information and testing empathy and cultural competence. They included the following: oral and written assessments; tasks in both French and English; different kinds of oral testing; different kinds of written tasks analysing French behaviour or analysing English behaviour from a French point of view; role-play between two people and mediation tasks with three people involved; discussion of ethnographic techniques and performance of these. In a few cases (five students) the validity of different assessment tasks could be matched against information elicited from in-depth interviews with the students.

In practice it was found that it was difficult to separate out the three different elements. Knowledge assessment often turned out to include elements of empathy. Empathy needed knowledge. Behaviour relied on awareness born of knowledge, and empathy and ethnographic techniques demanded a similar awareness. 'Empathy' and 'behaviour' both demanded qualitative assessment, that is to say, an overall impressionistic evaluation supported by some explanation from the students of their actions which could indicate their competence. 'Knowledge' invited a more quantitative assessment with specific criteria of accuracy, relevance and detail.

Oral assessment

Two kinds of oral examination assessment were used: a short role-play based on a selection of nine scenarios depicting cultural clashes or misunderstandings (see Appendix VI); and a more extended oral assessment with two role-plays chosen from four of the original nine, followed by questions on different aspects of French life and a short interview of the student by the teacher/assessor. In general the latter allowed for a more satisfactory assessment of cultural understanding since a wider range of information was covered and more opportunities existed for empathy to be demonstrated. The reduced number of situations in the second example and the option for students to prepare the situations beforehand led however to several of the students collaborating and producing the same responses.

As might be expected these oral assessments produced a variety of responses both in terms of knowledge and empathy. Knowledge on one level is fairly easy to assess in terms of accuracy, detail and relevance, although the weighting of these may be different. Thus the inclusion of 'almost everything I know about Brittany' in a role-play defending why one would wish to return to Brittany after living in Paris could gain marks for accuracy and detail but be questionable in terms of relevance:

A Bretagne il y a beaucoup de, très beaucoup de fermes. Une personne sur trois habite dans une ferme. Voici tous les pêcheurs dans Bretagne. Les traditions et par exemple la fest-noze. Toutes les âges, toutes les personnes allaient à la fest-noze. A la fest-noze la danse, la danse traditionnelle et la musique. Les personnes jouaient le binou.

[In Brittany there are lots of farms. One person out of three lives on a farm. There are all the fishermen in Brittany. The traditions and for example the special festival. All ages, everyone goes to the special festival. At the special festival, dancing, traditional dancing and music. People played the Breton bagpipes.]

'Knowledge' was also extended to include recognition of diversity and avoidance of stereotyping (although this could also be considered as a level of empathy as well); thus for example distinguishing between a view of Breton spoken by a large number of people

Interviwer:	Je veux parler du breton, en Bretagne. Il y a beaucoup de gens qui parlent breton?
Student:	Oui.
I:	Et toute la famille parle breton?
S:	Oui.
[I:	I want to talk about the Breton language in Brittany. Are there a lot of people who speak Breton?
S:	Yes.
I:	And the whole family speaks Breton?
S:	Yes.]

or by a few, mainly adult, inhabitants:

Interviewer:	Est-ce que tu vas parler breton là-bas?
Student:	Quelquefois mais seule[ment] avec mes parents. Mais avec mes amis je parle français.
[I:	Will you speak Breton there?
S:	Sometimes but only with my parents. But with my friends I speak French.]

Empathy is more difficult to assess. Shemilt (1984), in his comprehensive article on empathy, provides useful guidelines for teachers and pupils alike, both in identifying the nature of empathy and suggesting ways of distinguishing different levels of competence which could be assessed. In order to achieve a deeper level of understanding, a dual process is necessary: on the one hand to make things easier for pupils to understand (in Shemilt's words 'to render what is alien about the past mentalities sufficiently recognizable to the contemporary reader for him to accept them as his own'); at the same time it is necessary to make things more complicated or difficult, to foreground the discrepancies involved 'disconfirming pupils' expectations or predictions and, thereby, making them aware of logical intransitivities within their ideas' (1984: 44, 73). Shemilt suggests five developmental levels of understanding identified during classroom discussions of history:

Stage I: dry bones and a sense of superiority...

Stage II: assumptions of shared humanity and routine stress on motives...

Stage III: everyday empathy applied to history...

Stage IV: historical empathy...

Stage V: empathetic methodology (1984: 50–54).

Students thus move from disbelief and dismissal, through understanding of evidence and general rules of human behaviour to a transferred understanding of the context and how empathetic/historical methodology functions. These are expanded later into a criteria-related marking scheme incorporating 4 levels of empathetic and pre-empathetic understanding:

Level 1: No valid application of historical or empathetic understanding...

Level 2: Valid historical analysis but 'from the outside'. No evidence of empathetic understanding...

Level 3: Explanation 'from the inside', but only *everyday empathy*... reconstruction remains locked in twentieth-century world-view — no attempt to recreate an alien form of life and way of thinking...

Level 4: Genuine *historical empathy*... Genuine attempt to shed twentieth-century preconceptions and to recreate an alien world-view. Reward any answer that clearly attempts this even when less than completely successful. (1984: 75–6)

Shemilt thus differentiates between a kind of sympathy in understanding people and linking such empathy or sympathy to an imagined and detailed re-creation of historical circumstances and the effects they might have. Shemilt's use of the phrase 'alien world-view' suggests a comparison between cultures distant in time and cultures which are contemporary but distant in space. It was decided to apply these criteria to analysis of empathy with a French world-view.

None of the interviewees in the role-plays demonstrated total rejection of the French culture (Level 1): taking the part of a French person explaining their own culture is of course likely to preclude this possibility. The other three levels were present. Explaining from the outside (Level 2) was evident in answers where pro and contra arguments were advanced without representing how a French person might *feel*. For example, in explaining the lack of religious instruction in school, one student commented:

> Il n'y a pas de enseignement sur la religion parce que le autorité croit la religion détruit le éducation dans l'école. C'est détruire les personnes intellectuelles avec les mythes et la foi.
>
> [There is no religious instruction because the authorities believe that religion destroys education in the school. Myths and faith destroy intellectual people.]

She gives a valid account without explaining the connotations or associations of ideas with the concept of secular schooling in France and the role of the *école libre*, schools in which religion plays a very important role.

There were also examples of learners imagining themselves into the situation but using their own rather than a French experience (Level 3). Thus, for one student, the necessity of attending a grandmother's party was supported by a statement that

> Toute la famille devrait là et ils arrivent de toutes partes de France...et ma grand'mère, elle n'a pas vu toute la famille depuis cinq ans.
>
> [All the family should be there and they arrive from all over France...and my grandmother hadn't seen the whole family for five years.]

The student here transferred a family experience common in Britain (that families often have loose patterns of contact and see each other only occasionally) to the family experience in France where families generally keep in close contact with each other. Here then it would be quite unlikely that a grandmother would not have seen the family for five years.

Some students combined affective and cognitive elements in their role-plays to 'recreate an alien world-view', thus reaching Shemilt's Level 4. The following student described his attachment to Brittany in defending his desire to return:

> C'est simple pour moi. Je suis Breton, je parle breton, ma famille est Bretonne, toute ma culture est bretonne, alors je pense que, j'ai un sentiment, je suis chez moi en Bretagne. Ce n'est pas parce que je déteste Paris... Nos impressions de Bretagne, nos histoires, histoire, c'est dans mon sang, je pense.
>
> [It's easy for me. I am Breton, I speak Breton, my family is Breton, all my culture is Breton, so I think I have a feeling, I am at home in Brittany. It's not because I hate Paris... Our impressions of Brittany, our history, is in my blood, I think.]

He uses his knowledge of what is specific to Brittany and valued by Breton people to explain their rejection of Parisian life. The fact that he is asked to do so in a role-play allows him to articulate how he imagines Breton people feel in an immediate way. He can use the rhetoric of repetition in a direct expression of feeling which would not be available in an analytical description. This affective element accompanied a description of important traditions, tranquillity, a sense of community and the presence of the sea, farms etc. which were also cited as important factors.

One further dimension of empathy could be added to Shemilt's categories. As we have suggested in earlier chapters, intercultural communicative competence involves an awareness of difference and a consequent reflection on one's own culturally specific socialisation and limitations. A fifth level might be postulated in terms of the ability to recognise and articulate the difficulties involved not only in perceiving a situation from an insider viewpoint (Level 4) but also in recognising that one's own cultural standpoint, one's own existing values and expectations affect one's own perceptions. Only one student out of the 27 interviewed demonstrated this ability. In talking about the importance of attending the grandmother's celebration and taking the role of the French person she recognised that this might be difficult for an English person to understand:

> si je ne suis pas là... C'est très difficile d'expliquer parce que en Angleterre je crois vous n'avez pas d'occasions pourquoi toute la famille sont asseyées toute la table...grand événement, non seulement le mariage bien sûr, mais aussi pour un repas...les repas en France sont assez longs, en Angleterre, non?

> [if I'm not there... It's very difficult to explain because in England I think that there aren't opportunities for the whole family to sit round the table...a big event, not just a wedding of course, but also for a meal...meals in France are quite long, in England, not so?]

Although linguistic competence was not assessed in this experimental work, it was clear that in oral exercises linguistic competence in understanding native speakers was a crucial component. Comparing statements from the same pupils in oral examination, written examination (in French and English) and in evaluative interviews in English it was clear that silence and reduced communication in the oral examination did not mean lack of knowledge or empathy. One student, for example, who could only manage 'Il y a un boum toute la nuit pour ma grand'mère' [there was a party all night long for my grandmother] as a reason for attending a family gathering, was able to comment in English in her interview on the closeness of families at mealtimes and the importance of the occasion marked by the high numbers of family members attending and the care devoted to preparing and eating the meal. Linguistic competence of course forms an integral part of intercultural competence so in this area this student would achieve a low grading, but with respect to empathy and knowledge it is useful to have a range of other assessment channels where poor comprehension does not block demonstration of competence in other areas.

Written assessment

Written assessments offer this opportunity. In the two different terminal written papers prepared by team members for their pupils different kinds of questions were asked. One paper offered an essay question in French from a choice of four situations, each linking to one of the units studied (family, school, work and regional identity); the other paper provided six questions in English and French linked to the same topics but with all questions compulsory. The two papers are given in Appendices VII and VIII respectively. In the second paper, two questions asked for information, one on school and one on weddings:

(i) Expliquez en français (4 ou 5 lignes) les institutions ou les personnalités suivantes: l'école maternelle, le collège, le lycée, le conseil de classe, un surveillant, le baccalauréat.

[Explain in French (4 or 5 lines) the following institutions and persons:]

Vous vous appelez Geneviève et vous vous êtes mariée la semaine dernière. Ecrivez une lettre à une amie qui était malade et absente pendant la cérémonie pour lui décrire le mariage.

[You are called Geneviève and you were married last week. Write a letter to a friend who was ill and missed the service to tell her about the wedding.]

The second question also allowed for empathy to be displayed and this was an opportunity for students to demonstrate their awareness of the differences between a French and English wedding ceremony even though this comparison was not asked for.

Two further questions in English asked for students' views on French mealtimes and of a tourist video film on Brittany, encouraging students to explore their own reactions. Generally these questions allowed students to express a fuller response than the interchanges in the oral examination. Several students included comparisons with England in describing meals (even though this was not specifically asked for in the question). One student wrote for example:

A French mealtime can last for anywhere up to 3 hours, with many courses, and much wine being drunk in the process, the meal is never hurried and good homecooked food is always served, even small children may drink wine with their meal, if allowed to by the parents.

This is very different to our country where people eat at different times, eat different things and a meal can be finished within 10 minutes.

One student also explained the symbolic meanings of various elements seen in the Brittany film, for example:

These [religious] statues where [were] a sign that if your village's statue was larger than that of the next villages then your village was considered richer and superior.

The written medium here and the framing of the questions encouraged students to reflect on their own and the target culture. One problem however did persist, that of generalisation. The first example above suggests a single convention for mealtimes for all French families. Students were encouraged to reflect on the problem of generalisation and in the question on the Brittany film they were given the opportunity to reflect on modes of perception and description:

Write three or four paragraphs (in English) describing Brittany as seen in the video film. Do you think it is a full or accurate portrait of the region? Explain your reasons.

Interestingly one student replaces the stereotypes of the film with her own stereotypes, although recognising this at the same time:

I do not think that it is a totally accurate picture of Brittany as I am sure that parts of it around the coast are just like the Costa-del-Sol with hotels, flies, English pubs, lots of German tourists and glass-bottom boat trips.

In understanding another culture a multi-tier process is necessary: recognising existing hetero-stereotypes of that culture, forming new generalisations based on the insider conventions of that country, recognising the diversity within those conventions and finally the conventions that blinker learners' own perceptions and lead them to interpret in a particular way. In a discussion of 'cultural stereotypes', Brown (1987) points to the necessity of organising information learnt about a country into 'stereotyped images':

the cautious accumulation of stereotyped images can help a person to understand another culture *in general* [our emphasis] and the differences between that culture and his own. (1987: 125)

Most of our students demonstrated this intermediary stage of understanding. Recognition of diversity within a culture, with exercises such as those suggested by Zarate & Troutot (1990) (see Case 4 in Chapter 4), is a necessary further stage of development.

Two further questions which formed part of the written assessments deserve comment. These both specifically require the student to imagine themselves into a role, and to compare the two cultures (English and

French). One of the questions provides four quotations from French people working in schools in England which comment on cultural differences (school timetables in terms of hours, amounts of homework, subject specialisation versus 'broad education', and student/teacher relationships). Students are then asked to

> imagine that you have to explain some of the differences between a school in England and a *lycée* to a student from France who will be staying for a year in your school. To give a full picture you should discuss not only the physical differences but also differences in atmosphere and attitudes in English and French schools.

This generally produced full answers and good comparisons. Interestingly one student who wrote her answer first in French by mistake and then in English included some recognition of diversity in the English version (not included in the French version):

> The teachers [in English schools] usually get on with their pupils although there are some which are impossible to get on with. And there are some pupils who make it difficult for other pupils and also the teachers.

The fact that this pupil chose to write this question out again in English and included more revealing information in it indicates advantages in allowing pupils to write in English about their cultural knowledge.

A further productive alternative was offered by a different kind of written question, writing in French and imagining oneself as a French person reacting to an English way of life. This question was one of four in one of the examination papers and was chosen by 13 out of 14 pupils. Distribution of the questions beforehand allowed students to identify any vocabulary that was necessary and this perhaps reduced the problems caused by linguistic competence that were evident in other assessment exercises. The question focused on differences in family life:

> Etudiant(e) français(e) vous passez un an en Angleterre. Ecrivez une lettre à votre grand'mère française dans laquelle vous décrivez et expliquez quelques différences entre la France et l'Angleterre en ce qui concerne la vie familiale.

> [As a French student you are spending a year in England. Write a letter to your French grandmother in which you describe and explain some differences between France and England as far as family life is concerned.]

The written medium here allowed students more time and space to think themselves into the role of a French person and how they might react than in the oral examination where students are under constant pressure. The letter format also permitted an informality of expression which eased communication. Particularly useful in this exercise was the concentration on defamiliarising the familiar, imagining how our culture would seem to others, and this produced some high-level empathy. One student commented to her grandmother: 'Tu détesterais la famille anglaise parce que ils sonts plus distants qu'une famille française' [You would hate the English family because they are much more distant than a French family]; another imagined how a French person might react to eating trifle: 'Les anglais mangent quelquechose affreuse au répas de mariage qui s'appelle la bagatelle au xérès' [The English eat something terrible for the wedding meal called sherry trifle]. One particularly good answer focused on parents' attitudes, seeing how there might be similarities as well as differences:

> Je pense que c'est amusant que les parents en Angleterre sont pareil de la nôtre. Les deux ramenant tout à leur expériences de la vie, mais leur époque et la nôtre, ne sont pas comparables, c'est vrai!
>
> [I think it's funny that parents in England are the same as ours. Both of them bringing everything back to their experiences in life, but their time and ours can't be compared, it's true!]

In both oral and written assessment exercises formulae were used which were familiar to students: write a letter, a description, a discussion etc., but new elements were introduced which pertained particularly to the assessment of culture: comparisons with English culture, opportunities to demonstrate empathy, and the writing of answers in English.

Four other techniques were used which were presented to students as opportunities for language practice or discussion of the project. These exercises are thus more strictly speaking evaluative of the project itself but have also been used for assessment purposes internally. These were a mediation exercise, conducting an interview of a French native speaker, a presentation of questionnaire findings and in-depth interviews with selected students by researchers, in English.

A mediation exercise

The mediation exercise was carried out with three students. The exercise was constructed as one of mediating in a problem situation between the student's mother (played by an English teacher) and a French student on an exchange visit (played by Carole, a French 'assistante'). The problem situation to be resolved was the conflict between the exchange student wanting to wear trousers to school and the mother wanting her to wear a skirt.

This exercise provided an opportunity to assess both empathy and other aspects of intercultural competence. The mediating student needed to draw on a variety of competences. S/he needed cultural knowledge of France to understand the opinions or objections voiced. S/he needed empathy in using knowledge of cultural differences to explain difficulties in terms familiar to each participant from their own culture — the cognitive dimension of empathy. S/he also needed to be able to imagine how each of the two protagonists would be feeling and a certain degree of diplomacy to handle the situation agreeably — the affective dimension of empathy. A further dimension was added in considering the original model taken from Meyer's intercultural research with upper-secondary pupils in Germany (1991).

Meyer outlines three levels of cultural competence: monocultural, intercultural and transcultural. In Meyer's model the 'monocultural' level fails to recognise the factors important in the cultural context of the target language and interprets only in terms of the mother culture. Empathy, which is defined as operating on the level of understanding emotional experience, is not accepted as being of value. Attempts to mollify through omission or total acceptance of the target viewpoint are interpreted as the lowest level of intercultural competence. An understanding of different cultures through information culled represents Level 2 in 'intercultural competence'. What is missing in this intermediary level for Meyer is the ability of the mediator to relativise and understand himself and his own culture and to negotiate on the basis of this understanding. These abilities belong solely to the level of transcultural competence. Relativisation, cognitive evaluation of the validity of *different* viewpoints and the truthful transmission of these viewpoints between the participants are the key factors of this higher level. The final stage is seen as the ability of the mediator to locate himself in a cultural debate, to accept the validity of different cultural viewpoints and to use his imagination to provide a suitable solution which does justice to both. An important element is demonstration of feeling at ease with one's relationship to one's own culture while also recognising the validity of another culture: 'stabilising one's self-identity' (1991: 137). This is comparable with our own earlier suggestion of an addition to Shemilt's four levels of a fifth in which the learner recognises the difficulty of relinquishing temporarily one's own values in order to understand those of others.

The three examples of mediation filmed in the exercise could thus potentially be analysed in two different ways according to these models. In the event, it was only possible to use two of the examples since one student had such difficulty with the language, both in reception and production, that her levels of empathy or cultural understanding were almost impossible to disentangle from the linguistic misunderstandings. Here then, as was seen with the oral role-play, it was evident that in order for intercultural competence to be assessed, a minimum level of linguistic competence was also necessary.

In the mediation sessions with the two male students a definite progression was evident with both working towards some sense of personal responsibility and taking of initiative to provide solutions and an acceptance of the validity of the differing viewpoints. In both cases the French student suggested solutions (phoning the accompanying teacher from France as an outsider arbiter and wearing a dress instead of a skirt) but suggestions were also made by the mediators themselves. Discussions after the exercise provided insight into motivation for certain statements and allowed the students to reflect on what had taken place. This was a key factor in understanding their competence. In both sessions however there were also frequent examples of the student merely acting as translators or sometimes misunderstanding what the French student had said.

Although both students reached a compromise and demonstrated acceptance of different views; they achieved these goals through different routes. One focused at first on the practical problems of the French student not having a skirt with her (did other female students have skirts with them, should they buy one?) and moved on later to accepting Carole's attitude 'It seems that she just doesn't want to wear school uniform'. He did not at first explicitly accept Carole's point that 'je ne veux pas être comme tout le monde' [I don't want to be like everyone else], but offered in reply a practical solution of doing without a visit to a school: 'Tu passes aller à l'école' [You don't go to school]. Here then there is tacit acceptance of Carole's viewpoint but without exploring the clash between the desire for individual dress and the need for school uniform. At the end of the session he suggests two arguments that could offer a compromise: precedence and common sense — 'Dans le passé les étudiants pensaient qu'ils viennent [venaient] ici et ils jurent [juraient] que...on vont [irait] avec le jupe [en jupe]'... 'C'est pas une [un] problème...porter une jupe'. [In the past students thought they were coming here and they swore that they would wear a skirt. It's not a problem, wearing a skirt.] Here then there is the implicit suggestion that temporarily complying with convention will not ultimately damage Carole's personal principles. He establishes a sense of identity in a neutral position vis-à-vis Carole's intention not to wear a skirt or school uniform. There are indications of transcultural competence, following Meyer's model.

Another interesting facet was his relationship to the views put forward by his mother. Early in the exercise he cites his mother as an authority (which Carole fails to accept):

S: Mais ma mère, elle a dit, que…ici…
C: Moi, je m'en fiche de ce qu'elle m'a dit. Je porte mes vêtements.
[S: My mother said that…here…
C: I don't care what she said. I'm wearing my clothes.]

Towards the end of the interview Carole again challenges the validity of the mother's argument (that she believes that the teacher from France will also require Carole to wear a skirt) 'Je ne crois pas ta mère' [I don't believe your mother]. He challenges Carole's non-acceptance firstly by querying her statement and then asking for her reasons:

S: Tu ne crois pas ma mère?
C: Non.
S: Pourquoi?
[S: You don't believe my mother?
C: No.
S: Why?]

Again he has worked through to a sense of self-identity by demonstrating implicitly to Carole that his mother's arguments are worthy of consideration. He demonstrates to both sides that their arguments are valid. This allows for the present situation, in which each considers the other's viewpoint invalid, to be transcended.

He also shows his ability to empathise with Carole's values and expectations, to see things as she might see them. When his mother makes the point that 'English schools have a certain sort of atmosphere and that's what you have to do [wear uniform]', he anticipates in his 'translation' the way a French person might experience it: 'L'ambiance à l'école c'est très formal [formel] et on ne peut pas porter les vêtements comme ça, il faut, ici on doit porter un uniforme, une jupe. C'est tout, ça ne va pas'. [The atmosphere at school is very formal and you can't wear clothes like that, you have to, here, you have to wear a uniform, a skirt. That's all. It's not accepted.] He is thus recognising the cognitive structures which would make Carole interpret wearing a skirt as unacceptable formality. At the end of the interview he also indicates to Carole that he wishes to communicate as clearly as possible to her so that her views/difficulties do not come from a misunderstanding of the situation: 'Tu peux voir. Tu comprends?' [You can see. You understand?] This then suggests the kind of empathy desired by Shemilt where the student is able to put himself in the position of someone else and imagine their affective response. In the post-mediation discussion he pointed to his own desire to moderate Carole's statements: 'I don't think I said everything exactly the way that…not to say everything that Carole said so, as forcefully'. In transmitting, for example, Carole's assertion that 'Je ne crois pas ta mère', he adds a more neutral additional sentence explaining Carole's difficulty in a new situation 'She says she doesn't believe you. She says she can't believe it'. Some of the empathy demonstrated by the student was thus consciously recognised and the post-session discussion allowed him time to reflect and assess it.

The second student's interview operated on a slightly different axis showing less overt empathy but a stronger recognition of the equal validity of different viewpoints, moving closer towards Meyer's transcultural level. In the opening moments of the session he already exhibited a sense of confidence and challenge and self-identity by teasing Carole. In reply to her comment that 'Les garçons portent le pantalon', he enquires 'Tu es un garçon?' [Boys wear trousers… Are you a boy?] By introducing this in a lighthearted way he is able to show Carole that her argument as it stands is insufficient. Later in the session he uses a similar approach but on a more meaningful level: on two occasions he points out to Carole that her references to behaviour in France may not apply to an English context:

C: Si je suis Anglaise je portes l'uniforme, moi je suis française.
S2:   Ah oui, mais tu es en Angleterre maintenant…
C: En France…on se fiche de porter le pantalon.
S2:   Ah oui, en France, mais en Angleterre…
[C: If I'm English I wear a uniform, but I'm French.
S2:   Ah yes, but you're in England now.
C: In France…people don't mind at all about wearing trousers.
S2:   Ah yes, in France, but in England…]

Here then there is a recognition of appropriacy of different norms in different cultures which gives Carole the opportunity to relativise her own cultural identity. Indeed at the end of the session she shows signs of doing just that:

S2:   …en Angleterre [porter l'uniforme] c'est, je ne sais pas, c'est normal.
C: Qu'est-ce que c'est 'normal'? Ah bon, dis à ta mère que je porte pas une jupe mais…que je porte une robe.
S2:   …in England [wearing a uniform] is, I don't know, it's normal.
C: What's 'normal'? Oh well, tell your mother that I won't wear a skirt but I'll wear a dress.]

Interestingly here then Carole's thoughts on relativisation are followed by a compromise in terms of what she is then prepared to wear.

In his mediation between the two protagonists this student demonstrates his acceptance of the validity of the different viewpoints. He encourages

Carole to explain why headmasters in France are less bothered about whether girls wear trousers or not:

S2:   Pourquoi les directeurs…on ne [se] fiche pas…?
C: Parce qu'en France on pense que tout est dans la tête et que ce n'est pas les vêtements qu'on voit, c'est…
S2:   [to mother] It's just what's in the mind…that's all that people…
[S2:   Why do headmasters…they don't care…?
C: Because in France we think that everything is in the mind and it's not the clothes that you see, it's…]

In the post-session discussion he explained to one of the observers that he did try to help his mother understand Carole's viewpoint:

> You didn't actually help your mother to understand…that, why she was not going to wear a skirt, uniform rather.

> Well, I think I did tell her that in France that…the headmasters are more bothered about the academic…

In the discussion he also showed his acceptance and understanding of Carole's general stance: 'You can understand why she doesn't want to wear school uniform. I suppose I was trying to persuade her she's got to'.

The ambivalence towards the mother's point of view implicit in this statement is also one that was evident in his mediation activities. When transmitting the mother's view of the creation of a community feeling in the school, he suggests that this is a good feeling, showing his acceptance of it, but when pressed further is also unable to produce any further arguments:

M: Well, can you explain to her that it's different here. Explain to her why, you know, you've got to go… It's like work.
S2:   C'est quand on…on porte l'uniforme à l'école parce que il crée un bon ambiance…si les tous les étudiants portent l'uniforme, c'est très sympa, ils créent un impression de…je ne sais pas.
[S2:   It's when you…you wear a uniform at school, because it creates a good atmosphere…if all the students wear uniform, it's very pleasant, they create an impression of… I don't know.]

At the beginning of the session too, when asked for the reasons for compulsory uniform, he rather dodges the issue:

S2:   Carole, tu ne peux pas aller à l'école dans le [en] pantalon.
C: Pourquoi pas?
S2:   Je ne sais pas. C'est l'école qui donne l'explication.
[S2:   Carole, you can't go to school in trousers.
C: Why not?
S2:   I don't know. It's the school which gives the explanation.]

Thus his acceptance of validity on both sides is rather slanted towards Carole's point of view. His comments in the discussion — 'Mothers don't understand!' — is also revealing in this context.

One further positive point in this student's role as a mediator was his ability to take the initiative and think himself into Carole's situation, although again here the bias against his mother was evident. His mother, surprised at the lack of uniform in French schools, comments: 'Well, she must wear something suitable for school'. His mediating remark here takes into consideration Carole's norms of suitability rather than those of his mother: 'Hmm. D'habitude qu'est-ce que tu portes à l'école?' [What do you usually wear to school?]

If this second student generally proved stronger in terms of self-identity and the ability to accept the validity of Carole's arguments, there were also areas where he failed to pick up the importance of attitudes being expressed. The first student had failed to pick up Carole's expressions of individualism as important, concentrating on the practicalities of obtaining suitable clothes. The second student fails to pick up a similar point when Carole describes the aesthetic discrepancy between the French and English classroom: '[En Angleterre] ils créent une impression de tristesse, je trouve. En France c'est plutôt amusant. On a des couleurs différents'. [In England they create an impression of dullness. In France it's more fun. There are different colours.] When challenged on this point in the discussion it was clear that he had discounted the validity of this attitude:

Researcher: When Carole said...she was making the point about it was very sad, I wonder how you might be able to explain that...

S2:   That everyone wearing one uniform was sad... I don't think it's sad.

R: So that's why you didn't put much emphasis on that?

S2:   There didn't seem much point.

In both sessions then there were some points of view which were easier for the students to accept as valid. Generally both were able to produce counter-arguments and begin to relativise with some sense of self-identity and both showed signs of empathy, though in different ways.

In evaluating the session in terms of its efficacy as an instrument of assessment there are several factors to be considered. Meyer suggests that a single performance is not enough to evaluate or assess the competence of a student (1991: 142) and his own research included recordings of interviews for three successive years. The feasibility of such a programme with the time involved and the logistics of organising suitable participants would seem to preclude this as a viable possibility for a large upper secondary class. Meyer himself uses the exercise as a diagnostic test but questions whether these intercultural skills are 'the result of formal instruction' (1991: 155). He suggests that these exercises provide the opportunity for students to learn rather than to be tested, although of course these two activities do not preclude each other. A possible solution to the laborious task of setting up multiple active mediation tasks within which students could learn, could be to analyse video-recordings of other students' performances to allow students opportunities to reflect on what mediation involves. Exercises in answering arguments or understanding viewpoints could also form a preliminary basis for negotiation, although the more subtle skills of instantaneous response can of course only take place in direct experiential learning.

As an exercise in testing language skills it was clear that a certain minimum level of linguistic competence was necessary. The actual range of vocabulary was often very restricted. As one student said in the discussion, 'it was going over the same things all the time'. Nevertheless the situation did replicate the pressures of intercultural contact. Production of the target language in this context, even if only in a restricted sense, is likely to take place in a different way. The first student who experienced the pressure of the situation more, perhaps because of a deeper empathetic level, sums this point up well: 'It helps you learn words when it's rushed...a tense atmosphere'.

Clearly the mediation exercise was interesting for the students even if somewhat intimidating with the presence of an audience and a video camera. It could operate on several levels: simple translation, negotiation, diplomacy, empathy, establishing self-identity. As it stands it poses problems in terms of feasibility, but any modification in terms of length would destroy its value, since skills of understanding need developmental stages. With respect to the importance of including an experiential dimension in a cultural programme the exercise proved invaluable. However far a student has progressed in terms of understanding cultural differences, it is only in a direct interaction with someone from another culture that such intercultural knowledge can really flourish or show its true value.

Interviewing a native speaker

The interviews of native speakers which were carried out during a training day for ethnographic techniques (see Case 5 in Chapter 4) also provided a realistic context for assessment purposes. Students were helped to plan interview schedules and to reflect on good interviewing practice. The resulting interviews proved a useful source of assessing empathy in intercultural competence, with linguistic competence again playing a vital role.

Students were asked to draw up an interview schedule to explore the regional identity of the French native speaker interviewee. The interview could thus be assessed on two levels: the kinds of questions which had been planned beforehand in terms of their relevance to the topic and the sensitivity of the interviewer's reactions in the interview in responding to the statements from the interviewee.

Some questions disappointingly focused only on factual information concerning the place of residence rather than the interviewee's sense of identity: 'Où se trouve la maison dans le village? Qu'est-ce qu'on peut faire dans le village?' [Where is the house in the village? What can you do in the village?] Other students focused more on the distinctiveness of a particular region and the interviewee's own connection with it. For example, one student asked about the interviewee's native Britanny. Another student interviewing the same French person focused on the numbers of family members living in the region and the relationship to the capital. Questions demonstrating a higher level of empathy focused on the interviewee's consciousness of being French. One student asked: 'Dans quelles situations vous oubliez que vous êtes Français?' [In what situations do you forget that you're French?] Another: 'La France vous manque?' [Do you miss France?]

Clearly some pre-planned questions were necessary in this interview situation but the interviews divided into those where only the list of questions was asked, coming to an abrupt halt at the end of the list, and those where the interviewers responded to the interviewee. Here a level of intercultural competence is involved in being able to listen and respond. Three levels could be measured: total lack of response, some general response to interviewee, and particular response to statements relevant to the topic. Thus one student picked up an interviewee's point that she liked pubs in England and pursued this. Here there was evidence of empathy but the connection with regional identity was somewhat tenuous. On the other hand, with an interviewee who originated from the Midi and lived in Alsace, one student pursued the question of a border identity by asking if he spoke German. Disappointingly none of the students who interviewed this French person explored either the duality of living in a border region or feelings about identity, after having moved from one region to another. With another interviewee the question of sport and region was explored linking into the interviewee's Breton identity.

This was the first time for most of the students that they had interviewed a French native speaker. With the help of an 'assistant' or 'assistante' it should be possible to make this a more frequent teaching method and students could be alerted to the criteria on which they would be judged. Comments from students in subsequent evaluative interviews gave useful indications as to their awareness of what had been seen as necessary in these interviews with native speakers. In explaining his views on interviewing techniques, one student stressed an empathetic approach:

> Be careful that they're questions where you wouldn't take offence... Your wording...they might get the wrong impression.

Another student emphasised the framing of the question in a different way:

> If you ask the question and then give a choice of answers then she'd just pick one and leave it at that but if you just asked the question and left it open for her to continue then she'd talk for a few minutes. That was the best way of getting the conversation going.

It would be useful then to incorporate some kind of short evaluative discussion, as with the mediation exercise, or provide an opportunity for a written evaluation to allow students to demonstrate their knowledge of interviewing as well as an opportunity for putting this knowledge into action in an interview performance.

Questionnaire

Students encountered questionnaires in a similarly exploratory manner: with some preliminary explanation and discussion on the training day and, with one group, as an extended follow-on to a study of two questionnaires about school and schooling in editions of *Phosphore*, a magazine for French pupils in upper secondary.

The preparatory stages helped students to identify good and bad practice in setting out a questionnaire and illustrated methods of presenting information (the training day material is given in Appendix IV). Students in one school prepared their own questionnaires on 'school' in English, tried them out on ten of their peer group and presented their findings in French. This process was assessed on two levels: the framing and relevance of the questions and the level of skill in presenting the findings. As with the interview exercise this was the first time for the majority of pupils that they had undertaken such an activity. In this case it also involved a public presentation recorded on video and audio cassette and observed by an outsider. The results can therefore be seen as only a preliminary stage towards what should be a much higher level of proficiency after practice.

It was not evident in all of the presentations how the questions had been framed but this was explored further at the end of each presentation with a short discussion between teacher and students. The presentations themselves ranged from a mock interview, or interviews, replicating the questionnaire content, to presentations of statistics. None of the students provided any visual display of information and this too was discussed in the session afterwards with an evaluation of different presentational possibilities (OHPs, bar graphs, pie charts etc.). Comments from some of the students themselves also proved illuminating in terms of what had proved successful questions and how material could be presented. One student focused on the need for open questions:

> The ones that weren't successful were the ones that just gave out figures, like that said 'Do you like school?' Eight people said 'yes', two people said 'no'. They were a waste of time, you know...because you didn't get people's opinions, you just got people saying 'yes' or 'no', you didn't get reasons and whys. But the best ones were saying 'If you could change anything about the school, what would it be and why?' They were the ones that gave most feedback.

Another student commented on designing the layout of the questionnaire:

> It's a good way of showing you how to set things out, like giving boxes A, B, C, D etc., and which way to form your questions, what to start with and how to go, rather than jump into it...Before I thought you'd just be able to write a few questions down and that would be it, but it wouldn't be able to work like that.

These two students also offered comments on future presentational possibilities, one focusing on performance and the other on a written report:

> I would make it a lot more colourful because it was just a few words on a piece of paper, you know. I'd maybe just have a screen up and slides and stuff to point out to people. Bar graphs, pie charts and just generally more colourful.

> Well, you first of all just make a note of all the findings you've got and then I would have thought you put them in some form of paragraph or structure so the one follows each other, they're not jumbled, so you can read straight through it and not put too much babble in, just facts, so that people can understand and then maybe just draw a few graphs or whatever.

It would be quite feasible to translate this exploratory questionnaire exercise into a fuller assessment exercise, asking students to provide a written questionnaire on a particular topic and then either a written or oral presentation of a set of given questionnaire findings.

Evaluation interviews

It has been evident from the accounts above that evaluation interviews were valuable in providing additional supportive information for the exercises in assessment in which students were already involved. The interviews also revealed areas which had not been touched by the assessment exercises. Three particular areas were noticeable: students' own attitudes, the revelation of a kind of cultural unawareness, and cultural awareness at a deeper, more ambiguous level.

Students' attitudes to a culture are perhaps beyond the area of assessment in any case as has been discussed above. Certainly it was evident that the expression of such attitudes was far more forthcoming in an informal interview than in a formal examination situation. Thus one student, who was able to express some degree of empathy in her written work, commenting on the role of the French family: 'J'aime la vie familiale meilleux [mieux], c'est plus amicable!' [I like family life more, it's more friendly], also displayed a degree of ethnocentricity in interview: 'Personally I couldn't feel comfortable doing an exchange, I couldn't stand anyone else in my house apart from anything else'. Here then the interview added interesting information but could not perhaps be replicated in an assessment situation.

The remaining two areas could however be explored if suitable means of elicitation could be found. Failure to understand a culture was already evident in the assessment exercises insofar as students provided false information or misinterpretation. What the assessments missed was an indication of students' assumptions that some aspects of the foreign culture must be the same as their own: an assimilation of the unknown to the known. One student for example commented 'It's [the education system] very similar I should imagine because their baccalaureat is probably like the "A" levels'. The format of many of the assessment tasks sought to highlight comparison and difference and did not allow students to express their perceptions (often misguided) of similarity which surfaced quite frequently in the evaluation interviews. Some reframing of questions with a focus on similarity and difference could help to add this dimension to assessment.

The other layer of cultural awareness which surfaced occasionally in the interviews is more problematic in terms of assessment: namely, the understanding of a complexity of layers of behaviour or values, or the ambiguity of one's own position vis-à-vis another culture. One student, in talking about racial attitudes in France and England, recognised that racism could be much more complex than generally recognised, that as a white person one could be the victim of racism just as much as the perpetrator:

> Blacks, they're just as racist about the whites as the whites are about them.

Another student recognised that he had mixed views about French schools and about France in general which could not necessarily be separated out:

Well, I would if, sort of half of me would like to because I'd like to — I think it's a better education over there and better discipline, but half of me doesn't want to because I think it would be too hard and I've got the easy life here sort of thing, so I'd like to stop here...

If you compare the two, what they do and what you do, it makes you think, would you prefer the other way or would you like the English way.

Current 'A' level syllabuses encourage 'good organisation and control of material' as was seen in the analysis of syllabuses earlier. This can encourage a streamlining of arguments which present a neat cogent package for the examiner which is a far cry from the state of insecurity and anomie identified by Brown (1987: 135) and analysed in our first chapter. Billig explains in detail the range of schemata that any one person has at his behest and the differences in context which will encourage the choice of different options (1987: 236 and 242–43). Individuals for example may feel encouraged to adopt counter stances because of the strength or one-sidedness of the arguments presented, or may present extreme views in a group situation where more mitigated arguments are likely to be forthcoming. This complexity and ambiguity that students may be aware of is then fruitful in terms of cultural growth and decentring but at the same time may present considerable difficulty in terms of assessment.

Levels of Competence

Our discussion so far has concentrated mainly on techniques of assessment, on what it is feasible or desirable to assess and how specific techniques can be used in practice. Only by implication have we addressed the question of what level of knowledge and skill we should expect at various stage of teaching and learning. We have discussed how levels of competence can be defined and we have applied these definitions to the performance of learners in upper secondary education. We have also examined existing practices for public examinations in England at the end of upper secondary education. By implication, therefore, we have suggested that such learners can in principle reach the highest levels defined by Meyer for intercultural competence and by Shemilt for historical understanding.

Two questions deserve further discussion. First, are we justified in assuming that learners in upper secondary can reach the highest levels of competence as defined earlier? Second, what relationship is there between performance elicited by the kinds of techniques we have discussed and intercultural communicative competence as we have defined it.

The issue of levels for different stages of education is addressed by Campos *et al.* (1988). Drawing upon definitions of 'niveaux 1 et 2' already well known to some teachers of French as a foreign language in schools, they propose a third level which is appropriate to university study. In the course of their discussion they also address the relationship between the teaching of culture and the teaching of language.

At the first level, considered to be the equivalent in linguistic terms of 'threshold level' (Council of Europe, 1976), the learner needs information which allows him to identify the semantic field of the vocabulary he is using (Campos *et al.*, 1988: 122). They give as an example the following sentence: 'J'ai acheté des croissants pour demain en conduisant la petite à la garderie'. [I bought some croissants for tomorrow as I took the child to the day-care centre.] To understand this sentence the learner needs knowledge of the 'the socio-alimentary nature and role of the croissant and the socio-professional and family nature and role of the "garderie"'(our translation). There are two further semantic contents needed: the meaning of 'conduire' [to lead or to drive] and the identity of 'la petite' [the young female child]. Thus far Campos *et al.* are in accord with our suggestions in Chapter 2 that cultural learning is focused on vocabulary, and they too suggest that at this level linguistic and cultural learning are integrated, although they introduce a significant qualification in their statement: 'The teaching of culture at this level would not *necessarily* show itself to be different from that of language but the information that it would convey would be crucial' (our translation and emphasis). This level might be expected to produce, as Ager (1993: 81) suggests, 'stereotyped amazement: the production in the learner of astonishment that other people could be like that'.

The second level, beyond the 'threshold', continues the study of language but with increasing opportunities to handle written and oral texts which give the student an opening onto the culture of the country being studied (Campos *et al.*, 1988: 123). At this level teaching of culture can be distinguished from language teaching and provides learners, in parallel, with information not strictly linguistic 'allowing messages in the language to be understood and formulated' (our translation). With respect to the sentence quoted above, learners can focus on 'the socio-alimentary customs of the French and their education system' (our translation). Language becomes of secondary importance in comparison with understanding and producing texts. This level is to be expected at the end of upper secondary education as traditionally conceived in the *lycée*, the *Gymnasium* or the grammar school. It should in Ager's view 'assist the learner to move away from his own ethnocentricity and become aware of the arbitrary nature of his own culture' (1993: 81).

The third level corresponds to university study which is characterised by a critical dimension. The third level of cultural learning should therefore be distinguishable through the inclusion of a critical attitude, after the first period of 'learning' followed by the second level of 'deepening of knowledge'. At this level the study of culture should be clearly separated from language study, which should be concerned with linguistic and semantic analyses, whilst continuing to rely upon already acquired linguistic ability. This level should be reflexive, following a period of residence in the foreign country if this is possible, and should help the student to reflect as much upon his/her own cultural 'normality' as upon that of the foreign country (Campos *et al.*, 1988: 129).

We have cited the proposals by Campos *et al.* because they help us to focus on the theoretical issues of levels of competence and stages of education and also because they have implicit practical consequences. It is clear from their argument that they believe language and culture can be taught separately, particularly as language teaching focuses less on the acquisition of the foreign language and more on a study of the language as a system. Secondly, they appear to reserve for university study the characteristic of *critical* understanding of the foreign country and culture and relativisation of the 'normality' of the learners' own culture. This contrasts markedly with our own view of secondary education which is also evident in Melde's writing, for example, or in the aims of the National Curriculum for England and Wales (see Cases 1 and 2 in Chapter 4). Yet Campos *et al.* are writing on behalf of an association of university teachers (AUPELF: Association des université partiellement ou entièrement de langue française), as part of the analysis and interpretation of data supplied by 105 institutions in 21 European countries. In practical terms, the contrast in underlying assumptions between teachers in secondary and tertiary education has serious consequences unless some greater degree of harmony can be introduced.

Another aspect of the contrast is that Campos *et al.* define their levels of expectation of what learners should be taught in terms of institutions, whilst our own argument in Chapter 1 was based on theories of psychological development. Our position is that a comparative methodology combined with a defined body of knowledge is appropriate for all levels of education. The differentiation between levels should be made in terms of the complexity of the comparative analysis of a given cultural phenomenon and, secondly, in terms of a gradual increase in the detail of knowledge of cultural phenomena. In practice, the gradual deepening of analytical knowledge should be attained through a spiral curriculum which brings learners back to phenomena they have already discovered. Finally, we have argued that the separation of language and culture even at an advanced level is ill-advised and that the acquisition and study of 'key words' in particular and vocabulary in general is the hinge between the two.

The underlying assumptions of our position are that learners need to reach a certain stage of conceptual and moral development before they can fully benefit from a comparative methodology which relativises and suggests critical insights into both foreign and learners' own cultures. Nonetheless, as we said in Chapter 1, the teacher does not need to wait until learners have attained the requisite stage of development but should see their task as provoking development through comparative techniques. A spiral curriculum supports this approach since learners who did not grasp the critical relativisation of a given phenomenon during the first treatment have opportunity at a later and more mature point to re-consider the phenomenon in greater complexity and detail.

The implications of our position for assessment are not that one would expect different kinds of understanding and competence at 'threshold', upper-secondary and university levels, but that one would expect greater depth of complexity and detail. We suggested in the analysis of our own experiments in assessment and our account of Meyer's work that the highest level of intercultural communicative competence can be reached by learners in upper secondary. The postulation of comparable levels of historical understanding for the end of lower secondary education suggests that we might expect some pupils to reach the highest levels of intercultural competence there too; this is clearly an area for further research. This is supported in psychological terms, since developmental theory suggests that some learners will attain the requisite conceptual and moral stage before the end of lower secondary, although others may not.

The practical question of what to expect in assessment at any given point in secondary or higher education has to be answered in our view in practical terms. That is to say, that the practical issues of what time is available for teaching and, consequently, what selection is made of topics, will determine how much depth of knowledge can be expected of learners. On the other hand, whatever depth is reached, one would expect some learners to reach the highest levels of intercultural competence within the limits of what they have been taught. Thus, the techniques for eliciting performance for assessment should in principle be similar at all levels of education, although some techniques may be of more practical use than others according to assessment circumstances and the depth of competence expected.

The introduction of the terms 'performance' and 'competence' in the last paragraph leads to the second major question raised at the beginning of this section. The distinction between 'competence' and 'performance' is familiar enough to linguistics from both Chomsky (1965) and Hymes (1972). Smith argues that a similar distinction should be made with respect to Piaget's account of cognitive development: 'Inhelder and Piaget study children's performance so as to ground an attribution of competence on an empirical base' (1986: 62). Performance is subject to constraints brought about by specific circumstances of a given time and place, both external to the individual — and, for example, dependent on interaction with other individuals — and internal to the individual, such as lapses of memory, 'slips of the tongue', affective stress and so on. Performance is therefore of little interest to theorists — except as an empirical verification, as Smith suggests — and it is not surprising that Chomsky and others have expressly indicated their concern with competence as the more fundamental and generalisable concept and focus of study.

Similarly, language learning theorists have focused on 'communicative competence' in their attempts to define what it is learners are expected to acquire (e.g. Littlewood, 1981; Brumfit, 1984), just as we ourselves have discussed and defined intercultural communicative *competence*. Teachers, too, are wont to speak of competence, although in practice they deal most frequently with performance. For in the classroom they necessarily elicit and develop learners' performance,since their competence is an underlying and unattainable phenomenon. Teaching is therefore subject to constraints with respect to developing learners' competence, just as performance itself is constrained by internal and external constraints of a specific time and place. Teaching, in other words, is always indirect with respect to competence and when performance is elicited but appears to have no effect on underlying competence — in the form of learners' capacity to perform in the same way on a later occasion — teachers' frustration is frequently expressed as dissatisfaction with learners' 'motivation' or 'aptitude' or 'intelligence'.

Assessment suffers under the same difficulties. An assessor can only inspect and evaluate learners' performance as an indicator of their underlying competence. With respect to intercultural competence, an assessor must interpret a particular performance as an indicator of a level of competence, as we ourselves did earlier in this chapter. Zarate and Troutot, in the cultural textbook analysed in Chapter 4 (Case 4), also accept this indicator (1990: 33). Although an underlying level of competence is necessary for a corresponding performance, other factors need to be present to provide sufficient conditions for performance actually to take place. For example, in traditional written examinations, it is expected that external conditions should be conducive to good performance: a quiet, well-lit and well-aired room. Conditions internal to the individual at a specific time and place cannot usually be taken into account and one of the arguments for continuous assessment is that the significance of internal constraints of one specific time and place can be reduced by aggregating performance on a number of occasions.

Another aspect of this familiar problem is that during a performance, learners may exhibit competence at a number of levels. We saw in our experiments in 'mediation' that a student sometimes demonstrated competence at one level and sometimes at another during 'the same' performance. How should the student's level of competence be evaluated? What 'mark' should he/she be given for the whole performance? The traditional answer is to identify and evaluate parts of the performance and to aggregate and establish a mean for the whole. This may be defensible as a means of establishing an examination evaluation but it masks the fact that, if the constraints of a particular moment are reduced and sufficient conditions created, then a more direct exhibition of underlying competence can be achieved. And it is this underlying competence that examinations purport implicitly to measure.

These problems are not confined, of course, to the evaluation of intercultural communicative competence, nor to language and culture teaching *per se*. They are common to all forms of assessment. It is nonetheless important to review them again here as part of our discussion of the development of new techniques for evaluating a newly defined aspect of competence, namely the intercultural dimension of communicative competence. If learners' acquisition of the necessary condition of competence is to be assessed then the sufficient conditions for 'good' performance — i.e. as direct a reflection of competence as possible — have to be provided within the techniques of assessment. In our experiment with 'mediation', the external factors necessary for the experiment — the presence of observers, the use of video-recording — were inimical to good performance. It is therefore encouraging that even so, students managed to exhibit performance which we interpreted as indicating underlying competence at the highest level. That they did not do so consistently throughout the exercise is not surprising in the circumstances and should not be expected even in more favourable conditions. Even though an evaluation for examination purposes might have to establish a 'mean' performance at a lower level, both teacher and learner can take heart from the fact that momentary high level performance indicated the presence of a high level of underlying competence.

Conclusion

Assessment is often seen by both teachers and learners as a 'threat' to teaching and learning. Clearly, this chapter has only raised issues and speculated on possible developments in assessment. It is an inevitable fact of education systems that assessment in the form of examinations for public purposes will be influential on teaching and learning. It is important therefore to maintain the discussion of assessment alongside developments in teaching and learning intercultural communicative competence.

An essential development will be in the defining of levels of competence, and their relationship to techniques of assessment such as those discussed in this chapter. Some attempts have been made in this direction and van Ek (1986) has summarised some proposals made in the European context. The American Association of Teachers of French has suggested, within a discussion of professional standards for French teachers, two levels of 'cultural competence' (Goepper, 1989), and further work is in progress to define four levels (Kramsch, 1993). The questions are easier than the answers, particularly when contrasted with experience already available in assessing linguistic competence. Can cultural competence be assessed separately from linguistic competence? Can levels of cultural competence be refined to produce the finer 'steps' which have been defined for linguistic competence? Does cultural competence develop at the same rate as linguistic competence? Can linguistic competence develop whilst cultural competence remains fixed? And is it ethically acceptable to assess cultural competence?

It is inevitable that this chapter more than others must end with a series of questions. Teachers and researchers can all help to move towards answers, for the significance of assessment cannot be denied.

6 The Wider Context

It has been our purpose in this book to contribute to the developing integration of language and culture teaching and learning by exploring some theoretical issues and describing some case studies. In this final chapter we intend to raise our gaze from the immediate processes of the classroom to consider the broader significance of language and culture learning.

The growth of foreign language teaching in the twentieth century has been exponential. In the 'developed' world, language learning has been offered to more and more students in compulsory education at both primary and secondary levels and to increasing numbers in higher, further and adult education. The introduction of comprehensive schooling was crucial to language teaching because the fundamental principle of bringing the same curriculum to all pupils took foreign language teaching out of the realm of the elite — in the *lycée*, the *Gymnasium*, the grammar school — and offered the vast majority an opportunity to learn a foreign language for the first time. The rise in mass tourism in the second half of the century created a demand for languages in adult education which has not ceased to grow. Within Europe the mobility of students in further and higher education is another recent phenomenon creating demand for language learning. For a younger age group, new attempts to introduce foreign language learning in primary education are gaining ground, particularly in Western Europe. The programme of projected developments proposed by the Council of Europe is a clear indicator of future priorities and possibilities:

...special attention should now be given to the following new sectors:

- primary education (in countries which request assistance with new development programmes),
- upper secondary education,
- advanced adult education,
- vocationally oriented education and training

(Council of Europe, 1989: 10)

In the 'developing' world, the rate of growth is equally high, though the causes are not identical. The introduction of educational opportunities for more and more pupils — particularly when this includes growth in secondary education — has led to an increase in teaching the 'languages of wider communication' (Fishman, 1977); this means primarily English, with French and Spanish following some way behind. Political reasoning has led many education systems to see in foreign language learning for young people a key to future participation in the world community. In many cases however the inability to provide secondary education for all means that language learning is still the privilege of an elite minority.

The purposes and effects of language teaching differ significantly from one context to the next. Although policy statements about educational aims are sometimes remarkably similar in, say, a European and a Gulf country, the historically-determined context, the expectations of parents, children, teachers and politicians, and the role of the foreign language in the identity and political aspirations of each country differ beyond comparison. The role of European languages in the English school curriculum — within the context of Britain's relationship to the European Community and the changes in former communist countries — cannot be compared with the role of English in a francophone West African country, where economic factors, relationships with neighbouring anglophone countries and the need to produce English speakers in future generations dominate the agenda.

With respect to methodology and, lying behind it, psychological theory, the differences may not always be apparent. 'Communicative language teaching' is to be found in many disparate situations and has indeed often been introduced more quickly in developing countries. This may be because it is more appropriate there than in developed countries, or it may also be because recently founded education systems are more flexible and susceptible to advice from experts in methodology. Yet it is evident enough that every classroom is an inseparable part of a historically-located education system. Introduction to new methods ought to be carried out within an understanding of the whole system, and its purposes and characteristics.

It is for these reasons that preceding chapters have focused on the teaching and learning of language and culture within European education systems. Even here, of course, there are major differences determined by the historically contingent detail of school systems, of political and economic aspirations, of social structures and of national attitudes and expectations. The character of Britain as an anglophone country — and as the dominant anglophone country in Europe — has significance for language learning. The limited use of Dutch or Danish has significance in their respective countries. The position of French as a language of world communication has significance for France as a European country; and so on.

Nonetheless we believe that, with respect to the methodology, psychology and techniques of teaching and assessment discussed in preceding chapters, there is sufficient common ground for our earlier chapters to be relevant beyond their immediate origins.

Our allusion to the politics of developing countries is paralleled by the implicit political significance of comprehensive education, of student mobility in higher education and of the role of language teaching within the European Community. It is on the wider political and socio-economic role of language teaching that we shall focus in the rest of this chapter. In particular we shall draw together some earlier allusions to language teaching as political education. We shall reflect on the relationship of language teaching to multicultural education in societies with ethno-linguistic minorities. Thirdly, we shall consider the relationship between language teaching and social class, and to what extent language and culture learning can be expected to have differential impact according to the social class of the learners involved.

Language and Culture Teaching as Political Education

Although the phrase 'political education' has connotations of 'indoctrination' through its use as a description of teaching in communist education systems (Morison, 1987), it would be unfortunate if it were abandoned to that usage. For if 'education' is taken to include critical reflection on social and natural phenomena, then 'political education' can truly describe the critical understanding of native and foreign cultures and societies to which foreign language education contributes. For, as we suggested in concluding our first chapter, where foreign language education is successful in developing learners' grasp of otherness and their moral evaluation of their own and others' perspectives through cognitive and affective reciprocity, then the relationship with political education is created. On a basis of such understanding, learners no longer need to judge the actions and values of others from within their own world; they have the possibility of understanding and judging from within the perspective of others and their worlds. Our emphasis in Chapter 2 on the primacy of comparison as a methodological principle is closely related to the psychological potential. By making comparisons, learners are deliberately led into relativisation of their own perspective through prioritisation of the perspective of others. Comparison is not only a technique for highlighting similarities and differences as a means of making them more perceptible. It also serves as a step towards the acceptance of other perspectives, and the valuing of them as equally acceptable within their own terms. An evaluation of learners' own culture and society from that other perspective may then lead to critical distancing and decentring from it.

Doyé (1991, 1993) has drawn explicit comparison between political education and foreign language education. Referring to Gagel (1983), he identifies three stages in the former: cognitive, evaluative and conative. These lead to the acquisition of concepts and knowledge (cognitive), the clarification of values and the transmission of a capacity for political judgement (evaluative) and the teaching of the capacity and will to become politically engaged (conative/action-orientation). Doyé argues that foreign language teaching and political education coincide most clearly with respect to the cognitive dimension: the acquisition of concepts and knowledge from a foreign culture. Similarly, an evaluative dimension is inevitable in the analysis and comparison of societal norms and conventions and the unprejudiced reflection on learners' own society and its norms and conventions. Finally, he argues, the teaching of a capacity for political action is identical with teaching for 'communicative competence' when the latter includes acquisition of behaviour or action *vis à vis* members of other nations or societies.

It is at this point that teachers' responsibilities become clear. The degree to which learners turn a critical and evaluative gaze on their own culture and society from the vantage point of a new perspective will, in many situations, be influenced by the teacher. It is when he/she encourages both cognitive and affective decentring, thus reducing learners' affective tendency to accept the naturalness of their own cultural meanings and values, that the teacher has to consider the ethics of his/her position. The reverse of this coin is the teacher's position with respect to encouraging positive attitudes towards and affective engagement with the foreign culture and people. As we pointed out in Chapter 5, the encouragement of positive attitudes is tacitly agreed and sometimes explicitly documented as an aim of language teaching. Yet the ethical choices of teachers in both dimensions — attitudes to own and to foreign cultures — is seldom discussed. As McArthur says:

> A teacher's worldview or 'ideology' — if that is not too strong a term
> — is probably not much discussed because the matter is too delicate,
> dangerous or divisive, but it is there nonetheless. (1983: 88)

Melde's position is explicit and therefore helps to clarify the dilemmas. She takes her argument from Habermas's analysis of late-capitalist society and suggests that it is incumbent on language learners — and hence on language teachers — to become critical of their own and the foreign society (*in casu* German and French). She postulates three stages in reaching the aims of co-ordination of French and German perspectives and the social criticism postulated by Habermas:

(1) Understanding (*Begreifen*) of the French cultural world (*Lebenswelt*) and of the French (socio-political) system from within the internal French conditions and developments (appropriation of French perspectives);

(2) Understanding of Franco-German commonalities and differences as a pre-condition for Franco-German comprehension (*Verständigung*) with the aim of securing the future and self-determination in Europe (co-ordination of perspectives);

(3) Understanding of the necessity of defending and extending the communicatively structured cultural world which guarantees self-determination over communicative comprehension and the formation of political will in France and Germany. (Melde, 1987: 286, our translation)

She goes on to say that contradictions and conflicts, which reduce self-determination and political will, are the focus of private and public communication and function as the stimulus which breaks down the conception of learners' native culture as natural and taken-for-granted, thus beginning the process of decentring. This can only happen, she says, when learners are aware of the material and historical conditions which create such contradictions and conflict in society; hence the need for a social science observer perspective which provides the necessary information and analysis not evident in texts of private or public communication. Learners have to go beyond the text to understand the social conditions — and the forces which create them — out of which a text is produced.

Although Melde does not address the ethical dimension of teaching from this particular perspective, her explicit description of her concept of society and social criticism makes the political character of language and culture teaching quite open. It is through the methodology of comparison that she takes the responsibility first of creating acceptance of the other perspective and relativisation of one's own and secondly, of encouraging a critical analysis which goes beyond speakers' conscious knowledge of the socio-political context in which they produce texts for mutual understanding across cultural frontiers.

The value of Melde's approach for our purposes lies in the fact that she includes in a systematic and rational methodology an explicit political position. Clearly, whenever teachers compare social phenomena, explain historical contexts and describe material situations in their treatment of texts with students, they also introduce a political dimension to their teaching. If it is unsystematic and lacking in clarity to themselves and their students — neither analysed nor made conscious to either party — then they run the risk of unwilling and unknowing influence. The ethical dilemmas in such unconscious influence do not need further explication.

For teachers of Western European languages, this discussion may appear trivial. The common origins of moral values and political systems divert attention from ethical and political dilemmas. Since the learners' own society is similar in nature and values to that of the language and culture they are studying, the question of social criticism only arises if both societies are under scrutiny from a particular political standpoint, as in Melde's case. Yet in an experiment in teaching about British political institutions in French lower secondary schools (see Chapter 4), the comparison of a monarchy and a republic through consideration of the functions of heads of state and parliaments, already raises issues of critical distancing from either or both systems of government. Similarly, a comparison of attitudes, both private and public, towards immigrant communities in another unit of work for upper secondary pupils in France raises fundamental questions concerning social policies in both societies and causes reflective distancing. The teacher has in both cases to be aware of the implications of taking an overt position but even the selection and nature of presentation of texts implies a specific moral and political standpoint.

For teachers in England and Wales, the introduction of the National Curriculum brings these same issues onto the public agenda. The Statutory Order which gives the legal foundation to the National Curriculum requires a methodology which is based on comparison:

> In learning and using the target language pupils should have regular opportunities to:
>
> - consider and discuss similarities and differences between their own culture and those of the countries and communities where the target language is spoken. (DES, 1991: 26)

In the Programmes of Study, which indicate the aspects of culture which should be included, the Statutory Order requires that pupils should explore 'topics which deal with...social attitudes, customs and institutions which are relevant to them' and gives as non-binding examples 'attitudes towards religion, politics and society' (DES, 1991: 28). This makes it clear that the experiments being carried out in French schools would be entirely within the remit of the National Curriculum, and raise the same dilemmas and questions. The ethics of language and culture teaching cannot be dismissed; the contribution of foreign language and culture learning to political education cannot be ignored.

Cultural Learning and Multicultural Education

Since linguistic and cultural learning is an introduction to and an embracing of 'otherness' in foreign societies and language groups, its relationship with 'otherness' and with other language and culture groups within learners' own society appears evident enough. In general, however, the link has been established more in theory than in practice.

At a theoretical level there are two angles from which the contribution of language and culture teaching to learners' better understanding of their own multicultural, multilingual and multi-ethnic society can be discussed. In such societies — and almost all Western European societies are multicultural, as a consequence of economic migrations and for other reasons — the characteristics of individuals best able to live harmoniously with people of other ethnic groups have been compared with those pursued in foreign language and culture teaching. Doyé (1993) explains how the phrase 'intercultural education' — an American and German term — began as a concern to integrate minority groups, then became focused on educating majority groups for life in pluralist societies and, in a third stage, has been used by foreign language theorists and practitioners to describe the cross-national intercultural aims of language teaching. The concern common to all is to encourage the acquisition of psychological characteristics susceptible of generating harmonious relationships. Doyé, citing Thomas (1989), includes the following: lack of ethnocentrism, cognitive flexibility, behavioural flexibility, cultural knowledge, interpersonal sensitivity, and Doyé adds communication skill to these, as emphasised by Knapp, Enninger & Knapp-Potthof (1987).

As we argued in our conclusion to Chapter 1, there are sufficient theoretical grounds for believing that foreign language and culture learning has the potential to develop those characteristics. It is thus feasible to see language and culture learning as a significant — perhaps *the* significant — locus for education for international citizenship.

The second angle from which to consider these issues is that of curriculum policy. Churchill (1986) has identified six stages of curriculum policy with respect to linguistic and cultural minorities and most countries remain at one of the stages which is ultimately assimilationist, whatever the rhetoric of pluralism they profess. Nation-states and national governments use the curriculum of compulsory education to sustain national identity. Since this identity is rooted both historically and geographically, it is no surprise that history curricula reflect a national interpretation of history, and in extreme instances of totalitarian states the interpretation becomes a constructed legitimation of contemporary government. Even in democratic states, politicians become anxious if national history and geography is not central to the curriculum, as was evident in England during the establishment of a National Curriculum.

A less evident but potentially more powerful factor in controlling national identity is to be found in the language of instruction. Whenever there is a need to create or give particular support to national identity, governments impose a standard language through the system of schooling. The development of supra-national entities such as the European Union poses a threat to nation-states and their citizens' national identity. In the Netherlands, where nationalist identity is not a political or social priority, the response has been to allow other languages to be used as media of instruction. First there were languages of ethnic minorities in bilingual schooling, justified in terms of creating the best educational opportunities for young pupils — an argument which was refused in Britain as we shall see. More recently schools have been allowed to become monolingual in a language other than Dutch and the link between the language of education and national identity has been severed.

In Britain however the 'threat' of a supra-national European community has led to a re-affirmation of the primacy of the standard language. One minister for education declared that the English language is 'the essential ingredient of the Englishness of England' (cited in Jones & Kimberley, 1991: 17). More importantly a report on *Education for All* addressing the issue of multicultural education advised against the introduction of languages other than standard English as media of instruction. The authors prefaced their report by comparing a 'common language' with a common political and legal system as a means of giving society 'a degree of unity' and its members a form of 'corporate membership' (DES, 1985: 4).

In such a situation the curricular position of foreign language teaching is anomalous. It introduces an international dimension and a foreign perspective into a national curriculum. It is, as we argued above, politically subversive should the teacher wish to make it so. And it is as an extension of the international dimension that it can turn its focus inwards to consider the non-national, minority groups within the nation-state. By doing so, foreign language teaching can call attention to and legitimate the presence of other than the national language within the school curriculum. It can undermine the taken-for-granted naturalness of the standard language. This has been done in the English education system under the umbrella of 'language awareness' teaching, where language teachers have introduced pupils to minority languages, often the ones spoken bilingually by some of the pupils involved. Under the National Curriculum, however, this will no longer be encouraged in general and actively discouraged within foreign language lessons.

A third approach to multicultural education within foreign language teaching is a function of our emphasis on cultural learning. In Chapter 2, we suggested as part of our guidelines for a minimum cultural content, that learners should acquire understanding of social identity and social groups in the foreign culture. When this is realised in Western European circumstances — and we gave examples from Germany — ethno-linguistic minorities have to be included. When this is combined with a comparative method, as in the experiment in French upper secondary schools mentioned earlier, it is inevitable that students should consider both social policies and their own response to living in a multicultural society. In a classroom where some pupils are members of a minority, the initial distancing by focusing on the multicultural dimension of the foreign society may create a sense of security. Comparison with the home country immediately brings the issues into the classroom itself. Teachers and textbook writers have thus major responsibilities in ensuring that cognitive processes and affective responses are introduced carefully and deliberately in such highly sensitive issues. On the other hand, they should not, they cannot, simply avoid the issues of multicultural societies, for to do so is to withdraw from a coherent and complete process of cultural and linguistic learning.

The treatment of multicultural issues can thus be seen not only as a natural extension of learning about other cultures but also as an illustration of the kind of topic which makes most evident the political and ethical responsibilities discussed earlier. The selection of any topic which is the subject of social and political debate in the learners' own culture — irrespective of its standing in the foreign culture — will lead to distancing from and critical reflection on the native culture and society. This would also be the case for the topic 'social class'. In the following section we shall not pursue this particular approach — which would cause learners to reflect critically on the nature of social class influences in their own society and in their individual lives — but concern ourselves rather with the question as to whether foreign language and cultural learning *per se* has any significant relationship with the social class of learners.

Language Learning and Social Class

The relationship between success in language learning and learners' social origins has been given little attention. It would not be surprising however that there is a very strong relationship since a strong relationship can be found in all other aspects of education.

In one of the largest investigations of language learning, Burstall (1974) found consistent statistical relations between parental occupation and scores in language tests in both primary and secondary schools. Similarly

Lambert & Klineberg's (1967) international survey showed a strong relationship between social class and attitudes towards foreign peoples. Our own earlier research also found a clear link between social class and attitudes towards foreign people (Byram, Esarte-Sarries & Taylor, 1991). Further evidence can be found in studies of 'socio-culturally disadvantaged' learners of English as a foreign language in Israel (Olshtain et al., 1990) and of bilingual education in Hong Kong in which members of the lower socio-economic background are less likely to be successful (Yan Man Siu, 1988).

Some counter-evidence can also be found. In a small-scale survey of attitudes towards language learning — which has to be distinguished from attitudes towards foreign peoples and countries and also from achievement in language learning — Powell & Littlewood (1983) were surprised to find no significant relationship with social class. Saville-Troike (1984) also reports a study in which pupils matched initially for socio-economic status achieved differentially when receiving their schooling in a second language. One might expect that the large-scale developments in immersion programmes for second/foreign language learning in North America would provide evidence on social class. This is not the case as Holobow et al. (1991: 180) point out; they also suggest that the three available studies have limitations since 'none were longitudinal, and none of the student groups examined can be considered representative of working-class children from inner-city settings with extremely low socio-economic conditions'. Although Holobow et al. consider social class in their own study, it too has limitations in that they have so far reported only on Kindergarten and Grade 1 children and on their acquisition of interpersonal communication skills rather than the 'academic' and abstract use of the language in later stages of schooling. Nonetheless their study is noteworthy in concluding that 'the working-class and black students were able to benefit from this second language experience (partial immersion in French) as much as the middle-class and white students' (1991: 194).

Where a differential relationship is established, explanations are varied, even in this small set of research findings. Burstall had hypothesised that children coming to language study 'from a standpoint of equal ignorance' whatever their social background, might be less prone to differentiation by social class. She found however that this was not the case and explained it as parallel to other findings:

> Such children in no way approach a new learning situation on a footing of equality with children whose previous record of achievement has led to high aspiration and confident expectation of further success. Evidence from other studies...also suggests that children with parents

in higher-status occupations receive greater parental support when they approach new learning experiences than do those with parents in lower-status occupations (Burstall, 1974: 31).

For Burstall the key concept is that of parental support, considered to be more frequent in families of higher socio-economic status. This is complemented by teachers' expectations, over-estimating the abilities of those from higher socio-economic strata and under-estimating those from lower. This in turn has its effect on children themselves who can be 'depressed' by low expectations from their parents and teachers. In short, Burstall attributes the relationship between language learning achievement and social class to a general phenomenon in education, not specifically to language learning.

Olshtain et al. (1990) look for factors specific to the nature of language learning. They consider first the deficiency/difference debate on the language of children of lower-class parents, culturally disadvantaged children, citing Bernstein, Labov and others. They also consider Cummins' (1979) distinction between 'cognitive academic language proficiency' (CALP) which operates in cognitively demanding situations with little contextual support for language, similar to Donaldson's notion of 'disembedded language' (1978), and 'basic interpersonal communicative skills' in which cognitive demand is low and the language is highly contextualised, referring to the 'here and now' context. They conclude from their study that academic language ability in the first language — particularly awareness of language usage and register — is the strongest predictor of success in foreign language learning and that lower-class, disadvantaged students were less likely to have such ability. They also conclude that positive motivation and attitude is less important in the success of advantaged learners than it is in the success of disadvantaged learners, at least as perceived by their teachers. They carefully surround their conclusions with the statement that there are probably many factors involved in success, and their study needs to be refined and replicated. Its interest for us here is that it offers an explanation which is linguistic in nature and which could in principle lead to remediation within the education system, rather than simply hoping to change parents' and teachers' expectations and levels of encouragement. Olshtain et al. conclude:

> One possible implication is that we may need to strengthen the learners' academic proficiency in L1 to facilitate the learning of a foreign language in the school system'. (1990: 39)

Insofar as academic proficiency (CALP) or an ability to use 'disembedded language' is postulated as a contributing factor to academic achievement in general, it is evident that this explanation is similar to Burstall et al.'s in relating language learning achievement to achievement in other school subjects.

In a discussion of bilingual education and social class in Hong Kong, Yan Man Siu also refers to the academic language factor but speculates too on the issue of 'social distance'. He refers to Schumann's model of social distance between the language learner's group and the group whose language s/he is being taught. The greater the distance — measured on 8 parameters — the more difficult language learning becomes. Yan Man Siu then points out that, in Hong Kong, lower class Chinese students feel a greater distance from the English-speaking group in Hong Kong than do 'elite class Chinese', and that Schumann's model — normally applied to whole language groups rather than social classes within them — might explain the poor achievement in English and therefore in bilingual education in general among lower class Chinese learners.

This speculation could be transferred to foreign language learning: children from lower status socio-economic groups might experience a greater social distance from target language groups than do those from higher status groups. Were it to prove a significant factor, it would be interesting to identify the power of one of Schumann's parameters: 'congruence' between the cultures of the learners' group and the target language group. Were there to be a significantly greater distance between the culture of learners from lower social groups and the culture of the target language group as it is presented in the language class, there might be implications for practice of a concrete and feasible kind. It would be important, for example, to include in the portrayal of the foreign society images and information about all social classes and ethnic groups, different kinds of family structure, a range of employment and unemployment situations, and the stimulus to reflect on these issues and attitudes towards them, in the foreign and home culture and society. At the moment this has to remain speculative but it is important for language teachers to be constantly aware of the social class factor in their presentation of language and culture, in their selection and emphasis within a body of knowledge about the foreign culture. Social class is undoubtedly one of the most intractable factors in success in education in general but this does not excuse the language teacher from giving it constant attention.

Conclusion

The three issues we have raised in this final chapter are not unconnected. The injustices and inequalities suffered by individuals in education and throughout social life as a consequence of their social class or ethnic origins are still among the most significant political problems at the end of the twentieth century. They are inevitably highly visible to the critical gaze, created through comparative language and culture teaching, which turns learners' attention as much on their own society and culture as on the foreign one. For learners who themselves suffer injustices and inequalities, the issues are not merely academic, and language and culture teaching can give them the perspective from which they have a better understanding of their own situation.

Mennecke defines cultural awareness as 'the ability to see all culture, one's own and foreign, as the historically transmitted result of a community's history, mentality and living conditions' (1993: 43). It is a short step, for the disadvantaged, from this awareness to the action-orientation defined by Doyé, above, as the third element of political education. It is an equally short step to an action-orientation with respect to one's own society and its members, particularly if one feels disadvantaged within that society. The resulting attitude might best be defined as 'critical cultural awareness', not only a critical stance but also an action-orientation.

This view of language and culture teaching is a long way from the study of language as a system or the acquisition of skills to fulfil minimal communication needs which have been the two dominant approaches to language teaching. It would of course be misguided to believe that learning a foreign language and culture will liberate the disadvantaged from social injustice. There is nonetheless a potential for language teaching which can contribute to learners' better understanding of others and themselves, of other cultures and societies and their own, and that is a worthwhile purpose for any teacher, school and education system.

References

AGER, D.E. 1992, Language learning and European integration. Paper presented at the Colston Symposium, University of Bristol, April 1992.

ALLPORT, G. 1979, *The Nature of Prejudice*. Reading, MA: Addison-Wesley.

ALRED, G., BYRAM, M., ESARTE-SARRIES, V. and RUANE, S. 1992, Residence abroad and the cultural perceptions of foreign language students in higher education. Report to the Economic and Social Research Council on Project No. R 000 23 1196.

ANSUBAL, D. 1968, *Educational Psychology: A Cognitive View*. New York: Holt, Reinhart and Wilson.

ARRUDA, M., ZARATE, G. and VAN ZUNDERT, D. 1985, *Evaluer le regard touristique: Pour apprendre à voir*. Paris: BELC.

AUFDERSTRAßE, H., BOCK, H., GERDES, M. and MÜLLER, H. 1983. *Themen 1. Lehrwerk für Deutsch als Fremdsprache. Kursbuch*. Munich: Hueber.

AUPELF, The British Council, Goethe Institute 1988, *Culture and Language Learning*. Triangle 7. Paris: Didier.

BARTH, F. 1969, *Ethnic Groups and Boundaries*. London: Allen and Unwin.

BATSON, C.D. 1987, Self-report ratings of empathic emotion. In N. EISENBERG and J. STRAYER (eds) *Empathy, and its Development*. Cambridge: Cambridge University Press.

BAUMGRATZ-GANGL, G. 1990, *Persönlichkeitsentwicklung und Fremdsprachenerwerb*. Paderborn: Schöningh.

BAUMGRATZ, G., ALIX, C., BACHMANN, F., BÉCHAZ, J.-P., BEZLER, P. and SCHRADE, M. 1988, *Vivre l'école*. Paderborn: Schöningh.

BEHAL-THOMSEN, H. *et al.* 1993, *Typisch deutch?* Berlin: Langenscheidt.

BILLIG, M. 1987, *Arguing and Thinking: A Rhetorical Approach to Social Psychology*. Cambridge: Cambridge University Press.

BLEY-VROMAN, R. 1989, What is the logical problem of Foreign Language Learning? In S. GASS and J. SCHACHTER (eds) *Linguistic Perspectives on Second Language Acquisition*. Cambridge: Cambridge University Press.

BOSSELMANN-CYRAN, K. and WIGGER, A. 1988, 'Mit Micky Maus im Lilaland': Review of *Sprachbrücke 1*. *Info DaF* 15, 264-71.

BRISLIN, R., CUSHNER, K., CHERRIE, C. and YOUNG, M. 1986, *Intercultural Interactions: A Practical Guide*. London: Sage.

BROWN, H.D. 1987, *Principles of Language Learning and Teaching* (2nd edn). Englewood Cliffs, NJ: Prentice Hall.

BROWN, W.C. and LEVINSON, S. 1978, Universals in language usage: Politeness phenomena. In E.N. GOODY (ed.) *Questions and Politeness*. Cambridge: Cambridge University Press.

BRUMFIT, C.J. 1984, *Communicative Methodology in Language Teaching: The Roles of Fluency and Accuracy*. Cambridge: Cambridge University Press.

BRUNER, J. 1966, *Toward a Theory of Instruction*. Cambridge, MA: Harvard University Press.

BRYANT, B.K. 1987, Mental health, temperament, family and friends: Perspectives on children's empathy and social perspective taking. In N. EISENBERG and J. STRAYER (eds) *Empathy and Its Development*. Cambridge: Cambridge University Press.

BUCKBY, M. 1980, *Action! Graded French*. London: Nelson.

BURSTALL, C. *et al.* 1974, *Primary French in the Balance*. Slough: NFER Publishing Company.

BUTTJES, D. 1988, Kontakt und Distanz: Fremdkulturelles oder interkulturelles Lernen im Englischunterricht. In AUPELF, *Culture and Language Learning* Triangle 7. Paris: Didier.

BUTTJES, D. and M. BYRAM (eds) 1991, *Mediating Languages and Cultures: Towards an Intercultural Theory of Foreign Language Education*. Clevedon: Multilingual Matters.

BYRAM, M. 1989a, *Cultural Studies in Foreign Language Education*. Clevedon: Multilingual Matters.

— 1989b, Intercultural education and foreign language teaching. *World Studies Journal* 7 (2), 4–7.

— 1991. 'Background studies' in English foreign language teaching: Lost opportunities in the comprehensive school debate. In D. BUTTJES and M. BYRAM (eds) *Mediating Languages and Cultures: Towards an Intercultural Theory of Foreign Language Education*. Clevedon: Multilingual Matters.

— 1993a, Foreign language teaching and multicultural education. In A. KING and M. REISS (eds) *Multicultural Education and the National Curriculum*. Brighton: Falmer Press.

— (ed.) (1993b) *Germany: Its Representation in Textbooks for Teaching German in Britain*. Frankfurt a.M.: Diesterweg.

BYRAM, M. and BAUMGARDT, C. 1993. Deutsch Heute. In M. BYRAM (ed.) *Germany: Its Representation in Textbooks for Teaching German in Great Britain*. Frankfurt a.M.: Diesterweg.

BYRAM, M. and ESARTE-SARRIES, V. 1991, *Investigating Cultural Studies in Foreign Language Teaching*. Clevedon: Multilingual Matters.

BYRAM, M., ESARTE-SARRIES, V. and TAYLOR, S. 1991, *Cultural Studies and Language Learning: A Research Report*. Clevedon: Multilingual Matters.

BYRAM, M and LEMAN, J. 1990, *Bicultural and Trilingual Education*. Clevedon: Multilingual Matters.

CAIN, A. 1991, Comment se construit la connaissance en civilisation? L'étude des représentations que les élèves ont des pays dont ils étudient la langue. In A. CAIN (ed.) *L'enseignement/l'apprentissage de la civilisation en cours de langue (premier et second cycles)*. Paris: Institut National de Recherche Pédagogique.

CALDER, B., INSKO, C. and YANDELL, B. 1974, The relation of cognitive and memorial processes to persuasion in simulated jury trial. *Journal of Applied Social Psychology* 4, 62–93.

CAMPOS, C., HIGMAN, F., MENDELSON, D. and NAGY, G. 1988, *L'enseignement de la civilisation française dans les universités de l'Europe*. Paris: Didier Érudition.

CARLSON, E. 1956, Attitude change through modification of attitude structure. *Journal of Abnormal and Social Psychology* 52, 256–61.

CHOMSKY, N. 1965, *Aspects of the Theory of Syntax*. Cambridge, MA: MIT Press.

CHURCHILL, S. 1986, *The Education of Linguistic and Cultural Minorities in the OECD Countries*. Clevedon: Multilingual Matters.

CLANET, C. 1990, *L'interculturel: Introduction aux approches interculturelles en Éducation et en Sciences Humaines*. Toulouse: Presses Universitaires du Mirail.

CLIFFORD, J. 1988, *The Predicament of Culture*. Cambridge, MA: Harvard University Press.

CONDON, J.C. 1986, ...so near the United States. In J.M. VALDES (ed.) *Culture Bound: Bridging the Cultural Gap*. Cambridge: Cambridge University Press.

CORTAZZI, M. and JIN, L. 1993, Cultural orientation and academic language use. In L. THOMPSON, D. GRADDOL and M. BYRAM (eds) *Language and Culture*. Clevedon: Multilingual Matters.

COUNCIL OF EUROPE 1976, *Systèmes d'Apprentissage de Langues Vivantes par les Adultes*. Strasbourg: Council of Europe.

— 1989, *Draft Programme of Activities of the Council for Cultural Co-operation for 1989: Proposals for Further Action Regarding Language Learning and Teaching*. Strasbourg: Council of Europe.

CULBERTSON, F. 1957, The modification of an emotionally held attitude through role-playing. *Journal of Abnormal and Social Psychology* 54, 230–1.

CULLINGFORD, C. 1991, Children's attitudes to other countries. Paper given at a seminar on Stereotypes in the Depiction of British and German People in Contemporary Children's and Young People's Literature, Goethe Institut, London, November 1991.

CUMMINS, J. 1979, Cognitive, academic language proficiency, linguistic interdependence, the optimal age question and some other matters. *Working Papers on Bilingualism* 19, 197–205.

CURRAN, C. 1972, *Counseling, Learning: A Whole-person Model for Education*. London: Grune and Stratton Inc.

DES 1990, *Modern Foreign Languages for Ages 11–16: Proposals of the Secretary of State for Education and Science and the Secretary of State for Wales*. London: HMSO.

— 1991, *Modern Foreign Languages in the National Curriculum* ('Statutory Orders'). London: HMSO.

DICKINSON, A.K. and LEE, P.J. 1984. Making sense of history. In A.K. DICKINSON, P.J. LEE and P.J. ROGERS (eds) *Learning History*. London: Heinemann.

DONALDSON, M. 1978, *Children's Minds*. London: Croom Helm.

DOUGLAS, M. 1974, Taking the biscuit: The structure of British meals. *New Society* 19 December 1974.

DOYÉ, P. (ed.) 1991, *Großbritannien: Seine Darstellung in deutschen Schulbüchern für den Englischunterricht*. Frankfurt a.M.: Diesterweg.

— 1992, Fremdsprachenunterricht als Beitrag zu tertiärer Sozialisation. In D. BUTTJES *et al.* (eds) *Neue Brennpunkte des Englischunterrichts.* Frankfurt a.M.: Peter Lang.

— 1993, Neuere Konzepte der Fremdsprachenerziehung und ihre Bedeutung für die Schulbuchkritik. In M. BYRAM (ed.) *Germany: Its Representation in Textbooks for Teaching German in Britain.* Frankfurt a.M.: Diesterweg.

EDELHOFF, C. 1987, Lehrerfortbildung und interkulturelles Lehren und Lernen im Fremdsprachenunterricht. In G. BAUMGRATZ and R. STEPHAN (eds) *Fremdsprachenlernen als Beitrag zur internationalen Verständigung. Munich: iudicium verlag.*

EISENBERG, N. and MILLER, P 1987, Empathy, sympathy and altruism: Empirical and conceptual links. In N. EISENBERG and J. STRAYER (eds) *Empathy and its Development.* Cambridge: Cambridge University Press.

EISENBERG, N. and STRAYER, J. 1987, Critical issues in the study of empathy. In N. EISENBERG and J. STRAYER (eds) *Empathy and Its Development.* Cambridge: Cambridge University Press.

ELLIS, R. and ROBERTS, C. 1987, Two approaches for investigating Second Language Acquisition. In R. ELLIS (ed.) *Second Language Acquisition in Context.* London: Prentice Hall.

ERTELT-VIETH, A. 1990, *Kulturvergleichende Analyse von Verhalten, Sprache und Bedeutungen im Moskauer Alltag.* Frankfurt a.M.: Peter Lang.

— 1991, Culture and 'hidden culture' in Moscow: A contrastive analysis of West German and Soviet perceptions. In D. BUTTJES and M. BYRAM (eds) *Mediating Languages and Cultures: Towards an Intercultural Theory of Foreign Language Education.*

EVANS, C. 1990 *Language People.* Milton Keynes: Open University Press.

EVANS, E. (ed.) 1990, *Register of courses in European Studies in British Universities and Polytechnics 1990/91.* London: University Association for Contemporary European Studies.

FESTINGER, L. 1957, *A Theory of Cognitive Dissonance.* New York: Row.

FISHMAN, J.A. 1977, *The Spread of English: English as a World Language.* Rowley, MA: Newbury House.

FRITZSCHE, K.P. 1993, Multiperspektivität: eine Strategie gegen Dogmatismus und Vorurteile. In M. BYRAM (ed.) *Germany: Its Representation in Textbooks for Teaching German in Britain.* Frankfurt a.M.: Diesterweg.

FRY, H., MAW, J. and SIMONS, H. (eds) 1991, *Dealing with Difference. Handling Ethnocentrism in History Classrooms.* London: University of London, Institute of Education.

FURNHAM, A. and BOCHNER, S. 1982, Social difficulty in a foreign culture: An empirical analysis of culture shock. In S. BOCHNER (ed.) *Cultures in Contact: Studies in Cross-cultural Interaction* (International Series in Experimental Social Psychology 1). Oxford: Pergamon.

— 1986, *Culture Shock: Psychological Reactions to Unfamiliar Environments.* London: Methuen.

GAGEL, W. 1983, *Einführung in die Didaktik des politischen Unterrichts.* Opladen: Leske und Budrich.

GARD, A. and LEE, P.J. 1978, Educational objectives for the study of history reconsidered. In A.K. DICKINSON and P.J. LEE (eds) *History Teaching and Historical Understanding*. London: Heinemann.

GEERTZ, C. 1973, *The Interpretation of Cultures*. New York: Baric Books.

GIBSON, R. 1988, From Landeskunde to Cultural Studies: A skills and resource-based approach. In M. WRIGHT (ed.) *Dynamic Approaches to Cultural Studies*. Frankfurt a.M.: Lang.

GOEPPER, J.B. (ed.) 1989, *The Teaching of French. A Syllabus of Competence American Association of Teachers of French*. (National Bulletin, 15: Special Issue). October 1989.

GRICE, H.P. 1975, Logic and conversation. In P. COLE and J. MORGAN (eds) *Syntax and Semantics Vol. 3: Speech Acts*. London: Academic Press.

HALL, E.T. 1959, *The Silent Language*. New York: Anchor Books/Doubleday.

HAMMERSLEY, M. and ATKINSON, P. 1983, *Ethnography: Principles in Practice*. London: Tavistock.

HARRISON, B. 1990, *Culture and the Language Classroom*. London: Modern English Publications.

HASS, R.G. 1975, 'Persuasion or moderation?' Two experiments on anticipatory belief change. *Journal of Personality and Social Psychology* 31, 1155–62.

HÄUSSERMANN, U., DIETRICH, G., GÜNTHER, C., KAMINSKI, D., WOODS, U. and ZENKNER, H. 1991 *Sprachkurs Deutsch 1 (Neufassung)* (3rd edn). Frankfurt a.M.: Diesterweg.

HEIDER, F. 1958, *The Psychology of Interpersonal Relationships*. New York: John Wiley.

HERMANN, G. 1990, Foreign language learning and attitude change: An analysis of the issues. In J. FEUILLET and D. THOMERES (eds) *L'Enseignement des Langues en Europe de l'Ouest: Quels contenus? (Cahiers de l'EREL)*. 3. Nantes: EREL.

HOFFMANN, J.L. 1981, Perspectives on the difference between understanding people and understanding things: the role of affect. In J.H. FLAVELL and L. ROSS (eds) *Social Cognitive Development: Frontiers and Possible Futures*. Cambridge: Cambridge University Press.

HOLOBOW, N.E. *et al.* 1991, The effectiveness of a foreign language immersion program for children from different ethnic and social class backgrounds: Report 2. *Applied Psycholinguistics* 12, 179–98.

HOVLAND, C. LUMSDAINE, A. and SHEFFIELD, F. 1949, *Experiments on Mass Communication*. Princeton, NJ: Princeton University Press.

HOVLAND, C. and WEISS, W. 1951, The influence of source credibility on communication effectiveness. *Public Opinion Quarterly* 15, 635–50.

HOWITT, D. (ed.) 1989, *Social Psychology: Conflicts and Continuities: An Introductory Textbook*. Milton Keynes: Open University.

HUGHES, G. 1986, An argument for culture analysis in the second language classroom. In J. VALDES (ed.) *Culture Bound: Bridging the Cultural Gap*. Cambridge: Cambridge University Press.

HUNFELD, H. 1992 Hermeneutischer Fremdsprachenunterricht. In H. EICHHEIM (ed.) *Fremdsprachenunterricht, Verstehensunterricht, Wege und Ziele*. Munich: Goethe-Institut.

HYMES, D. 1972, On communicative competence. In J.B. PRIDE and J. HOLMES (eds) *Sociolinguistics*. Harmondsworth: Penguin.

IZZO, S. 1981, *Second Language Learning: A Review of Related Studies*. Rosslyn, VA: National Clearinghouse for Bilingual Education.

JANIS, I. and FESHBACH, S. 1953, Effects of fear-arousing communications. *Journal of Abnormal and Social Psychology* 48, 78–92.

JANIS, I., KAYE, D. and KIRSCHNER, P. 1965, Facilitating effects of 'eating while reading' on responsiveness to persuasive communications. *Journal of Personal and Social Psychology* 1, 181–6.

JANIS, I. and KING, B. 1954, The influence of role playing on opinion change. *Journal of Abnormal and Social Psychology* 49, 211–18.

JEFFERSON, G. 1989, List construction as a task and resource. In G. PSATHAS (ed.) *International Competence*. Norwood, NJ: Ablex.

JONES, C. and KIMBERLEY, K. 1991, *Intercultural Perspectives on the National Curriculum for England and Wales*. London: University of London, Institute of Education.

KIM, Y.Y. 1988, *Communication and Cross-Cultural Adaptation*. Clevedon: Multilingual Matters.

KING, A. 1990, *Degrees of Fluency: The Sixth Former's Guide to Language Degree Courses*. London: Centre for Information on Language Teaching and Research.

KNAPP, K., ENNINGER, W. and KNAPP-POTTHOF, A. 1987, *Analyzing Intercultural Communication*. Berlin: Mouton.

KOHLBERG, L., LEVINE, C. and HEWER, A. 1983 *Moral Stages: A Current Formulation and Response to Critics*. Basel: Karger.

KRAMSCH, C. 1991, Culture in language learning: A view from the United States. In K. DE BOT, R. GINSBERG and C. KRAMSCH (eds) *Foreign Language Research in Cross-Cultural Perspective*. Philadelphia: John Benjamin.

— 1993, *Context and Culture in Language Teaching*. Oxford: Oxford University Press.

KRASHEN, S. 1981, *Second Language Acquisition and Second Language Learning*. Oxford: Pergamon.

LADO, R. (ed.) 1958, *Linguistics Across Cultures*. Ann Arbor: University of Michigan Press.

LA FORGE, P.G. 1983, *Counseling and Culture in Second Language Acquisition*. Oxford: Pergamon Press.

LAMBERT, W., GARDNER, C. *et al.* 1968, A study of the roles of attitudes and motivation in second-language learning. In J. FISHMAN (ed.) *Readings in the Sociology of Language*. The Hague: Mouton.

LAMBERT, W. E. and KLINEBERG, O. 1967, *Children's Views of Foreign Peoples*. New York: Appleton-Century-Crofts.

LANGFORD, P. 1987, *Concept Development in the Secondary School*. London: Croom Helm.

LEE, P.J. 1978, Explanation and understanding in history. In A.K. DICKINSON and P.J. LEE (eds) *History Teaching and Historical Understanding*. London: Heinemann.

— 1984, Historical imagination. In A.K. DICKINSON, P.J. LEE and P.J. ROGERS (eds) *Learning History*. London: Heinemann.

LENNEBERG, E.H. 1967, *Biological Foundations of Language*. New York: John Wiley.

LEONTIEV, A. 1981, *Psychology and the Language Learning Process*. Oxford: Pergamon.

LEVENTHAL, H. 1970, Findings and theory in the study of fear communications. In L. BERKOWITZ (ed.) *Advances in Experimental Social Psychology* Vol. 5. New York: Academic Press.

LEVINE, D.R. and ADELMAN, M.B. 1982, *Beyond Language: Intercultural Communication for English as a Second Language*. Englewood Cliffs, NJ: Prentice Hall Regents.

LINCOLN, B. 1986, *Discourse and the Construction of Society: Comparative Studies of Myth, Ritual and Classification*. New York: Oxford University Press.

LITTLEWOOD, W. 1981, *Communicative Language Teaching*. Cambridge: Cambridge University Press.

LORD, C., ROSS, L. and LEPPER, M. 1979, Biased assimilation and attitude polarization: The effects of prior theories on subsequently considered evidence. *Journal of Personality and Social Psychology* 37, 2098–109.

McARTHUR, T., 1983, *A Foundation Course for Language Teachers*. Cambridge: Cambridge University Press.

McDONOUGH, S. 1981, *Psychology in Foreign Language Teaching*. London: Allen and Unwin.

McGUIRE, W. 1968, The nature of attitudes and attitude change. In G. LINDZEY and E. ARONSON (eds) *The Handbook of Social Psychology* (2nd edn), Vol 3. Reading, MA: Addison-Wesley.

McLAUGHLIN, B. 1987, *Theories of Second-Language Learning*. London: Arnold.

MEBUS, G., PAULDRACH, A., RALL, M. and RÖSLER, D. 1987, *Sprachbrücke 1*. Stuttgart: Klett.

— 1989 *Sprachbrücke 2*. Stuttgart: Klett.

MELDE, W. 1987, *Zur Integration von Landeskunde und Kommunikation im Fremdsprachenunterricht*. Tübingen: Gunter Narr Verlag.

— 1988, *La jeunesse face à l'enseignement: le système éducatif entre sélection et démocratisation*. Paderborn: Schöningh.

MELDE, W., AMMON, G., BENSE, U., WENDT, M. and ZAMZOW, M. 1987, *Le Languedoc-Roussillon: une région face à l'Europe*. Paderborn: Schöningh.

MENNECKE, A. 1993, Potentialities of textbooks for teaching cultural awareness. In M. BYRAM (ed.) *Germany: Its Representation in Textbooks for Teaching German in Britain*. Frankfurt a.M.: Diesterweg.

MEYER, M. 1991, Developing transcultural competence: Case studies of advanced foreign language learners. In D. BUTTJES and M. BYRAM (eds) *Mediating Languages and Cultures: Towards an Intercultural Theory of Foreign Language Education*. Clevedon: Multilingual Matters.

MILLS, J. and ARONSON, E. 1965, Opinion change as a function of communicators' attractiveness and desire to influence. *Journal of Personality and Social Psychology* 1, 173-77.

MINISTERE DE L'ÉDUCATION NATIONALE 1985, *Collèges: Programmes et instructions*. Paris: Centre National de Documentation Pédagogique.

MODGIL, S. and MODGIL, C. (eds) 1982, *Jean Piaget: Consensus and Controversy*. London: Holt, Rinehart and Winston.

MORISON, J. 1987, Recent developments in political education in the Soviet Union. In G. AVIS (ed.) *The Making of the Soviet Citizen*. London: Croom Helm.

MOSCOVICI, S. 1984, The phenomenon of social representations. In R. FARR and S. MOSCOVICI (eds) *Social Representations*. Cambridge: Cambridge University Press.

NATALE, S. 1972, *An Experiment in Empathy*. Slough: NFER.

NORA, P. 1984, Entre mémoire et histoire. In P. NORA (ed.) *Les Lieux de mémoire: I La République*. Paris: Gallimard.

ODLIN, T. 1989, *Language Transfer: Cross-Linguistic Influence in Language Learning*. Cambridge: Cambridge University Press.

OLSHTAIN, E. *et al.* 1990, Factors predicting success in EFL among culturally different learners. *Language Learning* 40, 1, 23–44.

OSTERLOH, K.H. 1986, Intercultural differences and communicative approaches to foreign language teaching in the Third World. In J.M. VALDES (ed.) *Culture Bound: Bridging the Cultural Gap*. Cambridge: Cambridge University Press.

OTTEN, E., 1992, Bilingual schools in Northrhine-Westphalia. Paper presented at the International Curriculum Development Conference, Szombathely, Hungary, May 1992.

PARTINGTON, G. 1980, *The Idea of an Historical Education*. Windsor: NFER.

PENFIELD, W. and ROBERTS, L. 1959, *Speech and Brain Mechanisms*. Oxford: Oxford University Press.

PETTY, R. and CACIOPPO, J. 1986, The elaboration likelihood model of persuasion. In L. BERKOWITZ (ed.) *Advances in Experimental Social Psychology* Vol 19. New York: Academic Press.

PFISTER, G. and POSER, Y. 1987, *Culture, Proficiency, and Control in FL Teaching*. Lanham, New York and London: University Press of America.

PHILLIPS, D. 1981, *Die Qual der Wahl*. Oxford: University of Oxford Department of Educational Studies.

PIAGET, J and WEIL, A.-M. 1951, The development in children of the idea of homeland and of relations with other countries. *Institute of Social Science Bulletin* 3, 561–78.

PICKERING, R. 1992, *Planning and Resourcing 'A' Level French: A Handbook for Teachers*. London: CILT.

PORTAL, C. 1983. Empathy as an aim for curriculum lessons from history. *Curriculum Studies* 15/3, 303–10.

POWELL, R. and LITTLEWOOD, P. 1983, Why choose French? Boys' and girls' attitudes at the option stage. *British Journal of Language Teaching* 21 (1), 36–44.

PRESTON, D. 1989, *Sociolinguistics and Second Language Acquisition*. Oxford: Blackwell.

RAI 1990, *Royal Anthropological Institute Teachers' Resource Guide*. London: Royal Anthropological Institute.

RALL, M. and MEBUS, G. 1990, *Sprachbrücke 1. Handbuch für den Unterricht*. Stuttgart: Klett.

REST, J.R. 1979, *Development in Judging Moral Issues*. Minneapolis: University of Minnesota Press.

RISAGER, K. 1991, Cultural references in European textbooks: An evaluation of recent tendencies. In D. BUTTJES and M. BYRAM (eds) *Mediating Languages and Cultures: Towards an Intercultural Theory of Foreign Language Education*. Clevedon: Multilingual Matters.

ROBINSON, G.N. 1988, *Crosscultural Understanding*. London: Prentice Hall.

SAHLINS, M. 1976, *Culture and Practical Reason*. Chicago: University of Chicago Press.

SAMPSON, E. 1971, *Social Psychology and Contemporary Society*. New York: Wiley.

SAVILLE-TROIKE, M. 1984, What really matters in second language learning for academic achievement? *TESOL Quarterly* 18, 2, 199–219.

— 1989, *The Ethnography of Communication* (2nd edn). Oxford: Blackwell.

SCHUMANN, J. 1978, Social and psychological factors in second language acquisition. In J. RICHARDS (ed.) *Understanding Second and Foreign Language Learning*. Rowley, MA: Newbury House.

SCHUMANN, A. 1986, *Etre français, rester breton: A la recherche de l'identité culturelle*. Paderborn: Schöningh.

SCHWARZ, H., TAYLOR, C. and VETTEL, F. 1989, *English G -A3*. Berlin: Cornelsen.

SEELYE, H.N. 1974, *Teaching Culture: Strategies for Foreign Language Educators*. Skokie, IL: National Textbook Company.

— 1984, *Teaching Culture: Strategies for Intercultural Communication*. Lincolnwood, IL: National Textbook Company.

SELIGER, H. 1988, Psycholinguistic issues in second language acquisition. In L. BEEBE (ed.) *Issues in Second Language Acquisition: Multiple Perspectives*. New York: Newbury House.

SELLAR, W.C. and YEATMAN, R.J. 1930, *1066 and All That: A Memorable History of England Comprising All the Parts You Can Remember*. London: Methuen.

SHAYER, M. and ADEY, P. 1981, *Towards a Science of Science Teaching*. London: Erlbaum.

SHEMILT, D. 1984, Beauty and the philosopher: Empathy in history and the classroom. In A.K. DICKINSON, P.J. LEE and P.J. ROGERS (eds) *Learning History*. London: Heinemann.

SMITH, L. 1986, Common-core curriculum: A Piagetian conceptualisation. *British Educational Research Journal* 12 (1), 55–71.

SMITH, P. (ed.) 1985–90, *Einfach toll!* Cheltenham: Stanley Thornes.

SOUTHERN EXAMINING GROUP 1989, *Chief Examiners' Reports for the General Certificate of Secondary Education Summer 1988 Examinations*. Guildford: Southern Examining Group.

SPRADLEY, J. 1979, *The Ethnographic Interview*. New York: Holt, Rinehart and Winston.

— 1980, *Participant Observation*. New York: Holt, Rinehart and Winston.

SUTHERLAND, M. 1986, Education and empathy. *British Journal of Education Studies* 34 (2), 142–51.

SWAIN, M and LAPKIN, S. 1982, *Evaluating Bilingual Education: A Canadian Case-study*. Clevedon: Multilingual Matters.

SWANN, Committee 1985, *Education for All: Committee of Inquiry into the Education of Children from Ethnic Minority Groups*. London: HMSO.

TAMBURINNI, J. 1982, Some education implications of Piaget's theory. In S. MODGIL and C. MODGIL (eds) *Jean Piaget: Consensus and Controversy*. London: Holt, Rinehart and Winston.

TAYLOR, C. 1971, Interpretation and the sciences of man. *The Review of Metaphysics* 25 (1), 3–51.

THOMAS, A. 1989, An action psychological approach to cross-cultural understanding. In P. FUNKE (ed.) *Understanding the USA*. Tübingen: Narr.

TINSLEY, R. and WOLOSHIN, D. 1974, Approaching German culture: A tentative analysis. *Die Unterrichtspraxis* 7 (1), 125-36.

VALDES, J.M. (ed.) 1986, *Culture Bound: Bridging the Cultural Gap*. Cambridge: Cambridge University Press.

VALETTE, R. 1986, The culture test. In J.M. VALDES (ed.) *Culture Bound: Bridging the Cultural Gap*. Cambridge: Cambridge University Press.

VAN EK, J. 1986/7, *Objectives for Foreign Language Learning. Vol. 2: Levels*. Strasbourg: Council of Europe.

VAN EK, J.A. and TRIM, J.L.M. 1991, *Threshold Level 1990*. Strasbourg: Council of Europe Press.

VANSTONE, J. and MENNECKE, A. 1993, Deutsch Konkret. In M. BYRAM (ed.) *Germany: Its Representation in Textbooks for Teaching German in Great Britain*. Frankfurt a.M.: Diesterweg.

WARNER, M. 1981, *Joan of Arc: The Image of Female Heroism*. New York: Random House.

WEBER, S. and TARDIF, C. 1991, Culture and meaning in French immersion kindergarten. In L. MALAVÉ and G. DUQUETTE (eds) *Language Culture and Cognition: A Collection of Studies in First and Second Language Acquisition*. Clevedon: Multilingual Matters.

WEST, J. 1992, The development of a functional-notional syllabus for university German courses. *CLCS Occasional Paper No. 32*. Dublin: Trinity College, Centre for Language and Communication Studies.

WIEGAND, P. 1992, *Places in the Primary School*. London: Falmer Press.

WILLEMS, G.M. 1992, The European dimension in education: Towards a concretisation of attainment targets in the education and training of language teachers. *ATEE News* September 1992 (Association for Teacher Education in Europe).

WILLIAMS, R. 1983, *Keywords: A Vocabulary of Culture and Society*. London: Fontana.

WINDES, R. 1961, A study of effective and ineffective presidential campaign speeches. *Speech Monographs* 28, 39–49.

WOODS, E.G. 1993, British studies in English language teaching. In M. BYRAM (ed.) *Culture and Language Learning in Higher Education*. Clevedon: Multilingual Matters.

WRIGHT, M. (ed.) 1988, *Dynamic Approaches to Culture Studies: Contribution to the 1st and 2nd Klagenfurt Symposia on the Teaching of British and American Studies at University Level*. Frankfurt a.M.: Lang.

WRINGE, C. 1989, *The Effective Teaching of Modern Languages*. London: Longman.

YAU MAN SIU 1988, Bilingual education and social class: Some speculative observations in the Hong Kong context. *Comparative Education* 24 (2), 217–28.

ZARATE, G. 1986, *Enseigner une culture étrangère*. Paris: Hachette.

— 1988 Que peut apporter l'anthropologie culturelle à la déscription et l'interprétation d'une culture étrangère dans la classe de langue? *AUPELF Culture and Language Learning* Triangle 7. Paris: Didier.

— 1991a, L'enseignement d'une culture étrangère. In A. CAIN (ed.) *L'enseignement/l'apprentissage de la civilisation en cours de langue (premier et second cycles)*. Paris: Institut National de Recherche Pédagogique.

— 1991b, L'immersion en contexte étranger: dispositifs de formation et d'évaluation. *Études de Linguistique Appliqué* 79, 49–61.

ZARATE, G. and TROUTOT, M. 1990, *Ma ville et celle des autres*. Paris: BELC.

ZIMBARDO, P., EBBESSEN, E. and MASLACH, C. 1969, *Influencing Attitudes and Changing Behaviour: A Basic Introduction to Relevant Methodology, Theory and Applications* (2nd edn). Reading, MA: Addison Wesley.

Appendix I

(i) *Les manifestations lycéennes*

Stéphane est lycéen à Brive. Il est en première. Il prépare un bac G de commerce. Ici, il parle des événements en France, et surtout de ce qui s'est passé à Brive, en 1990.

Au début de l'interview, il a expliqué que le 'déclic' à Brive était le viol d'une jeune fille, ce qui a souligné le manque de surveillants et de sécurité dans les lycées.

(a)   A Paris c'était aussi un élément comme ça, c'est un jeune homme qui s'est fait [tuer] dans une salle de classe, et c'était l'[événement] qui avait mis le feu au poudre, tout le monde râlait [depuis] un moment, mais là, ça c'était trop. Et il y a des coordinations [lycéennes], qui se sont créés, qui ont assisté les élèves à [arrêter] les cours, et à se [manifester], mais à Paris ça a été, ça a vite dégénéré. Puisqu'ils étaient vraiment nombreux. Alors, dans la [marche], sur la tête ils étaient pour et tout, mais dans la fin c'étaient des voyous qui étaient là. Alors ils [cassaient] les vitrines, ils volaient, [brûlaient] des voitures. Ça a donné vraiment une mauvaise réputation.

Et ça s'est passé au mois de septembre?

September, octobre, oui.

(b)   Pourquoi ça s'est passé cette année-là et pas l'année précédente?

Mais comme nous disons c'est beaucoup de petites choses qui se sont installées. Déjà dès la [rentrée] l'école d'architecture à Paris, n'avaient plus de [cours/locaux]. Les élèves étaient dans la rue pour étudier l'architecture. Dans les lycées comme [toujours] il y avait des problèmes. Il y avait des classes de trente-cinq élèves avec [vingt] chaises. S'il faisait qu'il y avait des élèves qui faisaient des cours [debout]. Puis il y a eu la [mort] de ce jeune garçon, qui a tout déclenché. C'était quelqu'un qui est venu…de l'extérieur dans l'école qui l'a [fait] ou quoi?…

On a jamais su et la presse a apparemment foncé sur ce sujet. Donc on ne sait pas bien ce qui s'est [passé], et on sait juste qu'une personne est [morte] dans une salle de classe. S'il y avait eu des surveillants ça ne [serait] pas arrivé.

(c) Et en France ce n'est pas la première fois que les étudiants manifestent. Les étudiants ont manifesté en mai '68, c'est là où il y a eu tous ces problèmes. Ils ont manifesté en '81 et ils ont [manifesté] cette année.

Il y avait une sorte de tradition.

Tradition, non, mais quand on en a [assez], et qu'on veut le [montrer], on manifeste.

Et ça c'était les étudiants [d'université]. Est-ce que c'est la première fois que les lycéens manifestent?

Non, en '81 les étudiants avaient manifesté aussi.

Qu'est-ce que, pour quelle raison, qu'est-ce que c'était la raison en '81?

Je crois que c'était toujours [manque] de matériel, manque de [personnel].

Et enfin '68, c'est bien [connu]. Bon, pour un lycéen français, ce n'est pas nouveau, il y a l'idée de manifester, ça existe.

Vocabulaire: Comment dit-on en français?

- pupil (student) co-ordinating committees
- to demonstrate
- to stop lessons
- murder
- to unleash, trigger off
- to have had enough
- lack of material and staff

Parlez

(1) Qu'est-ce qui a déclenché les manifestations à Paris?
(2) Quels étaient les problèmes dans les lycées?
(3) Comment est-ce que les lycéens ont réagi?
(4) L'idée d'une grève est nouvelle pour les lycéens?

Jeu de rôle

Stéphane explique à un ami anglais pourquoi les étudiants ont manifesté. Son ami s'étonne...

Appendix II

Anne-Sophie 17 ans ½ AMIENS

1 Janvier –	– Nouvel An chez mes grand-parents maternels avec mes parents et ma soeur.
9 Janvier –	– Nouvel An et anniversaire de ma soeur chez ma grand-mére paternelle avec mes parents, mes grand-parents, ma tante et son mari et mes cousines.
Pàquees –	– Chez moi avec mes parents, ma soeur, ma grand-mère paternelle et mes grand-parents maternels.
21 Aoút –	– Anniversaire de ma mère fêté moi avec mon père, ma soeur, & grand-parents maternels, ma grand-mère paternelle et des amis.
2 Septembre –	– Mon anniversaire, chez moi, avec mes parents, mes grand-parents maternels et ma grand-mère paternelle et ma marraine.
8 Octobre –	– Anniversaire de mon pére, chez nous avec mes grand-parents et grand-mère.
24 Décembre –	– Veille de Noël, chez moi, avec mes parents, ma marraine, ma grand-mère et grand-parents.
25 Décembre –	– Noël, chez moi avec mes parents, grand-parents et grand-mère.
31 Décembre –	– Veille de Nouvel An, au restaurant avec des amis et mes parents.

Appendix III

(iii) *Vidéothèque niveau supérieur, no. 47*

Dans un bus: l'emploi du temps d'un conducteur

Monsieur FILATRE: Je m'appelle Monsieur FILATRE Jean-Claude, je suis conducteur-receveur à la Société de Transport du Département du Calvados, et notre travail consiste à...surtout à faire du transport scolaire de la ligne et du ramassage d'usine aussi. C'est-à-dire, euh...prendre les enfants à leur domicile pour les emmener jusque dans leurs lycées et, pour les personnes de, des usines, de les prendre devant leurs domi...devant un arrêt bien spécifique et de les emmener à leur lieu de travail.

Notre journée de, de conducteur-receveur, euh...se détermine comme ça: le matin, nous avons une prise de service qui est aux alentours de six heures du matin, pour faire de la ligne et nous terminons notre journée aux environs de dix-neuf heures trente le soir. Pendant, euh...durant cette période, nous ne roulons pas toute la journée ; nous avons des coupures de deux heures le matin, deux ou trois heures, nous roulons pendant l'heure du repas où que les gens ont besoin de se déplacer, puis nous arrêtons de nouveau vers les quinze heures, pour repartir vers seize, dix-sept heures, sortie des é-, des scolaires, des gens qui travaillent, pour les re-, pour les reconduire chez eux.

Pour les personnes des usines, cela est autre chose parce que c'est des personnes qui commencent relativement de bonne heure, qui font les postes, donc ils commencent à cinq heures du matin, il faut se lever de très bonne heure, vers trois heures et demie du matin et notre journée se termine aux alentours de quatorze ou quinze heures.

Nous avons un avantage, c'est de, d'avoir un contact avec, euh...beaucoup de personnes de la clientèle, pouvoir dialoguer, discuter.

Bon, y a un p'tit inconvénient, c'est le temps de, de travail qui est très long, on est pris beaucoup de temps, mais à part ça, nous avons un travail qui est très agréable et on le fait avec plaisir.

Appendix IV: 'French Day'

Designing and Analysing Questionnaires

Session Notes

Aims:

- to teach the technique of formulating questions and designing questionnaires
- to teach simple scoring and analysis

Method:

- compare a 'good' and a 'bad' questionnaire

('bad' = questions with more than one question within them

= questions which are open-ended but leave space only for 'Yes/No'

= questions which require a graded scale but force a 'Yes/No'

= poor layout, creating difficulty for scoring)

- write a 1-page questionnaire which will allow you to find out about people's regional identity and relate it to their age, sex, place of birth and other factors you think are important
- use a pre-prepared example to show how to score and analyse
  - (a) use a score column
  - (b) use a coding sheet
  - (c) analyse by percentages of factors likely to be 'causes' (independent variables)

Questionnaire 'Les Vacances' (A)

(1) Nom ....   (2) Age ....   (3) Sexe ....

(4) Où avez-vous passé les vacances en 1991 et en quel mois?.....................

(5) Quel lieu préférez-vous pour passer les vacances?

      (a) au bord de la mer   (b) à la campagne   (c) en montagne

(6) Etes-vous d'accord avec l'opinion que les vacances scolaires sont trop longues   Oui ....   Non ....

(7) Que pensez-vous des vacances à l'étranger?

Questionnaire 'Les vacances' (B)

Chers amis

Nous sommes un petit groupe de lycéens qui font une étude sur les différentes façons de passer les vacances.

Nous vous demandons de bien vouloir remplir ce questionnaire qui nous donnera des renseignements importants. Le questionnaire restera anonyme et il vous faudra très peu de temps pour le remplir.

Veuillez le renvoyer dans l'enveloppe que nous vous donnerons à:

Mr M. Smith,
Newtown Comprehensive School,
NEWTOWN NT3 4LR.

Nous vous remercions d'avance de votre coopération et de votre aide.

Cordialement

Les lycéens de Newtown

'Les Vacances'

Veuillez cocher les cases ou écrire vos réponses sur les lignes pointillées.

Section A: Renseignements personnels

(1) Age: 10-20 ans
20-30 ans
30-40 ans
40-50 ans
Plus de 50 ans

(2) Sexe: masculin
féminin

Section B: Les lieux de vacances

(3) Où avez-vous passé les vacances d'été en 1991:

(a) au bord de la mer en France
(b) au bord de la mer à l'étranger
(c) à la campagne en France
(d) à la campagne à l'étranger
(e) en montagne en France
(f) en montagne à l'étranger
Autre (veuillez indiquer) ....

(4) En quel mois avez-vous passé les vacances d'été en 1991 ....

Section C: Les opinions sur les vacances

(5) Quel lieu préférez-vous pour les vacances? Indiquez votre premier choix (1) et votre deuxième choix (2).

    (a) au bord de la mer en France
    (b) au bord de la mer à l'étranger
    (c) à la campagne en France
    (d) à la campagne à l'étranger
    (e) en montagne en France
    (f) en montagne à l'étranger
    (g) Autre (veuillez indiquer) ....

(6) Indiquer sur l'échelle combien vous êtes d'accord avec l'opinion suivante

    'Les vacances scolaires d'été sont trop longues.'

Pas du tout	un peu	beaucoup	totalement	je ne sais pas

(7) Ecrivez en quelques lignes votre réaction à l'opinion suivante:

    'Les Français devraient passer leurs vacances en France parce que c'est le plus beau pays de l'Europe'

Pour coder les réponses							
No. du questionnaire	Age	Sexe	où 91	Mois	Choix	Vac. Scol.	Mots clefs

Interview Guidelines

The best way of listening is to ensure that the interview is not routine and predictable. (Start from ignorance.) If the informant is left to himself/herself, he/she is bound to tell you things that are new, unfamiliar, expressed in a different way etc. Creative listening is a constant process of picking up and building on what the speaker says.

- Make sure the interview situation is as comfortable as possible with recording equipment as invisible as you can make it.
- Adopt a friendly easy manner.
- Show interest by nodding, agreeing or making comments.
- Express ignorance, e.g. 'Je ne sais rien sur...' so that interviewee will help you out.
- Don't be afraid of pauses.
- Listen carefully to what the interviewee says and try to pick up what is important to them personally and culturally, so that this can be pursued. Try not to impose your own preconceptions.
- Repeating what someone has said or asking someone to explain something further can be good ways of finding out more.
- Use the interviewee's words either to restate their opinion or to formulate your own questions - 'La théorie, c'était...'
- Try not to talk too much yourself; murmurs of agreement can be a good way of belonging to the conversation without interrupting.
- Start interviews with factual, non-personal questions to put interviewee at ease and to establish context.
- Make your questions as open as you can so that you dominate the interview as little as possible.

Schéma de questions pour un entretien

Introduction

Nous voudrions vous parler de vos origines en France et de vos opinions sur l'influence des régions.

Première section: origines

Pourriez-vous nous dire où vous êtes né(e) et où vous avez été élevé(e)?

[Points à poursuivre:

- la région
- village, ville, grande ville
- combien de temps elle/il y est resté(e)
- est-ce que ses parents étaient du même endroit sinon, d'où]

Deuxième section: identité

Quand vous êtes en Angleterre, vous sentez-vous français(e)? Pourriez-vous le décrire?

[Points à poursuivre:

- dans quelles situations il/elle se sent le plus français(e)
- s'il/elle rencontre d'autres Français(es), est-ce qu'ils se distinguent par leur régions d'origine
- dans quelles situations il/elle oublie qu'il/elle est français(e)
- demander toujours des exemples et des détails]

Troisième section: l'identité de la région

Nous voudrions savoir plus sur votre région d'origine. Si vous aviez à décrire les caractéristiques principaux pour un Anglais, que diriez-vous?

[Points à poursuivre:

- la même question mais en décrivant la région à un(e) autre Français(e)
- demander des exemples des caractéristiques donnés]

Pour poser des questions

(1) Interrogatives

For example, 'comment', 'qui', 'où', 'quand'. 'combien', 'qu'est-ce que', 'pourquoi' 'quel', 'lequel', 'quoi', etc.

These all produce direct questions which may be more or less open (giving the respondant an opening to develop an idea or conversation in their own way) or closed (seeking a specific response).

> Où l'avez-vous vu pour la première fois?
> Qui l'a trouvé?
> Quand est-ce qu'elle est arrivée?
> Lequel des deux est arrivé le premier?
> Elle était comment, quand vous l'avez trouvé? Pourquoi l'avez-vous invité?

(2) Inversion of subject and verb:

> Avez-vous vu le match samedi?
> Voulez-vous téléphoner demain soir?
> Pourrai-je faire du ski là-bas?
> Ira-t-elle à Paris avec lui?

(3) Use of statements as questions

The difference can simply be indicated by punctuation/intonation:

> Tu viens avez moi?

Vous aimez le jazz?

Il n'avait rien dit à sa femme?

The listener can be invited to comment on a statement:

Il habitait là depuis longtemps, n'est-ce pas?

Elle est sympathique, hein?

J'adore les films de Truffaut; et toi?/ et vous?

Tu détestes les chats, n'est-ce pas?

Questions with 'n'est-ce pas?' often simply invite confirmation or agreement, though they may be contradicted; 'et toi?' allows a more open response.

(4) Asking opinions

This type of question tends to be 'open', allowing for a variety of responses, though it can be slanted in various ways.

Que pensez-vous de la géographie?

Tu ne trouves pas que la géographie est ennuyeuse?

Tu trouves que la géographie est intéressante?

Croyez-vous qu'on puisse améliorer les cours de géographie?

A ton avis, qu'est qu'il faudrait étudier en géographie?

Some are neutral; others, especially those which invite agreement or contradiction ('Tu ne trouves pas que…?'), point to the attitude or expectations of the questioner. Contrast the following:

Vous trouvez qu'elle est sympathique?

Vous ne trouvez pas qu'elle est sympathique?

Comment la trouvez-vous?

Participant Observation Guidelines

- Choose somewhere where it is easy to observe people (restaurant, library, shop).
- Choose somewhere where you can go several times preferably somewhere that you often visit.
- Choose somewhere where there are several things going on (which is used for different purposes).
- Try to work out the relationships between people you observe and to include as much of the whole picture as you can.
- If possible try to become part of the situation you are in so that you can begin to understand the context/the problems of that particular place.
- In your descriptions include your own reactions and problems and how you think your presence affects others - write as a personal diary.

- Write down the times of beginning and ending the observation and draw a plan of the place where you are observing.
- Write down all the details you can.
- Decide whether you can jot down abbreviated notes in the place itself or whether you will have to write these down somewhere else (by going to the toilet or afterwards). Try to write out as much as you can as close to the time of observation as possible. Include information about when you wrote down notes (how soon after, any problems that occurred etc).
- Decide beforehand with your teacher if your observation project is to be public or not.

Examples:

(1) A man in a newspaper shop is given a newspaper very quickly without him saying which newspaper he wants [impersonal? — because person is known? — because person in a hurry?]
(2) People's behaviour in trains (or other public places) in establishing their own personal space.
(3) Rules that operate in libraries as to places being kept for absent readers.
(4) Who sits with who? Who talks to who?
(5) What is involved in stopping a bus, getting on, paying fare?
(6) Listening to people in coffee breaks — jokes — who is actually important? what is actually important?

Exercises:

(1) All write down something about an experience shared and compare notes.
(2) Watch film — talk about what you see — differences.

In a work situation could look at:

(1) Are workers male or female?
(2) How do they dress? Are there differences?
(3) Which groups are formed — working? social?
(4) Who talks the most?
(5) Who seems to be in charge? Is he/she actually in charge?
(6) What kind of work is being done?
(7) How long do things take?
(8) In refreshment breaks who talks to whom? who sits with who?
(9) How much time is spent not working?

Appendix V: Exercises for Testing Knowledge

Topic: School

I Essay

(i) Simple description of part of the school system:

Décrivez un jour typique/l'emploi du temps d'un lycéen. Est-ce que c'est le même que celui d'un lycéen anglais?

(ii) Simple written explanation of part of the school system:

Expliquez le rôle du surveillant/Qu'est-ce que c'est un surveillant. [The premise here is that there is a difference in system, something unexpected but no relating of this to a deeper cultural structure is asked for.]

(iii) Explanation of cause and effect:

Expliquez le système bac et ses conséquences.

(iv) Evaluation of a system:

Quels sont pour vous les avantages et les inconvénients du système éducatif en France?

(Students are given the opportunity to describe and explain.)

II Short answer questions

A quelle heure la première leçon commence-t-elle?
Où les lycéens mangent-ils leur déjeuner?
La leçon dure combien de temps?
Quels sujets est-ce qu'on étudie en France qu'on ne trouve pas dans un emploi du temps d'un lycéen anglais?
Combien d'heures de sport est-ce qu'il y a?
Est-ce qu'on est au lycée le samedi?
Est-ce qu'on peut quitter le lycée pendant la journée?

(Desired information is given, students cannot guess answers, although the form of question may provide clues.)

III Information given in diagram or note-form:

(i) Faites deux 'time-lines' pour un jour typique - un pour un lycéen anglais, un pour un lycéen français. Commentez les différences."

(ii) Le surveillant

Qui est-il?	Qu'est-ce qu'il fait?"
1.	1.
2.	2.

(iii) Le système bac

Qu'est-ce que c'est?	Décrivez les conséquences.
1.	1.
2.	2.

(iv) Le système éducatif en France

Avantages	Inconvénients
1.	1.
2.	2.

(This use of note-form will encourage more relevant answers but is less good for testing their language. The 'organisation of essay' which gains marks in current 'A' levels is done for them.)

IV Gap-filling

(a) Le mot 'bac', c'est l'abréviation du mot................

(b) Il y a _____ différentes sortes de bac: ils s'appellent..................

(c) On doit étudier .... matières pour le bac.

(d) Tout le monde doit étudier .... et.....................

(e) Si on veut être médecin on doit choisir Bac ....

(f) Le bac est .... exigeant que 'A' level.

(Desired information is obtained, but only in the form of detail. This is poor for testing productive language and quite time-consuming to set. Students generally cannot guess answers.)

V True/false statements:

(i)   (a) La journée au lycée commence toujours à 8h.

        (b) On a toujours deux heures pour le déjeuner.

        (c) Les leçons durent quarante minutes.

        (e) Tous les lycéens du première et terminale prennent la philosophie.

        (f) Les lycéens français étudient plus de sujets que les lycéens anglais.

        (g) Les lycéens peuvent quitter le lycée quand ils n'ont pas de cours.

(This is a time-consuming exercise to set but easy to mark.)

VI Multiple-choice questions:

(a) Le surveillant est
      (a) un étudiant
      (b) un lycéen plus âgé
      (c) un professeur
      (d) un professeur retraité

(b) Pendant l'heure du déjeuner
     il: se promène dans les couloirs
            assiste à servir les élèves
            se promène dans la salle à manger
            prend son déjeuner

(c) Pendant les permanences
     il: corrige les devoirs
            discute du progrès des lycéens avec les professeurs
            fait ses devoirs
            garde les élèves

(Again, time-consuming to set but can be easy to mark. Some answers can be disputed. Both exercises V and VI can answered by guessing.)

Appendix VI

(iii) Oral exams

Role Play (A)

Vous êtes Français(e). Votre correspondante vous invite à passer une semaine avec un groupe de jeunes au bord de la mer. Malheureusement c'est l'anniversaire de votre grandmère. Elle aura 70 ans et si vous n'êtes pas là...

Discutez la situation, expliquez le problème et essayez de trouver la solution.

Role Play (B)

Vous êtes Français(e) et vous allez vous marier avec un(e) Anglais(e). Il y aura un mariage à l'église suivi par un buffet. Votre famille française n'est pas contente.

Expliquez le problème et essayez de trouver une solution.

Role Play (C)

Votre correspondante anglaise a décideé de rester au café après l'école. Elle ne veut pas rentrer à la maison manger avec la famille. Elle veut aller au cinéma après avoir mangé un sandwich au café.

Expliquez les réactions de votre mère et essayez de trouver une solution au problème.

Role Play (D)

Votre correspondante anglaise suggère un séjour en Grèce ensemble au mois de mai — tout est moins cher au printemps. Vous êtes lycéen(ne) en première.

Est-ce que vous pouvez manquer deux semaines de cours? Quelle est la réaction de votre entourage (famille/amis) en France? Essayez de trouver une solution.

Role Play (E)

Votre correspondante ne comprend pas pourquoi il n'y a pas d'enseignement sur la religion ou sur la vie personnelle et sociale en France. Elle trouve qu'il est important de discuter ces choses en classe.

Expliquez et justifiez le système français.

Role Play (F)

Votre correspondante anglaise trouve que les profs à votre lycée sont très distants et très sévères.

Essayez d'expliquer pourquoi et dites ce que vous faites si vous avez des problèmes au lycée.

Role Play (G)

Votre correspondante anglais est au chômage. Il vous semble qu'elle ne prend pas la situation au sérieux. Discutez son attitude avec elle et expliquez ce que vous feriez à sa place.

Role Play (H)

Vous discutez votre choix de carrière avec votre correspondante anglaise. Vous trouvez un peu bizarre qu'elle ait l'intention de travailler comme agent de police...

Role Play (I)

Votre ami ne comprend pas pourquoi vous voulez retourner vivre en Bretagne. Expliquez et justifiez votre décision.

Appendix VII

Préparez une question de la Section A et une question de la Section B.

Section A

(1) Les plaisirs et les inconvénients de vivre dans un immeuble parisien.
(2) Ecrivez une lettre à un(e) ami(e) français(e) dans laquelle vous essayez de la/le persuader de renoncer à fumer.
(3) Imaginez que vous venez d'avoir votre permis de conduire et que vous partez en vacances avec votre famille (en France bien sûr!). Décrivez vos expériences au volant.
(4) Un système Minitel pour l'Angleterre. Discutez le pour et le contre.

Section B

(1) Vous êtes un(e) élève français(e) de 18 ans et cette année vous allez passer votre baccalauréat. Décrivez votre scolarité à partir de l'âge de 11 ans et vos ambitions pour l'avenir. N'oubliez pas d'expliquera quelques différences entre les systèmes français et anglais.
(2) Etudiant(e) français(e) vous passez un an en Angleterre. Ecrivez une lettre à votre grandmère française dans laquelle vous décrivez et expliquez quelques différences entre la France et l'Angleterre en ce qui concerne la vie familiale.
(3) Animateur/trice à la radio française, vous suivez quelqu'un(e) pendant une journée de travail. Racontez vos expériences et vos réactions.
(4) La situation: vos parents français ont choisi de vivre dans un petit village breton. Votre père est instituteur et votre mère travaille dans un musée. Bretons de naissance ils avaient décidé de rentrer au pays pendant les années 70. Ils parlent breton à la maison, vont aux fest-noz etc. Vous êtes lycéen(ne) à Quimper et vous voulez étudier à Paris. Imaginez la discussion avec vos parents et écrivez seulement les paroles des trois personnes.

Appendix VIII

First Year 'A' Level: Summer Exam 1992

You are advised to spend an approximately equal amount of time on each question. (30 minutes)

TOPIC 1: La Famille

Question One

Vous vous appelez Geneviève et vous vous êtes mariée la semaine dernière. Ecrivez une lettre à une amie qui etait malade et absente pendant la ceremonie pour lui décrire le mariage.

Question Two

Write a couple of paragraphs (in English) to explain the significance and importance of mealtimes for a French family.

TOPIC 2: L'Ecole

Question Three

Expliquez (en français) — 4 ou 5 lignes — les institutions ou les personnalites suivantes.

(a) L'école maternelle   (d) Le Conseil de Classe
(b) Le Collège   (e) Un Surveillant
(c) Le Lycée   (f) Le Baccalauréat

Question Four

Here are four quotations from French people who have been working in schools in England.

(a) ...il y a beaucoup plus d'horaires en France qu'en Angleterre. Je trouve ça incroyable de finir à trois heures, par exemple.

(b) ...vous avez deux extrêmes, le système anglais, où on ne donne pas assez de devoirs et le système français ou on en donne trop.

(c) ... en France vous avez 'broad education' ... en Angleterre on specialise trop tôt.

216

(d) En Angleterre, tous les professeurs ont l'air de voulour être les amis des etudiants.

Using these statements as starting points, imagine that you have to explain some of the differences between a school in England and a 'lycée', to a student from France who will be staying for a year in your school. To give a full picture, you should discuss not only the physical differences but also differences in atmosphere and attitudes in English and French schools.

TOPIC 3: Le travail

Question Five

Looking for a holiday job, you look through the pages of a newspaper which a friend has brought back from France.

Choose one of the jobs on offer and write (in French)

(a) Letter of application
(b) A Curriculum Vitae.

TOPIC 4: La Bretagne

Question Six

Write three or four paragraphs (in English) describing Brittany as seen in the video film. Do you think it is a full or accurate portrait of the region? Explain your reasons.

Index